While the literature relating to Scottish
significantly in recent years, the influe:
its early modern history has been neglec
with Scottish influence on the formation of North American national
identities. Alexander Murdoch's fascinating new study explores Scottish
interactions with North America in a desire to open up fresh perspectives on the subject.

Scotland and America, c.1600–c.1800:

- surveys the key centuries of economic, migratory and cultural
  exchange, including Canada and the Caribbean
- discusses Scottish participation in the Atlantic slave trade and the
  debate over its abolition
- considers the Scottish experience of British unionism with respect to
  developing American traditions of unionism in the US and Canada.

Incorporating the latest research, this is essential reading for anyone
interested in the dynamic relationship between Scotland and America
during a key period in history.

Alexander Murdoch is Senior Lecturer in Scottish History at the
University of Edinburgh and was formerly Researcher for the Scottish
State Archives. His previ-

Scotland and America, c.1600–c.1800

Alexander Murdoch
The University of Edinburgh

First published 2010 by
PALGRAVE MACMILLAN

Palgrave Macmillan in the UK is an imprint of Macmillan Publishers Limited, registered in England, company number 785998, of Houndmills, Basingstoke, Hampshire RG21 6XS.

Palgrave Macmillan in the US is a division of St Martin's Press LLC, 175 Fifth Avenue, New York, NY 10010.

Palgrave Macmillan is the global academic imprint of the above companies and has companies and representatives throughout the world.

Palgrave® and Macmillan® are registered trademarks in the United States, the United Kingdom, Europe and other countries.

ISBN: 978-0-230-51657-1 hardback
ISBN: 978-0-230-51649-6 paperback

This book is printed on paper suitable for recycling and made from fully managed and sustained forest sources. Logging, pulping and manufacturing processes are expected to conform to the environmental regulations of the country of origin.

A catalogue record for this book is available from the British Library.

A catalog record for this book is available from the Library of Congress.

10 9 8 7 6 5 4 3 2 1
19 18 17 16 15 14 13 12 11 10

Printed and bound in Great Britain by
CPI Antony Rowe, Chippenham and Eastbourne

In memory of Elizabeth J Murdoch 1920–2003
And for her granddaughters
Anna Elizabeth Rylance Murdoch
and
Lydia Catherine Rylance Murdoch

Contents

Preface

This book has many different origins, but chiefly it grew out of my
attendance as a postgraduate student at the 'Scotland, Europe and the
American Revolution' – Scottish Universities' American Bicentennial
Conference at the University of Edinburgh in June 1976 and, secondly,
my offering two decades later an honours course at the University of
Edinburgh following my appointment as a Lecturer in Scottish History
under the title 'Scotland and America'. This in its initial incarnation
focused on the eighteenth century, but I later expanded its remit to
the extremely long eighteenth century of 1603–1917. I adopted the
latter date at the suggestion of Professor Rhodri Jeffreys-Jones in
acknowledgement of the USA's late entry into the First World War, with
all that this subsequently entailed for the twentieth century. He would
no doubt be gratified to read the analysis of Kathleen Burk in her book
Old World, New World: The Story of Britain and America (2007) 'that there
was no decided change in the relationship until 1917, and that the
usual date of 1914, in the context of Anglo-American relations, is not
a significant signpost' (411). Although this book has been written in
a belief that the relationship of Scotland to America was significantly
different from that of Britain as a whole, there is no doubt that the First
World War altered Scottish relations with America, and vice versa, in
1917 rather than 1914.

I am responsible for all the shortcomings of this addition to an
extremely varied literature on the subject, but I have many acknowl-
edgements to make in relation to anything positive a reader might take
from what is offered here. I owe a great debt to Dr Robert J Cain as
former Director of the Colonial Records of North Carolina project of the
North Carolina Office of Archives and History, who employed me as the
researcher for its Scottish Records Program (in the American spelling)
from 1986 to 1990. I am also grateful to all my former colleagues in
the American Studies programme at what was then Nene College and
is now the University of Northampton from 1991 to 1995 for sharing
their robust views on just how we would define that enterprise, and to
the support I received from colleagues with whom I taught British and
European History there. On taking up my appointment at at Nene, it
was my pleasure to join the committee that at that time directed at the
university to promote American Studies and who had just introduced

an undergraduate degree programme in the subject. Although that degree has now been withdrawn by the university, American Studies still flourishes at Edinburgh as part of the teaching of degrees in History and English Literature as well as through flourishing postgraduate programmes in American History, Canadian Studies and Transatlantic (literary) Studies.

Some of the students who took the Scotland and America course at Edinburgh have gone on to postgraduate study, including Sonia Baker, John Beech and Matthew Dziennik, who graduated with degrees in Scottish Historical Studies, Scottish Ethnology and Scottish Historical Studies, and History respectively. Other students I remember as making particularly constructive contributions to the course include Kirsteen Foster, Kevin O'Donnell, Chris Peck and Chris Rae. Martin Casey distinguished himself by returning books when the next intake of the course needed them most! During the academic year 2001/2002 I was fortunate to be allowed to teach a more specialist version of part of the course under the title Scottish Settlement in the American South and gained much from the work of David Ellis, Caroline Parkes and Mark Mulhern, who explored the different perspectives they brought from American Studies and Scottish Historical Studies in a constructive manner that taught me much. Tom Devine, Professor of Scottish History, made a substantial contribution to the teaching of the course during the academic year 2006/2007, and I hope in the future that it might seminar drawing more widely

x *Preface*

Dickinson, Owen Dudley Edwards, Dr Marjory Harper, Professor Ged Martin and Dr Nicholas Phillipson. It has been a pleasure in completing this survey to draw on a series of remarkable research monographs that have made an outstanding contribution to the subject recently. This is a better book than it would have been previously because it has been able to draw on the findings of Dr Douglas Hamilton (2005), the Rev. Dr Iain Whyte (2006) and Dr Douglas Watt (2007). I owe a special debt to Dr Eric Graham and Dr Whyte as honorary postdoctoral fellows in Scottish History in the School of History, Classics and Archaeology at Edinburgh for their enthusiasm and assistance in helping to organize the Scotland, Slavery and Abolition Conference held at New College at the University of Edinburgh on 10 November 2007. Lastly, I must record my thanks to the School of History, Classics and Archaeology for granting me research leave for the academic year 2008/2009 to try to bring this project to a conclusion, to Christina Hussell of Computing Services at the university for support in meeting the publisher's requirements for submission and to Sonya Barker of Palgrave Macmillan for her patience as commissioning editor for the book.

Introduction

Much of what has been written about Scotland's relations with America has been concerned with uncritical ethnic chauvinism. Like many other ethnic groups in America, Scottish-Americans claim a significant importance for themselves in helping to make America, and Scots naturally focus on this when thinking about their country's exchanges with America, neglecting the very considerable impact of America in making modern Scotland. This book is a survey of what we know about this complex subject to date, excluding the entirely unexplored history of cultural exchange between Scotland and America in the twentieth ... Most work has been carried out on the eighteenth century, ...oon Enlightenment

peace negotiations that followed its conclusion, his claim about the importance of 'Scotch-Irish' blood' was meant as much of a joke as Voltaire's observation in the eighteenth century that 'today it is from Scotland that we get rules of taste in all the arts, from epic poetry to gardening.'[2] Clearly Wilson's Presbyterian background was an important part of his upbringing and personality as his education at Princeton and later experience as president of that university. In his 'Scotch-Irish' speech, he identified his Scottish predecessor as president of Princeton, James McCosh, as well as the great Scottish Presbyterian leader of the nineteenth century, Thomas Chalmers, as major figures in the tradition he claimed to represent. Later he would write to Andrew Carnegie (in seeking funding for Princeton) that 'the Scots blood that is in me makes me wish to renew the traditions of John Witherspoon's day in the old place.'[3] It is important to remember, however, that Wilson was not a Scot like McCosh or Chalmers or Carnegie, let alone John Witherspoon.

Ironically, Wilson when at Princeton reformed and modernized it by leading it away from the Presbyterian seminarianism that had made it 'Scottish'. Wilson appealed to the legacy of Witherspoon and McCosh for Carnegie's cash, but he looked to the German universities of the nineteenth century as a model for the academic excellence to which he aspired for Princeton. It was they, and not Scottish universities, whose specialist curricula had provided the model for his own postgraduate education as a historian at Johns Hopkins University.[4] In contrast, there clearly was a very material American influence on Scottish education by the end of the nineteenth century in the form of Andrew Carnegie's decision to establish the Carnegie Trust for the Universities of Scotland in 1901. Although his own formative education took place in the United States rather than in Scotland, by establishing a Scottish trust, Carnegie supported the idea of the national importance of the Scottish educational system, although he was criticized at the time for forcing change on the Scottish universities. By 1904 the Carnegie Trust funded the studies of half of all students at Scottish universities, and had become 'practically a ministry for Scottish universities', and in the process doubled their income.[5]

Carnegie's intervention in the Scottish education system illustrates how relations between Scotland and America began to alter significantly after the end of the American Civil War. Although expansion of the British Empire would have a significant impact on Scotland in the second half of the nineteenth century, much of that empire was American, particularly Canada and the British Caribbean. Combined with growing US influence on Scottish and British public life as issues of democratic reform, republicanism and federalism became increasingly important; the balance in the cultural exchange between Scotland and America began to shift to the expanding and dynamic North American continent, including Canada. As the Scottish population stagnated, that of North America continued to grow exponentially, and given Scotland's long links with America it should be no surprise that the effect on the country was as great as that in Ireland. This book represents an attempt to focus on the issue of the importance of adopting a comparative approach to examination of Scottish exchange with America that does not privilege claims of national or ethnic superiority, but instead employs them to explore complex issues of national development and ethnic diversity in a transatlantic context. Unlike the Irish or other European (or Asian, Caribbean or South American) immigrants to the United States in the nineteenth century, those who were 'British' (including Wilson's 'Scotch-Irish') believed that they had a kind of prior claim on America through ethnic connections with its traditional elite and the first European settlers there. It is now obvious how simplistic their views were, but it distinguished their experience of America, just as it disguised the growing impact of America on Britain, Scotland and Europe as a whole.[6]

Most of this book is about Scottish contact with America in the ʼnineteenth and eighteenth centuries, although it seeks to look forward ... Scotland and America in the

identity for itself by its opposition to constitutional as well as absolute monarchy. It embarked on egalitarian democracy (for men) in public life early in the nineteenth century in a manner that would provide an influential alternative model for political reform in Britain. All of these issues mark the United States as worthy of the particular attention it receives in the last chapter of this book, and are worthy of exploration in much greater depth in future research.

Thus the book has been organized in two unequal parts. In Part I, the reader is provided with a survey of our current knowledge of Scottish trade and settlement in America in the seventeenth and eighteenth centuries, as both became focused on the western hemisphere rather than Europe in a manner that laid the basis for the great expansion of both in the nineteenth century. The two defining episodes in increasing Scottish contact with America were the contrasting failure of the Company of Scotland expeditions to Darien in Panama at the turn of the eighteenth century and success of the Scottish merchants trading out of Glasgow in achieving dominance in the tobacco trade with America in the third quarter of the eighteenth century. It is clear, however, that the failure to establish an independent colony at Darien was far from the end of Scottish trade in the Caribbean, which remained a significant destination for Scottish merchants and emigrants into the early nineteenth century. Equally the tobacco trade with the mainland American colonies of Virginia and Maryland on the Chesapeake Bay was far from the only point of contact for Scottish merchants and emigrants on the North American mainland in the seventeenth and eighteenth centuries. This much broader contact between Scotland and America in the eighteenth century in particular provided the basis for the more complex issues of cultural exchange between Scotland and America that are considered in Part II.

The key subject that links emigration and trade with cultural exchange is slavery. It is only recently that this has become apparent to most scholars working on research that relates to Scottish contact with America. Of course, it has long been known that the major American commodity trades in sugar and tobacco (and, later, cotton) all involved plantation production that depended on slave labour imported from Africa and later on their descendants born into hereditary bondage in the Caribbean and the American South. Even at Darien in 1700, the colony's leaders requested shipments of African slaves to carry out heavy manual labour." Yet from a Scottish perspective, until recently these were issues that were viewed as part of American and Caribbean history rather than Scottish history. It was the wealth generated by colonial trade and its impact on Scottish modernization that was viewed as Scottish, and for a number of historians of Scotland, colonial trade was responsible for only an insignificant part of the wealth generated by the economic advances the country experienced in the eighteenth and nineteenth centuries.[8] That view has come under considerable revision recently.[9] This has not been the result of significant additional research on Scotland's trade with America in the eighteenth century but reflects new perspectives arising from the changing nature of Scottish society in the early twenty-first century as it has become more diverse ethnically, more confident and less insular.

There has been important new academic research that has increased awareness that however small Scotland's direct involvement in the slave trade and the use of slavery in the British Empire had been, it is important to acknowledge that there were links between Scotland and this painful legacy of imperialism. This is particularly important because over the course of the eighteenth and nineteenth centuries, as Scotland became more integrated into Britain and the British Empire, Scottish national identity became mediated increasingly through culture rather than politics or, indeed, economics. This was the legacy of the successful adoption of European Enlightenment culture in Scotland by the end of the eighteenth century and formed the basis of the now largely forgotten self-styled 'democratic' public culture of nineteenth-century Scotland.[10] That is why in this study Chapter 3 on trade at the end of Part I con- ... involvement in the transatlantic slave

Recognition of the injustice of human slavery illustrated a relatively neglected aspect of the influence of Enlightenment culture on Scotland. It was also present in the history of Scottish awareness and concern with the native peoples of America. The changing nature of this contact (remotely as well as directly) was founded on a different kind of trade and a different moral issue than those involved in slavery, although of course in the seventeenth century, in particular, many 'Indians' were also enslaved. The trade was first in animal furs and skins in return for gunpowder and alcohol, and later was in the land occupied by native peoples who could no longer resist a growing settler population. European ideas about savagery and civilization changed over the course of the eighteenth century in a manner that increased willingness to acknowledge the virtues of 'savage' tribal societies previously dismissed as such in the sixteenth and seventeenth centuries. Did the changing nature of cultural relations between Gaelic-speaking Highlanders and Lowland Scotland during the early modern period give Scots distinctive insights into the cultural encounters they experienced with native peoples in the Americas? It is clear that this was an aspect of Scottish contact with America that had an impact on the Highland Scottish experience of modernization and change that occurred over the course of the eighteenth and nineteenth centuries.[13]

In both the case of the issue of slavery in the British Empire and the place of native peoples within it, one of the distinctive aspects of Scottish experience of contact with America was its national religious culture and its identification with Presbyterianism. As Presbyterian congregations grew and multiplied in North America, so they came to exert an important influence in Scotland. The transatlantic Protestant evangelical movement of the eighteenth century had a profound impact on cultural and social change in eighteenth- and nineteenth-century Scotland. Not all Scots were Presbyterians, but equally Presbyterians in Scotland had to acknowledge that many Presbyterians were not Scots. They also had to recognize that they had more in common with many fellow Protestants in America, even if they were not Presbyterians, than they did with the established Church of Scotland that developed as the British state church in Scotland during the eighteenth and nineteenth centuries. When Presbyterianism augmented in the nineteenth century under the impact of economic and social change in Scotland, American influence on Scottish religious culture increased, drawing more and more into international and transatlantic networks of Protestant evangelicals whose concerns came to have a significant impact on the great moral issues of the abolition of slavery and the promotion of world missionary work that increased in importance in Scottish public culture over the course of the nineteenth century.[14]

If British North America and the British Caribbean were important parts of Scottish cultural exchange with America in the eighteenth and nineteenth centuries after 1783, the influence of the United States grew ever more important as its population and economy expanded to the point that it attracted a substantial majority of Scottish emigrants. This book concludes with a chapter that considers the argument that Scotland exerted a disproportionately large influence on the formative years of the United States that made an enduring mark on its character. Similar suggestions have been made in regard to Canada. Both have some merit, but the conclusion of this study is that in both cases emphasizing the contribution of one particular national, ethnic or tribal group in the development of a country does not tell us as much as a more challenging but ultimately more rewarding comparative approach. The creation of the Atlantic world and the expansion of its networks played a crucial role in the creation of modern Scotland. Equally, to consider Scottish contact with America as too small in scale to be of significance is to underestimate its impact. Scotland benefited from a geographical position that was peripheral in European terms, but placed it at the centre of the Atlantic networks that created the modern world. This was something that would come to define the   nation in modern times.

Part I

Scottish Trade and Settlement in America

1
Scotland and America in the Seventeenth Century

Introduction

In 1622 Sir William Alexander received a charter from James VI of Scotland to found a Scottish colony in the North American lands lying between New England, where English settlement was in its infancy, and the long established English fishing stations on the island of Newfoundland.[15] Later, in 1628, James's son Charles I granted Alexander a second charter giving him (in theory) a claim to all the lands between English and French territories in North America.[16] Alexander was one of the many Scottish courtiers who followed James ⋯⋯ of England in 1603. In the pamph-

of our men, but have enriched few,' while 'the necessities of Ireland are neere supplied, and that great current which did transport so many of our people is worne drie'.[18] Alexander was not correct about the future of Scottish emigration patterns in the seventeenth century. Many more Scots were about to die in the Thirty Years War in Europe and many more Scots would emigrate into Ireland than ever would travel further westward before 1700.

Alexander did, however, understand James VI's concern about the 'civilitie' of Scotland. In his *Basilikon Doron*, intended as a manual of kingship for his eldest son, James had argued that if the Scottish Crown could establish plantations in the Highlands and Islands of the country they would 'within a short time ... reform and civilise the best inclined among them, rooting out or transporting the barbarous and stubborn sort, and planting civility in their rooms'.[19] If plantation in the Highlands failed to achieve this, then exportation of its savage population to America in the seventeenth century would both promote British empire there and remove them from Scotland. As Charles I put it in a letter to Alexander regarding his renewed efforts to establish New Scotland in 1629, colonists from the Scottish Highlands would assist in 'debordening that our kingdome of that race of people which in former times hade bred soe many trubles ther'.[20] None of this came to pass. Alexander's scheme to sell baronetcies of Nova Scotia to aspiring gentry who wanted a title failed as a means of raising the finance for further colonization, and by the time of his death in 1640 Scotland had descended into the maelstrom of the British wars of the three kingdoms. Only the name of New Scotland survived, in its Latin form, and was revived in the eighteenth century when what was by then the French colony of Acadia became 'British'.[21] In the eighteenth and nineteenth centuries large numbers of Scottish immigrants would add a significant Scottish element to the population of Nova Scotia. Ironically, many of these immigrants came from the Scottish Highlands that Sir William Alexander had convinced Charles I (briefly) would be the ideal source of population for an American New Scotland. However, by 1632 plans to establish a new Scotland in the seventeenth century had been abandoned in the interests of peace with the French, who re-established their presence in the land they called Acadia. Nova Scotia would not be established until the eighteenth century but it did eventually become the kind of British colony James VI and William Alexander would have wanted. Scotland's empire would be created out of the edifice of British unionism James VI did so much to create and promote as part of his reign in both England and Scotland.

Charles I did not share that vision, and the result was catastrophe across Britain and Ireland. By the time of Sir William Alexander's death in 1640, civil war and anarchy had rolled across all three of the Stuart kingdoms. After the execution of Charles I, the legacy he left ensured military conquest of both Scotland and Ireland by the English republican regime led by Oliver Cromwell. Scotland was defeated and occupied every bit as comprehensively as Ireland had been, but for Cromwell the Presbyterian Scots of the covenants, although misguided, were still part of the Godly Revolution to which he had devoted his life.[22] The Irish, by contrast were a threat and, along with Wales and the Scottish Highland clans, provided the basis for a possible Stuart counter-revolution that had to be guarded against at all times. Catholic Gaelic-speaking prisoners from Ireland sent to the West Indies became a threat to stability there, whereas the planters valued the Presbyterian Lowland Scots sent to them after Cromwell's victories at Dunbar and Worcester.[23]

We do not know much about it, but Scottish assimilation into the Cromwellian Protectorate after the comprehensive defeat of Scottish armies at Dunbar (1650) and Worcester (1651) had repercussions that made it possible for Scotland to participate in the Atlantic economy of the seventeenth century in a manner that had been closed to it during the reigns of the early Stuart monarchs of Britain. Although the Covenanting Presbyterian regime in Scotland had been defeated, the victorious English military regime recognized their previous role during the Anglo-Dutch war of 1652–54.[25] Although at other points in the seventeenth century the English Navigation Acts were applied against Scottish merchants as well as the Dutch, the Act of the 1650s did not affect the Scots, as they were now subjects of the expanded Cromwellian Commonwealth.

There is little evidence that Scottish merchants were able to take much advantage of this opportunity. Thomas Tucker reported to the Commonwealth government in England in 1655 that trading voyages from Scotland to the Caribbean had been discontinued because the returns had been poor.[26] The only entry in the Dumbarton Register of Ship Entries that relates to tobacco refers to it as imported in a ship from Rotterdam. Another entry from the earlier year of 1648 records the importation of 20,000 pounds of tobacco in a Glasgow-owned vessel arriving from Martinique in the Caribbean.[27] Scots sent as convict labour to the West Indies after the defeats at Dunbar and Worcester were sent in English ships. Although some prisoners had been sent to America after the Scottish defeat at the battle of Preston in 1648, *The Proceedings of the Council of State relating to Scotland during the period of the Commonwealth* of 19 September 1650 'authorized the transportation of 900 Scots prisoners to Virginia and 150 to New England.'[28] Some of these men moved to other colonies when they completed their indentures. One later Scots immigrant to East Jersey in 1685 wrote back to Scotland that he had met a fellow 'countryman, who was sent away by Cromwell to New England; a slave from Dunbar, living now in Woodbridge [East Jersey] like a Scots laird, wishes his countrymen and his native soil well, though he never intends to see it.'[29] David Dobson has argued that it was 'no coincidence that the Scots Charitable Society was established in Boston on 6 January 1657 "for the relief of Scotchmen" as this was around the time that many of the Dunbar and Worcester veterans would have been ending their years of servitude'.[30] Although other Scottish prisoners taken at Dunbar and Worcester were offered to the French and the Venetians for service in their armies against the Turks, it was those sent to the western hemisphere who would contribute to the process whereby more Scottish merchants after the restoration of the Stuart monarchy (and a separate kingdom of Scotland) in 1660 looked westward beyond Ireland for profitable trading under the impact of continued disruption of the longstanding Scottish trading links to France, the Netherlands and the ports of the Baltic Sea by chronic political instability in Europe.

T C Smout in commenting on the expansion of Glasgow's trade in the seventeenth century, identified the years after 1642 as the beginning of

Glasgow's ascendancy in Scottish trade, commenting that increasing access to a British market allowed the town's merchants to consolidate their existing trade and gain access to markets that previously had been 'completely outwith the horizons of normal Scottish trade'. Through this they entered 'the wider Atlantic, sending their ships to the Spanish Atlantic Islands (the Canaries, the Azores and Madeira), to the English Caribbean (especially Nevis, Montserrat and Barbados) and to the mainland plantations of North America (Carolina, Virginia and Maryland, New Jersey, New York and Massachusetts)'.[31] Did they begin to do this because integration into the Cromwellian Commonwealth/Protectorate had made possible what had been impossible under the early Stuarts?[32] Did the Cromwellian period open up regional economic avenues for trade from Glasgow to Ireland and the west of England as well as the north Atlantic through the west of Scotland to the rest of the nation?

However it happened, it was a gradual process in which established merchants were encouraged to try to enter the Atlantic trade, and received returns that were substantial enough for them to persist with the experiment. After 1660 this brought them into conflict with the English Navigation Acts, but the lack of clarity in this legislation (and perhaps enough shared interest with fellow Protestant dissenters in England, Ireland and New England) enabled them to find niches where trade was possible. Smout wrote that 'at least after 1673 the traders that

re-establish the Scottish kingdom of 1603–38, complete with absentee monarch. No wonder that the Scottish poet and former courtier Thomas Urquhart of Cromarty died of laughter on hearing the news of the Restoration.[34] 'Disaggregation', to use an ugly modern term, allowed the restored Stuart monarchy to govern Scotland (and Ireland) without reference to an English Parliament. This meant that the Scottish Privy Council under the Stuarts had no interest in enforcing the English Navigation Acts in Scotland. The Glaswegian merchant Walter Gibson, 'who sailed his vessels disguised as English ships and imported Nevis sugar straight home to the refineries on the Clyde,' flourished despite the Navigation Acts.[35] Scottish proposals that the Restoration English Parliament grant trading privileges to Scotland 'ran up against English fears about the competitive edge enjoyed by the Scottish carrying trade, the close Scottish trading links with the Dutch and, above all, the perceived Scottish threat to vested coal and salt interests in the north-east of England'.[36] When this idea was revived by London merchants seeking access to cheap Scottish coal and salt in 1674, the project failed again because 'the Scots opted for colonial expansion rather than closer ties to English domestic markets.[37]

The arrival of James, Duke of York and Albany, in Scotland as King's Commissioner in 1679 encouraged those Scottish merchants and members of the aristocracy and gentry who saw colonial trade as the panacea for Scotland's economic difficulties to embark on serious planning to encourage it. James had been posted to Scotland by his brother because of opposition in the English Parliament to his status as heir to the throne in the so-called 'Exclusion' crisis, at a time when mercantilist economics were rapidly reducing the options open to smaller European kingdoms and trading centres seeking access to colonial trade. York, or rather Albany, to give him his Scottish title, sought to use his position in Scotland to demonstrate his ability to govern. His Scottish title was used to name the frontier settlement established on the New York frontier once he had assumed authority over that colony and what became East and West New Jersey following their conquest from the Dutch.[38] The Scottish Duke of Albany's time in Scotland was a relatively short period in what one might charitably term a varied career. His role in Scottish public life was not always to be so positive as he was the instigator of the ill-starred Scottish Jacobite movement that so blighted the history of early modern Scotland. Albany arrived in Scotland as the natural leader of the Royalist interest and between 1679 and 1682 he experienced some success in developing this position, and he continued to acknowledge his connection with Scotland after his return to England. Indeed, his younger daughter Anne's determination to achieve a successful parliamentary union between England and Scotland may well have been rooted in her experience of living with her father in Scotland at this time. James undermined his own position by his assault on the political elite in Scotland after 1686 in pursuit of an agenda that historians are still trying to define. It certainly included toleration for Roman Catholicism, but did not directly involve the issue of overseas colonization.[39]

One of James's initiatives while he was in Scotland, however, was to explore the possibility of introducing mercantilist economic policies. To that end he convened a committee of trade to advise the Privy Council of Scotland 'anent the causes of the decay of trade and what they should propose for the remied thereof'.[40] Leading Scottish merchants were summoned to make recommendations to the Privy Council that were recorded in a 'Memorial concerning the Scottish plantation to be erected in some place of America' submitted to the Privy Council in 1681. This is a document which demonstrates considerable knowledge about the western hemisphere, and acknowledged the influence of 'William Colquhoun, now resident in Glasgow, who hath been a planter amongst the Carribe Islands these 20 years and thereby hath acquired a considerable fortune that hee hath now settled here in this country'. Colquhoun, it was claimed, was 'the onelie persone fitt for giving information for further encouragement to the settleing of a colony'.[41] All

and void it of very maney both idle and dissenting persones.' This is not that dissimilar to the recommendations of Sir William Alexander in relation to New Scotland in 1629. For the Stuart monarchy, plantations were about trade and increasing wealth that would bring them tax revenue, but they were also about the disposal of 'idle and dissenting persones' who were a potential source of unrest in England, Scotland and Ireland.

Following James's departure from Scotland in 1682, never to return again, efforts to carry out the recommendations of the Privy Council's committee of Trade in Scotland by undertaking plantations in Carolina and East Jersey (but not Jamaica) would involve both the aim of expanding trade and the exportation of dissent.[46] Merchants seldom leave records of their spiritual lives and the expanding literature of religious Protestant dissent in the seventeenth century seldom included reflections on trade and finance. Yet these were not separate worlds. As David Harris Sacks has written about Bristol during this same period, 'the capitalism born in coping with the new demands of the Atlantic economy and the new conditions of politics in the Restoration was not only a set of beliefs but a system of organization for carrying them out, a way of doing as well as seeing – a distinct form of life'.[47] For Scotland, RH Campbell has written with considerable insight that 'there is no question that the influence of the religious tradition [in Scotland] was widespread, so that even those who rejected or actively opposed it were often as much its products as those who were among its supporters. The religious tradition may then have to be credited with much that might seem at first sight to have little contact with it'.[48] For Campbell, the issue is not the disruptive effect of covenanting Presbyterianism on seventeenth-century Scotland, 'but whether its disruptive elements were potentially conducive to economic growth or not.' He argued that although Presbyterians were associated with opposition to the Stuart monarchy, they also represented a 'religious tradition ... [that] provided an encouragement to devote effort to work and achievement.'[49] There is evidence that the merchant community in Glasgow that led the way for Scotland's entry into the Atlantic economy was very much identified with that religious tradition.

The Scottish attempt to take on land settlement in East Jersey no less therefore involved the great Scottish Quaker Robert Barclay of Urie. Originally this was land granted by the Duke of York (and Albany) to two English aristocrats after the Dutch had been expelled from the area, divided between them into East and West New Jersey. Later East New was purchased by consortia dominated by members of the Society of

Friends, most of who were also involved in William Penn's efforts to found a colony to the west of New Jersey under a royal charter creating the separate proprietorial colony of 'Pennsylvania'. While West Jersey became connected with Pennsylvania, the proprietors of East Jersey recruited further investors, six of whom were Scottish, one of whom was Robert Barclay of Urie.[50] As Barclay and some of the other Scottish proprietors of East Jersey were from the north-east of Scotland there was a distinctive Scottish regional character to the settlement they promoted. Not all of the colonists were Quakers, but the efforts of Barclay and his colleagues coincided with William Penn's efforts to create a colony in Pennsylvania based on the principle of religious toleration. It is important to remember, however, that merchants and landowners who were members of the Society of Friends were as concerned with the rewards of profit in this world as by the prospect of spiritual salvation in the next.[51] East Jersey, like Pennsylvania, was a proprietorial colony whose owners hoped to benefit from their privileges and investments. William Penn was close to James politically, particularly after he became king as James II and VII in 1685. Given the political catastrophe that overtook James, it is impossible to prove whether he believed genuinely in religious toleration or if he wished to use the issue as a means of advancing the causes of Roman Catholicism and the absolute power of the monarchy in Britain and Ireland. Before his suc-

After 1690 few additional Scottish indentured servants and other colonists arrived in East Jersey. As the servants who had arrived from Scotland completed their indentures many of them became landowners in their own right through purchase of land from the proprietors or tenants of farms offered to them for rent. Although the arrival of Scots settlers introduced a distinctive Scottish ethnic element to the colony, they were not a majority of the population, which contained a significant 'Dutch' and 'English' population, many of them American-born people who had migrated from New York and New Jersey in search of land to take up on favourable terms. The 'Scottishness' of East Jersey was to a great extent top down as from 1685 to 1705 approximately two-thirds of the board of resident proprietors in East Jersey were Scots.[54] This had a marked effect on the pattern of landholding in the province, which was much more conservative and dominated by larger landowners, including the resident proprietors, and had much more in common with New York and Pennsylvania than New England. Much of the population in New Jersey nevertheless had originated in New England, and they had been welcomed into the colony by proprietors eager to increase the value of their lands by encouraging an increase of population. What made the East Jersey settlement unique in Scottish terms was that it survived, partly because it was established in an area where settlement of a European creole population already had been established.

Scottish proprietors also could relate their efforts to the broader efforts led by conservative Quaker interests to colonize West New Jersey and Pennsylvania in a manner which was distinctive in terms of government and to a degree in terms of economic policy. East Jersey became part of a coastal region of North America that began to develop at a rapid rate in the eighteenth century, compared to the experience of both Virginia and New England, as major centres of British settlement began to integrate with each other economically, socially and, ultimately, politically. In East Jersey the original Scottish proprietors became absorbed over time into a native-born colonial elite, while many if not the majority of the descendants of the Scots indentured servants sent to the colony in the 1680s intermarried with families of different ethnic origins to establish the common population pattern of British American colonies of an ethnic inheritance that included several European traditions rather than one.

The experience of the Scottish Carolina colony attempted about the same time as East Jersey provided a contrast in that as interesting in the main it failed, although it shared similarities more in common with the New

Scotland project in the early seventeenth century or the catastrophic failure of the Darien scheme at the end of the century. Like both of these unfortunate enterprises, however, Port Royal in Carolina (named Stuart's Town by the Scots) was part of the process of greater Scottish participation in the Atlantic economy. Stuart's Town was associated with the idea of encouraging Scottish Covenanting Presbyterians to leave Scotland for Scottish proprietorial colonies in America at a time when the Stuart monarchy, as it had with Penn in Pennsylvania and Barclay in East New Jersey, wished to encourage American plantations under British authority without the monarchy assuming direct responsibility for any of these enterprises. It was a concept that in Carolina would survive the fall of the Stuarts, but which no proprietors or their heirs were able to sustain in a manner satisfactory to them in the eighteenth century.

There is no doubt that those at the heart of the Carolina enterprise were associated with Covenanting Presbyterianism, and more specifically Covenanting Presbyterianism of the south-west Scottish heartland of the movement. Initial interest focused on securing a grant in the lands of James, Duke of York and Albany, on account of his Scottish connections, but by the time a 'Carolina Company' was formed in 1682 they were in negotiations with the English proprietors of the lands in 'Carolina' south of Virginia.[55] The members of the company were wealthy noblemen, lairds and merchants of south-west Scotland with

the advice wee have had at London it will be our great advantage and greatly for the support of all that is there already planted' in Carolina.[59] Cochrane argued that 'Southward of all that have yet planted' the Scots would 'be as near the Spaniards as possibly wee can be that we may have a present trade with them'. There are echoes in this text of the arguments about the potential for free trade at Darien advanced almost 20 years later when the issue of colonization of land claimed by, but not occupied by, the Spanish was raised again. In both cases, were the Scots thinking of trade with Spanish settlements, or of following the example of the Dutch, French and English in seeking to tap into Spanish colonial wealth in the Caribbean by force?

The Carolina Company was intended to be a commercial attempt to found an independent settlement under the general authority of the English proprietors, although at the time negotiations became caught up with the political fallout in England over the purported 'Rye House' plot to assassinate Charles II and his brother. This was seized upon by Charles II as a means of attacking the Whig/Dissenting opposition to his regime, particularly in the English Parliament, but there were repercussions in Scotland as well. Scots associated with the Carolina colonial project had gone to London, ostensibly to negotiate with the Carolina proprietors over the terms on which they would pursue their colonization project, but at least some of them were involved in discussions over the possibility of organizing an assassination attempt on the lives of Charles and James. The entire affair illustrated the stark choices facing Scottish Presbyterian Whigs under the Stuart regime. Armed conflict had led to conquest and hardship earlier in the seventeenth century, but the endless jockeying over the toleration issue appeared incapable of delivering a solution to the problems many Presbyterian Scots had in acknowledging allegiance to the Stuart monarchy. The Stuarts, on the other hand, were interested in encouraging American colonization projects as a means of physically removing potential opponents from their British and Irish kingdoms. If opposition Presbyterian Whigs were willing to leave Scotland to attempt plantations in North America on the model of New England, then that was far preferable to their travelling to the United Provinces of the Netherlands, where they would add to the potential military strength of a colonial rival rather than help develop overseas plantations under the authority of the British monarchy. In fact, some of those who initially did subscribe to the Carolina Company, including some who emigrated there for a time such as Hugh Erskine, third Lord Cardross, did subsequently choose exile in the Netherlands.

The model for colonization pursued by the Carolina Company was similar to that pursued by the East Jersey proprietors. Both differed from English schemes only in targeting Scotland as a source of the indentured servants who would provide the labour, at least initially, for the colony. The 'Overtures for Incouradgement of Servants' drafted for the company in 1682 stipulated that indentures would be for a term of three years and that their transportation costs and maintenance would be borne 'by yr [their] masters', who would be the undertakers of the company who emigrated to South Carolina or their agents.[60] At a time when Covenanting Presbyterians taken prisoner by the Scottish government were being sentenced to transportation to America, these relatively generous terms were intended to enable the company to offer good conditions to such prisoners it accepted from the government. As the government lacked the capacity to incarcerate prisoners for any length of time, transportation to the plantations was an attractive option to them for the disposal of such prisoners. When Walter Gibson's ship the *Carolina Merchant* sailed for Carolina in 1684 with Lord Cardross, William Dunlop and other intended planters, among the servants who made up the majority of those on board were 35 prisoners who had been accepted from the government, but who probably were indentured on the same terms as the other servants.[61] Given that the government prisoners shared the same Covenanting Presbyterian principles as the other members of the party, this is hardly surprising.

their investment. Stuart's Town was destroyed by the Spanish before this point became an issue, but subsequently in Carolina more generally, as elsewhere in British North America, it was rare for proprietors to collect quit rents sucessfully, with the possible exception of the early years of the Scottish plantation in East Jersey.[64]

Although additional ships were sent there by Scottish merchants in the 1680s Stuart's Town did not last long as a Scottish plantation as a Spanish expedition destroyed it in 1686.[65] Although the proprietors of South Carolina in London had been encouraging, the Governor and Council at Charleston did not welcome the Scots, to the point of hostility toward the Scots' assumption that semi-independent (at least) authority had been granted by the proprietors for a separate settlement. In addition the Scots had a different approach to relations with native peoples with whom they came in contact, although this appears to have brought them into conflict with the Spanish at St Augustine in Florida as well as the Carolina authorities at Charleston. Thus the fears expressed in the 'Memorial concerning the Scottish plantation to be erected in some place of America' considered by the Privy Council of Scotland just five years previously proved to be only too well founded.[66] Some of the survivors of Stuart's Town returned to Scotland, but others remained in Carolina at Charleston, where they provided much of the impetus for the foundation of the first Presbytery of Carolina, which would correspond with fellow Presbyterians in Scotland for many years after the fall of the Stuart monarchy in 1688–89.

As in East Jersey, the Carolina settlement added to the early Scottish diaspora in the Americas. It was overshadowed in the seventeenth century by the far larger number of Scots who left their country for Ireland, for England and for continental Europe, but their departure still marked the beginning of a social change in the pattern of Scottish emigration that would transform the country irrevocably as it became enmeshed in an Atlantic economy. What the Scots at Stuart's Town failed to achieve, as the Scots in East Jersey failed to achieve, was the establishment of the kind of separate Scottish plantation identified as an objective by the Scottish Privy Council and its advisers in 1681. The Privy Council memorial had suggested that exploratory voyages from Scotland should be carried out not only to survey possible sites of colonization, but to contact 'all those places [sic] in America 'where many Scots gentlemen of quallitie and present planters there doe reside to take informatione from them ... especially considering that there are many Scots men already planted in these Islands'.[7] The writer of the memorial was confident that the Scots already scattered across the European colonies in America had 'longed these many yeirs' for a 'Scotts plantatione'. He was confident that they would be glad to remove themselves and their families to any place appointed,' and that they would 'be a considerable beginning to the said plantation, they being people acquainted and seasoned with these countries' whose support would 'save much of the expense which the erecting of such a plantatione may occasion'.[68]

Stuart's Town was destroyed before it could attract Scots from other European colonies in America. East Jersey, centred near its towns of Perth and Woodbridge, survived, but its proprietors after the regime change in British and Irish politics in 1688–89 changed their strategy from recruiting Scottish indentured servants and free colonists to a willingness to accept anyone on their lands who could afford to rent or buy them. These terms were less generous than those of proprietors elsewhere in America, which acted to preserve the Scottish character of their lands until this changed, as it did within a generation. The great Scottish experiment in post-Stuart colonization in America at Darien would involve similar issues, and its comprehensive failure would determine the character of Scottish contact with America over the two centuries that followed.

Darien and its discontents

While Scotland had been involved in 'Colonial schemes' before the

Darien thus is a history with two halves at the centre of Scottish and American history; the short, nasty and brutal history of an emphatic failure to sustain a colonization project in America, in contrast to the colony marking the scale of the ambition that led to the beginning of a modern, 'Atlantic' and 'American' Scotland. The latter perspective has been associated with British unionism.[70] Failure at Darien included both defeat of the first Scottish expeditions by the environment they encountered, leading the minority of colonists who survived death through disease and malnutrition to abandon the colony, and military defeat by the Spanish of the second expedition, forcing the survivors to make terms and surrender the site of the colony in 1700. Failure and defeat established that to survive in the harsh economic climate of European mercantilism at the end of the seventeenth century, Scots had to concede that the political independence of the ancient Scottish kingdom maintained (mostly) by its aristocratic elite since the medieval wars of independence was no longer tenable. There was no point in asserting political independence if the kingdom lacked the ability and resources to defend that independence. Early Scottish attempts at establishing American plantations underlined that fact.

Of course Scottish independence had been undermined since 1603 by the fact that there was no resident monarch in Scotland, although the background to Darien was the achievement of political autonomy by the Scottish Parliament following the change of monarch in 1689. The Company of Scotland Trading to Africa and the Indies was chartered by the Scottish Parliament without reference to William of Orange as monarch of Scotland. This has led some to ascribe the failure of the Scottish expeditions to Darien to the failure of William of Orange to act as king of Scotland in promoting and defending the project. For them, William was the reason for the Scots' lack of success, rather than a harsh American environment, inept leadership or Spanish opposition. Thus Darien did not demonstrate the need for greater union for Scotland, specifically a British union, rather it demonstrated that Scotland needed to assert greater political autonomy to ensure that it was not reduced to the subordinate colonial status in relation to England that would make it a second Ireland.

David Armitage has argued that 'the attempt to settle a colonial empor ium at Darien, and with it to bring Scottish commercial independence from England, ended in defeat, disaster and despair,' but also argued that the debate surrounding the Company of Scotland generated the most sophisticated and wide-ranging controversy in seventeenth before the debate on the union with the English Parliament.[71] Before turning to a discussion of that debate, however, the 'defeat, disaster and despair' itself should be discussed. Douglas Watt has made the case against the management of the Company of Scotland and its directors. The company was an outstanding success in terms of convincing many people in Scotland that its projects for colonial settlement in America represented Scotland as a nation and thus made investment in the company an act of patriotism. Although naturally most of those with money to invest in Scotland were from its landowning and mercantile elite, the public debate over the Company of Scotland's projects represented the beginning of the formation of a broader arena of 'public opinion' in Scotland. This was not absolutely new. The impact of the sixteenth-century Reformation and the expansion of print production clearly had involved the expansion of 'public' culture, but by the end of the seventeenth century greater numbers of people in Scotland were being drawn into it, particularly in urban areas. It was nothing like the public sphere of the very largest urban centres in Europe such as London and Paris, but it fuelled a national debate on the future that marked a key stage in the modernization of Scottish public culture. In the words of Douglas Watt, 'The Scots experienced the destructive force of the new financial world more acutely than any nation before them.'[72] It should be added that this financial world had grown through the expansion of the Atlantic economy and its influence on Europe during the seventeenth century. There are three aspects to consider in seeking to understand

best-selling book by William Dampier published in 1697 under the title
A New Voyage Round the World. In 1699 an associate who had travelled
with Dampier in Panama, Lionel Wafer, published *A New Voyage and
Description of the Isthmus of America* containing detailed descriptions of
Darien and the native people in its vicinity, with whom he had lived
for a time after becoming injured during a buccaneering expedition
to the Caribbean in 1681. Some of the directors of the Company of
Scotland contacted Wafer in early 1698 and arranged for him to travel
to Edinburgh to discuss Darien's suitability for plantation and trade
with them. Wafer stayed with Andrew Fletcher of Saltoun at his East
Lothian estate near Haddington and convinced those who spoke to him
that the Company of Scotland should invest its capital in an expedition
to take possession of Darien. He appears to have offered to accompany
such an expedition, but to have set financial terms for this that were
considered excessive by the directors. William Paterson did go as a volunteer, and was elected to the expedition's governing council in place
of someone who had withdrawn from the voyage. Paterson survived
the failure of the colony, although his wife did not, and he returned to
Scotland. His account of the expedition to the directors of the company
emphasized weak leadership in the council and poor provisions as the
reason for the expedition's failure, along with his judgement that the
trade goods sent to the expedition were overpriced. Those who organized the expedition had no knowledge of the market in the Caribbean
for the trade goods which were intended to provide profits for the settlement.[73] Indeed, it is unclear how the Scots anticipated trading, unless
their real intention was to carry out buccaneering attacks on Spanish
ships and settlements.[74]

What Paterson did not blame for the failure of the expedition was
the inhospitable nature of the site of the settlement, which remains
unsettled and inaccessible to the present day.[75] Paterson remained an
advocate of British settlement at Darien, responding to the final failure
of the Scots to establish themselves there by petitioning the Board of
Trade in London, urging them to attempt to succeed where the Scots
had failed. Paterson was a visionary, but successful exploitation of the
potential of Panama as a major element of world trade had to await the
twentieth century and an enormous commitment of resources by the
government of the United States as part of its own imperial expansion.
Previous attempts by a commercial company to contol a canal across
the isthmus in the nineteenth century failed just as comprehensively as
the Scots attempt at settlement at the end of the seventeenth century.
When riches were achieved in Panama, however, the day at Darien was

a long way from the zone that became an essential cog in expanding world trade during the twentieth century. That was centred on the existing pattern of settlement dating back to Spanish colonization.

Thus the directors of the Company of Scotland who saw foundation of an American colony as fundamental to its success had seriously miscalculated its potential for success. Paterson's eloquence and conviction, Dampier's visionary account of potential wealth and Spanish weakness in the Caribbean in his best-selling book (seven impressions from 1697 to 1715 and translations into Dutch, French and German) and Wafer's pre-publication accounts of the riches to be exploited at Darien all convinced them that this was the place where the company should be. Scotland, the directors of the Company of Scotland believed, would achieve the wealth it required to survive as a nation in America. The Scots had been drawn in by a classic account of the riches of America, in contrast to the exhausted lands and resources of the old European world. Paterson was not alone among survivors of the first expedition in praising it. Captain Robert Drummond of the company's ship, the *Caledonia*, wrote to the directors in praise of the climate, and a journal kept on one of the first expedition's ships followed the well-worn trope of more than two centuries of European colonization of the Americas by listing a bewildering array of natural riches: 'The Soil is rich, the Air is good and temperate, the Water is sweet, and everything contributes to make it healthful and convenient'.[76] Even more importantly, however, it was provision in the Act that the King should support, by force if necessary, the ambitions of the Company of Scotland. 'I have been ill served in Scotland,' William declared in response, 'but I hope some remedy may yet be found to meet the inconvenience that may arise from this Act'.[78] This was before it had been decided that the directors of the company would pursue American colonization. Many of the directors and subscribers of the Company of Scotland believed that trade with Africa and the East Indies on the model of the English East India Company or the Dutch East India Company was the course which should be pursued. Doing so, however, would certainly arouse the opposition of East India Company shareholders in London, and would hamper efforts to raise capital for the company there. The original intention of the company was to raise substantial sums there, and in pursuit of this, the London-based directors of the company were joined by three further directors from Scotland so that the company court of directors could formally meet in London.[79] When the subscription book was opened on 6 November the target amount of £300,000 was pledged in just over a week. After Parliament's protest to the king, however, the money that had been paid as part of subscription (25 per cent of the total) was returned to subscribers.

William of Orange had taken his eye off Scottish affairs, as had his favourite adviser, the Earl of Portland. A new Scottish ministry anxious to win popularity had approved an Act establishing an international trading company, which became perceived as a threat to established mercantile interests in London once its existence became known there. William Paterson, forced to resign as a director of the Bank of England only months after being at the forefront of the campaign to persuade the English Parliament to charter it, had misled an inexperienced Scottish ministry into seeking to cash in on popular belief that colonial trade would solve Scottish economic problems. Once it became clear how badly he had miscalculated, Paterson and his fellow directors had a lot of explaining to do in Scotland. English economic 'nationalism', expressed through the Westminster Parliament, would transform the Company of Scotland into a symbol of Scottish sovereignty and a vehicle for the political ambitions of those who had approved the Act, chartering it in Scotland after the king dismissed them from office. Much of the case they would make was that English opposition made it impossible for the company to succeed. Failure was not the fault of Paterson or the directors of the company, or a sign of Scotland's economic and political weakness; it was instead the result of the English opposition. This included preventing the Scots from identifying alternative sources for capital subscription, to replace that lost in London, when the Scottish directors sent three of their number to Amsterdam and Hamburg. In Amsterdam, the same kind of jealousy of the company emerged as that which marred its efforts in London, as Dutch East India merchants in particular sought to discourage potential investors. Whether William of Orange, as Stadholder of the Netherlands, and those who supported his interests there were behind the opposition to company agents is not clear, but no money was forthcoming.

In Hamburg, English opposition was made manifest. The English diplomat Sir Paul Rycaut was based in the city at this time and filed regular reports on the activities of the company's agents, who were also in the city to supervise the completion of two ships being constructed there for the company. William Paterson was one of those agents, and dismissed Rycaut's opposition, intent on marketing the company as focused on trade to the Orient rather than American colonization. Rycaut's activities proved decisive in defeating the Scots' plans, however. On the instructions of William III, he submitted a memorial to the senate of Hamburg disowning the Company of Scotland which later 'was published several times in English translation by the justly indignant Scots'.[80] On the other hand, the company's own (English) agents in Hamburg cautioned against over-ambition. William Paterson had convinced his fellow Scots that 'the keys to the universe' were there for them to take if they would just dare to take them, but some experienced authorities continued with their plans for an expedition to exert their authority over the site claimed by the Scots. When two Scottish deserters from the second expedition were apprehended and interrogated by Spanish forces, plans for an immediate attack on the Scots were made to prevent them from establishing themselves.

In February 1700 Alexander Campbell of Fonab arrived at Darien to take military command of the colony, with a sloop he had purchased in Barbados bearing further supplies.[82] He had fought in the Low Countries with William of Orange's armies against the French but had been reduced to half pay with the advent of the peace treaty of 1697, and like many other demobilized Scottish soldiers, offered his services to the Company of Scotland as a colonist on its expeditions. A few days after his arrival Campbell led 200 Scots and some native auxiliaries to seize the initiative against the Spanish, apparently on receipt of intelligence from natives sympathetic to the Scots. As in 1699, an advanced party against the Scots was attacked and driven off, this time at a hill called 'Toubacanti', with relatively few losses of life on both sides. Modest as the encounter was, the Scots celebrated it as a victory. In Scotland there were celebrations in the streets of Edinburgh when news of (an exaggerated) victory reached the country. At Darien the euphoria dissolved when 11 Spanish ships appeared off New Caledonia at the end of the month, landing troops to attack the colony on 1 March and driving the Scots back into their fortifications 17 days later. By 31 March the Scots had agreed articles of capitulation, and by 11 April they boarded their ships for departure to Jamaica, where a substantial number of the survivors decided to remain, establishing a connection that would grow and expand considerably in the years following the union. The defeat of the second expedition and its forcible expulsion from Panama had occurred without the aid of the added force of 5000 soldiers dispatched from Spain that arrived in Panama in the summer of 1700. Those who had been confident of Scottish ability to displace the Spanish had been proven wrong. Without English support the Scots were no match for the Spanish, and with William of Orange determined to ensure that Spain should not enter into an alliance with France, there was little hope that he would use the resources of his kingdom of England against Spain to promote the trading interests of his kingdom of Scotland.

Yet in final defeat the expeditions to Darien marked the establishment of a powerful connection between Scottish efforts to escape their circumstances, promoters and the idea of America as the means by which they would do so. Defeat in Darien, however, did ensure that for Scotland North America (including the West Indies) became the focus in Scottish engagement with the problems and the possibilities presented by the western hemisphere. Public debate in Scotland was founded on reaction to English opposition, and the subsequent efforts by the King to demonstrate that of his three kingdoms in Britain and Ireland, the parliament and the people of his wealthiest and most populous kingdom dictated his economic and political priorities. This debate generated ideas about America in Scotland that emphasized an inclusive, integrationist political economy rather than a national identity defined by dynasty and kingship or ethnicity and kinship. Paradoxically, defining the desire to participate in Atlantic trade in such terms ended up portraying the Company of Scotland and its Darien expeditions as an enterprise that redefined Scotland in terms of inclusive, outward-looking, integration with European Atlantic trade. Given Paterson's experience of the Netherlands, it does not take much imagination to identify the model for Scottish ideas about Atlantic trade. Through eventual parliamentary union with the Westminster Parliament, the Scots would incorporate the broader free-trading ideology of the Dutch in the seventeenth century into the developing British empire of the eighteenth century. The debate over Darien in Scotland anticipated the debate over union with England that developed after William of Orange's death in 1702, and much of that debate concerned Scottish access to Atlantic trading networks.

First, English and royal opposition turned the Company of Scotland

English authorities to accept his vision, he was left with an idea that he could sell only in the country of his birth, capitalizing on the advent of unprecedented parliamentary sovereignty for the Parliament of Scotland as an unexpected by-product of political changes in Britain and Ireland from 1688 to 1692.

Recent research on the manner in which capital for the Company of Scotland was raised has concluded that, analysing its history in relation to the more general history of financial institutions in Scotland and Europe, the Company of Scotland provides an early example of 'financial mania', similar to the 'South Sea' and 'Mississippi' bubbles in England/Britain and France in the period around 1720 (the latter of which also involved speculative investment in anticipated profits of trade with American colonies). John Law as a young man in Edinburgh witnessed the Company of Scotland mania, which he drew on in later life as the financial Controller-General of France who presided over the 'Mississippi Bubble' financial mania.[83] The difference was that after the initial subscription was completed in Scotland there was not enough money left to fund speculative investment in Company of Scotland shares while English as well as European investors remained unable to invest or unconvinced of the company's potential. So the Darien phenomenon of 1696 was very modern, but it was also highly specific to Scotland. After all, congregations of the Church of Scotland prayed for the success of the company's expeditions, ministers and their families invested in it and six ministers of the kirk accompanied its colonists to Panama.[84] It also brought experience of the effects of financial mismanagement to a very broad section of Scottish society.

Although the subscription books record 1267 individual subscribers and 53 institutions, it is likely that investment in the company involved a greater number of people because some of the individual shareholdings were shared. For example, the £1000 subscribed by Maxwell of Pollock was a pooled investment with the lairds David Bogle of Kelburn and William Cunningham of Craigends.[85] Institutional shareholdings represented members of incorporations of trades or the town councils of royal burghs. One striking feature of the subscription lists of the Company of Scotland are the number of women involved. Of the individuals named in the subscription lists, 91 were women. The financial value of their subscriptions was only 5 per cent of the total, but many were widows or daughters with money to invest. Some servants also appear.[86] So while the movement to invest in the Company of Scotland was hardly a mass phenomenon, it involved a significantly larger number of individuals in a much smaller society than similar financial organizations in England such as the Bank of England or the English East India Company, despite England's much larger population and money supply. Thus the formation and failure of the Company of Scotland had a revolutionary impact on Scottish perceptions of America because, while earlier Scottish 'colonial schemes' directed to America had involved small numbers of investors and colonists, a much larger number of people in Scottish society invested in the Company of Scotland. Despite the utter failure of its American expeditions, investment in American trade and participation in the American economy came to characterize economic and social change in Scotland over the course of the eighteenth century. There are strong reasons to believe that this was partly the result of the social and cultural impact of the national debate in Scotland over the Company of Scotland and the Darien expeditions. That debate was over what should happen to the Scottish claim to Darien and to those in Scotland who had lost all the money they had invested in the Company of Scotland through the destruction of its capital base after the failure of its expeditions, but the events expanded Scottish contact with America, including ideas and awareness of America among many Scots who would never go there.

As Bridget McPhail has put it, 'if the Company of Scotland left the New World unscathed, its failure changed the Old World forever,' meaning that failure in Darien led to negotiations for parliamentary union with England which in turn, so the powerful British narrative goes, created

seventeenth century, as they aggressively expanded attacks on Spanish interests in the western hemisphere and established Virginia, New England, New France and New Netherlands in North America. With native peoples eliminated in so much of the Caribbean as early as the seventeenth century, perhaps what distinguished Scottish efforts was their focus on the central American mainland. Spain had originally claimed North America and established its garrison at St Augustine in Florida in defence of that claim, but in the seventeenth century it had to recognize that it could not sustain it against English, French and Dutch incursions. Yet the Scots chose the Caribbean as the focus of their efforts at colonization because it was perceived as offering greater opportunities for generating wealth.

Darien was different in that it was an attempt to establish permanent settlement on the mainland in an area marked more by activity by pirates and buccaneers than by colonial settlement. Both Dampier and Wafer, the publication of whose influential books coincide so exactly with the Scottish expeditions to Darien, had been accused of involvement in piracy. The leaders of the Spanish expeditions against the Scots were instructed to treat the colonists as pirates unless they could produce royal instructions from William of Orange as their king authorizing their actions.[88] In the event they were allowed to surrender with military honours, presumably because the local Spanish authorities did not want to prolong their siege of New Caledonia as they did not intend to occupy it. The seventh article of the surrender agreement stipulated that local native people who had cooperated with the Scots were not to be molested following the Scottish withdrawal. Darien would be left to return to its 'natural' state in the absence of any European settlement.

Failure at Darien was complete with the surrender of the second expedition. For many devout Scottish Presbyterians, failure in Darien was a sign of God's displeasure with the nation. One of the most famous Covenanting Presbyterian ministers of the church, Alexander Shields, died in Jamaica after taking part in the surrender of the colony to the Spanish. How had the Scots failed to serve God's purpose in Panama? Francis Borland, another of the ministers on the second expedition, returned to Scotland to see out his days as a parish minister in Lanarkshire, writing a 'History of Darien' that was published in Glasgow in 1779, at the height of the American Revolution that proved to be so heavy a blow against the monopoly trade in tobacco that had become such a rich commodity for Glasgow merchants in the eighteenth century. For Borland, the Scots had demonstrated their unworthiness before God in the swamps of Panama, and the failure of the colony was a judgement of God against the nation.[89]

During the parliamentary session of 1700 the opposition argued that the kingdom's claim to Darien should be reasserted by the nation's parliament.[90] Addresses were presented to Parliament calling upon it to respond to the humiliation of the nation, not just at Darien but also in failed harvests and widespread poverty at home. Eventually an address to the King was agreed by Parliament, which requested that the King recognize the legality of the Company of Scotland's efforts to colonize Panama, but it was not an Act of Parliament that proclaimed this as the company's right. William Paterson later repackaged his vision of colonial triumph for Scotland into a British project for the expansion of its trading empire at the expense of Spain, calling for Darien to be colonized again. The Scottish Member of Parliament, William Seton of Pitmeddon, in his pamphlet on *The Interest of Scotland*, argued that failure on so many fronts left a union of the parliaments of Scotland and England as the only way forward, a union which would secure Darien against the Spanish and their French allies.[91] Scottish unionism, however, projected equal partnership of two ancient and independent kingdoms, despite their disparity in population and wealth. The Company of Scotland's claim to Panama became part of justifying that claim.

As late as 1738–41, when Admiral Edward Vernon took Portobello

Company of Scotland shareholders for their losses. By guaranteeing Scottish access to American commercial markets, it also laid the basis for the reinvention of the country in the eighteenth century. At the time, British empire was specific to America. Later this would change, but in the beginning, colonial trade meant North America, which over the course of the eighteenth century became the crucible whereby the project of a united Britain was defined.

2
Emigration in the Eighteenth Century

Scotland exported a high percentage of its population (mostly young men) in the seventeenth century, but most of them went to northern Europe.[93] That pattern was reversed over the course of the eighteenth century. By the end of the eighteenth century North America was the principal destination for Scottish emigrants and would remain so for all of the nineteenth century. This change occurred slowly, accelerated during the extraordinary decade before the American Revolution, with the main destination beginning to shift to Canada in its aftermath. It grew out of the changing pattern of Scottish overseas trade. If Scottish emigration to England made the greater impact on the country over

English ideas of Jacobite Highlanders, as it does about Scotland and America.[97] A different kind of evidence regarding Scottish emigration to America was the establishment of St Andrew's societies. The St Andrew's Society of Charleston was established as early as 1729. That for Philadelphia was founded in 1749 and for New York in 1756 although a 'Scots society' had already been formed in the latter in 1744.[98] Very different are the remarkable 'narratives' of 'Peter Williamson', who appeared in Edinburgh in 1757 claiming to have been kidnapped as a 12-year-old boy in Aberdeen in about 1742 for shipment to America as an indentured servant. Williamson published a pamphlet based on what he claimed were his adventures in America in order to raise funds for pursuing a legal action in the Court of Session in Edinburgh against those he accused of being responsible for 'kidnapping' him. He went on to open a successful coffee house in Edinburgh and establish the city's first penny postal service. When he died there in 1799, he left instructions that he was to be buried in the costume he wore during a period of captivity with the Delaware Indians of Pennsylvania in 1754, and his pamphlet, *French and Indian Captivity* remained in print for many years after his death. We do not know if he was 'truthful' in his narrative, given the many alterations he made to the text of his pamphlet in editions published during his lifetime, but he was able to obtain detailed testimony from many people in the Aberdeen region regarding the kidnapping and captivity of boys who were then sent to America, and this was printed as evidence in support of his Court of Session action.[99]

In 1739 more than 100 men, women and children were kidnapped on the isle of Skye by seamen who had come in a ship from Glasgow specifically to take on a cargo of people to sell as indentured servants in America. Sir Alexander MacDonald of Sleat and Norman MacLeod of Berneray had encouraged merchants from Glasgow to send ships to Skye to kidnap human cargo from their estates, presumably for a financial consideration. The facts of the case that brought this 'trade' to the attention of the government became difficult to determine after a substantial number of those taken captive escaped from a ship bound from Scotland to North America or the Caribbean when it stopped at Donaghadie in the north of Ireland to take on provisions. The local authorities intervened and reported the case to London, where it attracted the interest of the Lord Chancellor, who demanded explanations from the Scottish legal establishment in Edinburgh, aghast that 'Britons' could be taken from their beds in the middle of the night to be sent for sale in America.[100] MacDonald and MacLeod managed to deny all knowledge, at a time when the writ of the law in Scotland did not run at large. Edmund Burt, an Englishman serving with General Wade's garrison in the central Highlands in the 1730s, recorded that he was aware of Highland chiefs selling people from their estates to merchants under the pretext that they were criminals sentenced to transportation. 'It has been whispered,' wrote Burt, that 'their Crimes were only asking their Dues, and such-like Offences; and I have been well assured, they have been threatened with hanging, or at least perpetual Imprisonment, to intimidate and force them to sign a Contract for their Banishment.'[101]

Early settlement in New York

In the 1730s the first organized settlements of Scots in North America after the union of 1707 were attempted, all related to American colonial efforts to populate lands then on the frontier. In New York, efforts were made to attract Protestant settlers from Europe who could be settled north of Albany in areas that were beginning to become contested between New York, native American confederations and French agents sent south from Quebec to expand the boundaries of New France. In 1732–34 the Royal Governor and his council advertised that they had 'purchased' 100,000 acres near Lake George from native American tribes and that settlers who would take up unimproved land there

own passage on ships that Campbell chartered for them. A small minority were indentured servants recruited to work land that Campbell planned to take up on his own account, but he had also arranged for the emigration of many additional people because he had been promised 'headright' to land, specifically from 1150 to 1500 acres for each family 'of which 1000 Acres were to be allowed to himself.'[104] The number of acres Campbell's family later claimed was to be made available to him under this agreement was 100,000 – the entire tract that had been advertised in 1732. They had to concede, however, that no legal record of this agreement was kept, although in 1757 it had been discussed in William Smith's *History of the Province of New York*, published in London. In this work Smith, a prominent New York lawyer and later judge, discussed Lachlan Campbell's efforts to bring immigrants to take up the Lake George land grant and described his failure to secure a grant under the promised scheme as resulting from the jealousy and dishonesty of government officials in New York at the time. By 1757 Campbell was dead, but Smith's book may have encouraged his eldest son, who had served in the Royal American Regiment during the Seven Years War, to journey to London to petition the Board of Trade to order the current Governor of New York to honour the promises that Smith had written were made to his father. The son had already obtained a much reduced grant of 10,000 acres from the Governor and the Council of New York in 1763, as had representatives of '140 families of the people who had emigrated', in the form of 47,000 acres, within which the township of Argyle was chartered in 1764, subsequently to become known as 'the Argyle Patent.'[105] The expenses involved in surveying and taking up the lands meant that some of the families had to sell their share of the grant. However, because the land was associated with Scottish Gaelic-speaking settlement, soldiers who had fought with the Scottish Highland regiments and had become acquainted with the area during the British attacks on Ticonderoga and Crown Point also took up land there under the terms of the Royal Proclamation of October, 1763, offering 'land without fees to those who had served in the war against France, and wished to stay in North America'.

Smith, however, would have been aged nine when Campbell first arrived in New York, although he argued in correspondence with Cadwallader Colden, Governor of New York from 1763, that he had become convinced of the justice of Campbell's case from studying contemporary records and from conversations with his family, as well as accounts from others who had been members of the Council of New

York when Campbell had negotiated with them.[106] Colden had been Surveyor General for New York when Lachlan Campbell claimed his land, and argued that Campbell had not recognized that the New York lands near Lake George were promised to others. Both Smith and Colden were colonial officials who speculated in land, as did many in the British American colonies. Smith published a pro-emigration pamphlet, *Information to Emigrants*, in Glasgow in 1773, at the height of Scottish emigration to America, and his interest in encouraging a steady stream of emigrants to northern New York, which could not fail to raise the value of lands held there by himself and others, no doubt contributed to the origins of this publication.[107]

However, Smith did not specifically refute Colden's claim that the families Campbell had persuaded to come to New York opposed Campbell's petition for a large land grant as a reward for bringing them to the colony. Colden wrote that those Campbell had brought with him to New York proclaimed that 'they had left Scotland to free themselves from the vassalage they were under to their Lords there & they would not become vassals to Laughlin Campbel in America.'[108] Although Colden may have been involved in efforts to get title to some of the land himself, the rapidly changing political situation from 1763 to 1776 meant that grants made under the authority of the Crown held little validity. What is clear is that Lachlan Campbell's early attempts to attract Gaelic-speaking Scottish settlers to northern New York to help

appears to have first been discussed by Oglethorpe and the Georgia trustees after the former had returned to London from Georgia in 1735. They commissioned Lieutenant Hugh Mackay and a Captain Dunbar to recruit Highlanders for Georgia from the area north and west of Inverness. Dunbar was the son of an Inverness merchant named John Dunbar and captain of one of the ships that took Highland colonists direct from Inverness to Georgia.[110] Whether he was 'George Dunbar, gentleman in Inverness-shire,' who obtained a grant of 500 acres in Georgia from the trustees in September 1775 is difficult to determine. Lieutenant Hugh Mackay held a military commission and became an officer in the regiment Oglethorpe was authorized to raise in Britain for the defence of Georgia and which arrived in the colony in 1738. He presumably was related to Mackay tacksmen and gentry in Ross-shire and Sutherland and was able to work with them to recruit colonists there. Patrick 'McKay of Cyderhall', 'gentleman in Sutherland,' also received 500 acres in Georgia in September 1735. Among those from the Great Glen west of Inverness who were given land grants were John Mohr Mackintosh, nephew of William Mackintosh of Borlum, a prominent Jacobite general in the 1715 Jacobite rebellion. A number of MacGillivrays, Mackintoshs and other clansmen taken at the siege of Preston by the British army in 1715 had been transported from Liverpool to Charleston and it appears that Inverness merchants were able to recruit colonists and indentured servants for Georgia from the area occupied by the Clan Chattan confederation, of which these clans were members, because there had been contact between Charleston and Inverness after the arrival in America of those transported to Charleston in 1716.

The Georgia trustees received offers from Scotland to recruit further colonists, including one from Daniel McLachlan (or MacLauchlan), who proposed that the trustees commission him to organize the recruitment of more Highlanders with the promise that 'we should have in a very few years as many trussed up Plaids in Georgia as in the Highlands of Scotland'.[111] McLachlan had received a call to become minister of Ardnamurchan in Argyll in May 1733. After being inducted into the parish in September 1734 he applied for leave of absence to go to Edinburgh but went to London, where he published *An Essay upon Improving and Adding to the Strength of Great Britain and Ireland by Fornication*.[112] It was reported to the synod of Glenelg on 2 August 1737 that McLachlan had recanted 'all the prophane passages of his stupid and wicked book', and 'was to have himself transported with a parcel of McLachlans to Georgia, tho' the Trustees of that colony had not allowed or counte nanced Mr McLachlan's going there with them.' According to another source, Mclachlan emigrated to Jamaica instead. Not everyone who departed for Georgia was a volunteer. The synod of Ross of the Church of Scotland recorded testimony in their minutes in 1740 that related to charges of drunkenness and immorality brought against the minister Donald Fraser, including that he had made threats to Marjorie and Christian McCadie that he would have them transported to Georgia if they repudiated his sexual advances.[113]

The Scottish Highland colony at 'Darien' or 'New Inverness' essentially succumbed to the pressures of war, although the parish eventually established in its environs was called 'Saint Andrew', after the name of the fort the Highlanders had erected nearby. War had come to Georgia as part of wider conflict between Britain and Spain in 1739, and in Georgia Oglethorpe organized an attack on the Spanish garrison at Saint Augustine. By that time the regiment Oglethorpe had been authorized to raise in Britain for the defence of Georgia (the 42nd Foot) had arrived there and was camped near Darien. In 1740 Oglethorpe recruited Highlanders from Darien to accompany him on his expedition to St Augustine, which failed after a skirmish in which most of the Highlanders were killed or captured.[114] The end of the war in 1748 was followed by the disbandment of Oglethorpe's regiment, which had provided a market for farm produce raised by those still living at Darien, and this meant the end of Georgia as a colony managed by Parliamentary trustees.[115] The fame of the Darien colonists arose from a remarkable petition against the introduction of slavery in Georgia drawn up in their name in January 1738 (old style), just before the Stono slave rebellion in South Carolina which caused such fear in southern mainland British colonies. David Brion Davis has written that who wrote it, 'by combining the ideal of natural rights with Biblical and ... philosophism, ... struck a chord that would reverberate the anti-slavery movements and culminate in Lincoln's Second Inaugural Address.'[116] The [...] statement that it was not to adopt slavery in Georgia that aroused such admiration and others included the statement that it was 'shocking nature, that any Race of Mankind and their Posterity should be to perpetual Slavery,' and that 'it is freedom and that to an degree us, what a Scene of Horror must it bring about!'[117] It has that the text displayed familiarity with the work of various philosophers such as Francis Hutcheson, who had suggested 'that absolute bondage might be contrary to the general promote human happiness.'[118]

The fact that it had been arranged for a Presbyterian clergyman to accompany the colonists to Georgia indicated that the influence of the Church of Scotland was significant in the settlement, but that minister (John Macleod) denounced the petition and left Darien to become a Presbyterian minister in slave-holding South Carolina at Edisto Island. Oglethorpe himself owned slaves in South Carolina, although opposing its introduction in Georgia, and he was Deputy Governor of the Royal African Company. Yet, late in life he would write to Granville Sharp (in 1776) 'that slavery was contrary to the Gospel as well as to the fundamental law of England.'[119] On the other hand, it has been established that in 1755 one of the signatories of the Darien anti-slavery petition, 'John Mackintosh-Bain', applied for an additional land grant under 'headright' on the basis that in addition to his wife and four children, he had in his household 'three White Servants and eight Negroes ....'[120]

Whatever the reasons for the inclusion of the eloquent moral denunciation of slavery in the petition, it did influence another remarkable statement against slavery by the residents of St Andrews Parish, led by Lachlan McIntosh, son of the leading signatory of the 1738 petition and a slave-owner. Passed by a 'congress' held at Darien in support of the 'manly conduct of the loyal and brave people of Boston and Massachusetts Bay, to preserve their liberty', it also stated that 'to show the world that we are not influenced by any contracted or interested motives, but a general philanthropy for all mankind, ... we hereby declare our disapprobation and abhorrence of the unnatural practice of Slavery in America ....' Slavery was declared to be 'a practice founded in injustice and cruelty, and highly dangerous to our liberties (as well as lives)' and that it was 'debasing part of our fellow creatures below men, and corrupting the virtue and morals of the rest.'[121] Was the text intended to be read by, or read to, slaves as well as the citizens of Darien? In 1774 there had been a serious slave rebellion in St Andrews Parish. A group of fewer than a dozen slaves on the plantation of 'Captain Morris' killed their overseer, his wife and a boy, as well as wounding a carpenter on the plantion. They then wounded the owner of a neighbouring plantation, Angus M'Intosh, and attacked the house of Roderick M'Leod, killing his son. Two of the ringleaders were condemned to be burned alive once the rebellion had been put down. Was the text composed to prevent slaves from joining free black Loyalist military units, such as those already being formed by Governor Dunmore in Virginia, as well as to answer the charges of hypocrisy levelled at Georgia 'Patriots' by Loyalist colonists?[122] One point is certain. Lachlan McIntosh did not free his slaves and nor did any of the other members of the Darien 'congress'. By 1775 there were 18,000 slaves in Georgia, and no matter what McIntosh thought about slavery as an abstract concept, he was not willing to attack the wealthy slave-owning planters who dominated Georgia politics.

Another early settlement of Highlanders was established in the Cape Fear River Valley of North Carolina in 1739, just after the settlement in Georgia and the attempted settlement in New York led by Lachlan Campbell. In 1729 Archibald Campbell, one of the factors on the Duke of Argyll's estate in south-west Scotland, wrote 'that several persons in Kintyre in imitation of there neighbours in Irland show a great Inclination to go to new England to settle there.' The Irish example of emigration to America which began in the late seventeenth century was well known in that part of Argyll adjacent to the centre of the emigrant trade in the north-east Irish ports of Belfast and Larne. Just as Lachlan Campbell of Islay was looking for lands to colonize in America and chose the New York frontier, so those who organized the emigration from Argyll to North Carolina were owners of small estates, like Neill MacNiell of Ardelay or his associate Duncan Campbell of Kilduskland near Lochgilphead. Their reasons were no doubt the same as Lachlan Campbell's, and a substantial number of the people they brought with them came from Islay. Small landholders were being squeezed by the big estates, particularly if they were tacksmen, but even those who owned a small estate might consider selling out to larger landowners and looking for new lands to purchase on more advantageous terms in North America or the West Indies. Campbell of Kilduskland had sold his estate in the 1720s and gone to Jamaica, but returned to Scotland to participate in a new venture to take up land in the Cape Fear Valley.[123]

The governor of North Carolina by the time they arrived in 1739 was a Scot, Gabriel Johnston. Johnston had nothing to do with the Highlands but he was keen to encourage settlement in the hitherto underdeveloped Cape Fear River Valley in North Carolina that bordered on the boundary with South Carolina. This lack of development was partly because before the smallpox epidemic of the 1720s the Cherokee posed a significant threat to anyone settling too far upriver and partly because Cape Fear (often rendered 'Cape Fair' in Scotland by those recruiting colonists) had acquired that name as a result of the hazardous weather conditions prevalent at the mouth of the river. Johnston was to play an important role in the development of the port of Wilmington, named after the political patron in England who had been responsible for his appointment, at a more sheltered location further up the river than the first port established in the area at Brunswick.[124] In 1740 Johnston was able to persuade the North Carolina assembly to grant a ten-year exemption from taxation for the Scots, and the governor and his council made land grants of 14,479 acres to 22 men, the largest award of 2643 acres being given to Duncan Campbell of Kilduskland. Most of the approximately 90 families who made up the majority of the group did not receive land grants initially, but arrived as indentured servants bound for a period of service to those who held their indenture (usually three to seven years), which enabled those who brought servants with them to claim additional land under 'headright'.[125]

The settlement remained small in scale, but there appear to have been subsequent migrations to the Cape Fear Valley in 1742, as there is a reference to planned emigrations by 'a great many more highlanders from Argyle' in the journal of the Society in Scotland for the Propagation of Christian Knowledge (SSPCK) in January 1742, by which time Duncan Campbell of Kilduskland was back in Scotland.[126] It is certain that the scale of settlement remained small at this time. The recruitment of additional indentured servants in Argyll in 1754 for the Cape Fear Valley settlement can be documented from a number of sources. It is clear that about this time the wealthiest leader of the 1739 migration, Campbell of Kilduskland, had arranged to sell his lands in North Carolina and that the recruitment of additional indentured servants in Scotland was related to this. A ship engaged in the Jamaica trade with the Campbell of Black River family in St Elizabeth's parish there was used. A list of servants who had accepted indentures was submitted to the Sheriff Court in Argyll in an attempt by the landowner concerned, Campbell of Jura, to prevent the emigration. As several of the men listed in this document were recorded in the Cumberland County North Carolina tax list of 1755, it is clear that this particular emigration did take place, but it also demonstrates the very small scale of settlement in these initial emigrations from Argyll to both Jamaica and North Carolina, just as the number of emigrants recruited from the northern Highlands for Georgia was several hundred rather than several thousand. The significance of these emigrations was not in their immediate demographic impact, but in the initial points of settlement they established, which attracted much larger numbers of emigrants from Scotland after the end of the Seven Years War with France in 1763.[127]

It is telling that the Scottish colony in East Jersey established at the end of the seventeenth century developed so differently after 1725 in comparison with those settlements established on the New York, Carolina and Georgia frontiers during the same period. Indeed, it became a source of settlers migrating overland to the south-eastern American frontier that opened up so comprehensively after the victory in the Seven Years War. New immigrants were coming to north-eastern New Jersey during this period from the north of Ireland, but also from the south-western Lowlands of Scotland, the region in which the commercialization of agriculture and expansion of mercantile activity increased most in the middle of the eighteenth century. Once New Jersey became a royal colony, its location in the region between the two most rapidly growing ports and cities of North America – New York and Philadelphia – encouraged rapid expansion of both population and commerce as the frontier of settlement moved west. This meant that ethnicity was less of a factor as individual immigrants and families assimilated and intermarried among the existing population. Those most easily identified accumulated wealth, and with it elite social status. They owned land, but they were engaged primarily in commerce, including land speculation. They relied on ethnic and family ties in business activities and retained little of the feudal conceptions of land ownership and tenancy that had characterized the early settlement. When popular disturbances and riots broke out on larger estates in opposition to rising rents, it was families of Scottish descent such as that of James Alexander who led the defence of proprietorial authority. Those families with significant economic and political influence in eighteenth-century New Jersey, particularly the larger landowners, often traced their descent partly or wholly from the Scottish settlers who had arrived in the seventeenth century. By the third generation, however, most of these families were identified less with Scottish ethnicity than with their elite status.[128]

Expansion of American settlement after 1754

It may be that the 'persistent localism' TH Breen defined as a founding characteristic of early English settlement provides a useful model for understanding the pattern of settlement in the Carolinas and Georgia when settlement in that region began to expand in the 1730s and 1740s.[129] That changed after British victory in the Seven Years War and the removal of most French support for native American resistance to the expansion of 'British' settlement westward from the traditional centres of colonial population on the coast. In both northern and western New York and the south-eastern North American mainland, lands that had previously been contested were opened up for settlement, although this very development would lead to tensions within this newly expanded British North American empire. After 1763 the rush to invest in frontier lands led speculators to look for settlers wherever they could find them and this led to substantial increases in emigration from Scotland as well as other parts of Britain and Ireland during this period. Some Scottish immigrants, particularly Highlanders, moved to take up lands that become available for settlement only after 1763, while others in the Middle Colonies in particular entered a more highly developed economic and social environment that presented them with much more complex challenges of assimilation and adaptation. Scots generally during this period became associated with loyalty to British authority in a society in which other groups were increasingly coming to challenge it, and this would have a major impact on the very different experiences of immigration of individual families and groups who left Scotland for America between 1763 and 1776.[130]

The foundation of the quantitative analysis on which Bernard Bailyn erected his narrative of British emigration to North America between the end of the Seven Years War and the outbreak of the American Revolution was a register of emigrants compiled by British Customs officers in 1774 and 1775 on the instructions of a British government heavily lobbied to take action by Scottish landowners and politicians.[131] The data is British but the register itself arose out of Scottish anxieties. If British society after 1763 was not in crisis, it certainly was in acute transition. The emigration of large groups of Highlanders in Scotland led by their tacksmen for destinations in North America was presented by the Lord Advocate of Scotland, Henry Dundas, as threatening to empty the country of the very population who had provided the manpower to win the North American war of 1754–61 with the French. A similar concern among landowners in Scotland was that the cheap labour they needed to 'improve' their estates commercially would be allowed to emigrate to North America and lead to higher labour costs in a country where wages had always been low, when they were paid at all.[132]

Although there was widespread emigration of families from an agricultural background in the north of Ireland and the north of England as well as Scotland, it is clear that the issue of agrarian change was most acute in Scotland. and that there, in a society in which the peasant population had become accustomed to mobility, it was easier to recruit emigrants in numbers for settlement in America than elsewhere in

Britain and Ireland. Jonas and Thomas Brown of Whitby in Yorkshire attempted to take up a land grant on the Georgia frontier on advantageous terms by recruiting the emigrants they needed to meet the requirements of the colony to establish settlements. Whether enlisting indentured servants or free emigrants, they were more successful in Orkney and Caithness than in Yorkshire. When the Browns' associate William Manson tried to recruit indentured servants to enable him to take up a land grant in his own right in Georgia, initially he focused his recruiting efforts on Newcastle, where he had more success in attracting discontented and distressed artisans willing to enter into emigration than agricultural labourers. For the latter he turned to Scotland.[133]

At the core of the Scottish reaction to the post-war emigration frenzy was a sense of both anxiety and elation at the challenges, dangers and possibilities opened up by British victory in America and the Peace of Paris in 1763. Archibald Menzies published a pamphlet/broadside in 1763 which advocated expanding settlement in North America following the peace.[134] Menzies was from a family of Perthshire Jacobite gentry, and was appointed as General Inspector of the Annexed Estates in Scotland in 1764, partly as a result of the attention attracted by his pamphlet. During his tenure of the inspectorship, Menzies referred to virtually all of the tenantry he encountered on the estates confiscated by the British government in punishment for their owners' participation in the 1745 Jacobite rebellion as 'ignorant, awkward and lazy', although he did also note that labour was becoming scarce on the estates because of emigration, whether overseas or to the Lowlands.[135] In contrast his pamphlet suggested that, on the basis of what he had seen when travelling to the eastern Mediterranean as part of the Grand Tour, the population there would form the perfect recruiting ground to populate new lands in Florida.[136] The implication was that this would avoid loss of population in Scotland. Other members of the Scottish landed class were also associating North American colonization with the 'improvement' of the Scottish Highlands after the end of the war with France. John Swinton, Sheriff-Depute of Perthshire, in making his case (successfully) to be made a Commissioner of the Annexed Estates, wrote that rather than allowing population from the Scottish Highlands to emigrate to 'Canada' more should be done to employ them in their own country: 'I mean there is really a Canada at home si sua bona NORUNT.'[137]

Another East Florida Society member, Sir Archibald Grant of Monymusk in Aberdeenshire, however, wrote to his kinsman Sir Alexander

Grant in London about the potential he could see in Florida land grants: 'Since ever I could read on these subjects, I have been convinced, and am daily more and more confirmed in opinion, that America will at a periode, I don't presume to say when, be the grand seat of Empire and all its concomitants.' Grant thought that Highlanders were the very stuff of colonization overseas (echoing Sir William Alexander): 'people ambitious, avaricious, or some how uneasy or whimsical' who in numbers 'ramble to army, or somewhere abroad', could provide the population required for expanding British overseas colonization. He was wrong about Florida, but not about the importance of emigration from the Scottish Highlands to the future of British North America.[138] However Richard Oswald, who did acquire land in Florida in partnership with one of Grant's London relations, was less sanguine about Scots Highlanders as a source of emigrants by 1767, writing that it was very difficult to obtain indentured servants in Scotland as 'the People have all employmt, & are not so fond of going abroad as formerly'. He invested in slaves for his Florida plantations.[139]

Slavery may have made economic sense in East Florida, but not to the frontier lands in North America previously contested with the French and their Native American allies. In North Carolina, with the end of the Cherokee war, those who obtained land grants in the region were able to attract substantial numbers of emigrants from the Scottish Highlands, just as happened in New York in the Mohawk Valley and around Lake George. It appears clear that this success in attracting emigrants from Scotland to both areas was partly driven by the personal experience of Scottish soldiers who had served there during the Seven Years War and had either returned to Scotland and given personal testimony regarding the desirability of these lands or written to friends and acquaintances in Scotland in glowing terms about them. One example of this is a letter preserved in the Robertson of Kindeace Papers in the National Archives of Scotland, from Kenneth McLeod, a soldier in Captain Robertson's company of Montgomery's 77th Regiment and dated 23 April 1760. McLeod wrote to James Fraser, the minister of Alness, while his company remained in New York waiting for Montgomery and his Carolina detachment to return from their expedition against the 'Gerieckes' [Cherokees]. The letter may well have been dictated by McLeod, for it is formally written in a very legible hand with the exception of an annotation at the bottom of one page adding that 'if my Friends pleases to Write me and send the Letter so I will not pay any thing for it – .' On the inner folds of the paper used to make an envelope for the letter are lines extolling the virtues of living in America: 'this is a good Country to live in the Country people are all free holders The few that pays Small Rent is but a trifal they Live Independent of their Liards and all men here are alike.'[140]

On the face of it this seems to be a text recording the words of a soldier in the ranks of Montgomery's regiment about landholding in New York, but the last line of the text quoted above adds; 'I have [crossed out] My master done Captains Duty Last year and am appointed the Same this year but No more pay than a Lieutenant's and the oldest In the Reidgment'. As the letter records that 'I am with a good master Lieut Robertson of our own Country' and is preserved in a box of correspondence relating to the Robertson of Kindeace family of Ross-shire, there is a strong possibility that McLeod's officer wrote the letter. How much of the text records McLeod's actual message and how much is it a text written by Robertson that somehow represents what McLeod wished included in the letter? Yet, however problematic the letter as a text in terms of authorship, its message is very clear: 'I recommend to you to Come to this Country'. Is this McLeod calling his people from feudal bondage in Scotland to a New World or is Robertson (and perhaps McLeod as well) thinking of developing the land in America promised to soldiers under the King's bounty as a reward for their service in America? After all, this was land that would need settlers to realize its value.[141]

Similar issues relate to some well-known sources relating to emigration from the Scottish Highlands to the Cape Fear Valley of North Carolina. Alexander McAllister wrote from Cape Fear to his 'Cusin', Angus McCuaig in Argyll on 29 November 1770 that 'if you cam hear if god Speres you' he could leave to each of his children 'apice of land which is mor than they can expect Where they are this is the best poor mans country I have heard in this age.'[142] There is a contrast in this text with the letter McAllister wrote to his brother Hector about the same time, reproaching him for being 'a great hindrance to many a poor man in your pretending always to Com & never come as you have ben in this Country & must know more about it than those that is Strengers to the ways of it.' However if Hector did intend to return and take up 'Troy', the plantation he owned on Cape Fear, 'if you find your Self in a capacity of purchasing a few Sleves [slaves] it would be more to yr advantage than Servents if not Servents is when one can do no better wher there is Sleves [slaves] one Carful hand would be very nesicry [necessary].'[143] Although McAllister uses the language of justice for the poor and the opportunities that awaited them in North Carolina, writing to James McAllister in Argyll about a year later that 'I don't

Dout but the land holders will put ther one [own] Constructisions on ther letters but let them construe as they will if ther will prissit [persist] in the augmenting ther rents I belive in a few years som of ther land may ly weast [waste].'[144] In his letter to his brother McAllister writes, as Oswald did of East Florida, as a plantation owner concerned about the supply and cost of the labour necessary to work his plantation.

Highland emigrants in New York also became associated with Loyalism, although this was not always the case. John Strachan, who arrived in New York from Paisley in 1774 at the age of 16, became a private in Captain Zealy's company of Colonel Klock's Second Battalion of Militia in the Palatine District of Tryon County, and Thomas McClumpha, from Galloway, served in Colonel Fischer's Third Tryon County Regiment from the Mohawk District.[145] Neither of these men were Highlanders, however, and in New York and Pennsylvania even more than North Carolina, Scottish Highlanders became associated with loyalty to the authority of the Crown on the eve of and during the American Revolution. As the northern New York frontier lands around Crown Point became the epicentre of the war between the British and the French in North America during the 1750s, so it became a priority for settlement after the end of the war in 1763 and the object of the royal proclamation of October 1763 promising land grants on the New York frontier to British veterans of that war. Many of the survivors of Montgomery's 77th Regiment of Foot, decimated at the siege of Havana in 1762, knew the region as fertile and open for settlement, and it became known for Scottish settlement, although by no means all settlers were Scots.[146]

Glengarry and Scottish Canada

The Scottish settlement in America about which we know most was that which originated in the central Highlands of Scotland and was established on lands owned by Sir William Johnson in the Mohawk River Valley, perhaps because some of those who organized emigration there had served in the region with the British army during the war with the French on the New York frontier. This was an emigration that was typical of those from the Scottish Highlands in that it was led by tacksmen, but unusual in that most of the emigrants were Roman Catholics and very many of them bore the surname Macdonell. Many were from the Glengarry estate and the others from lands adjacent to it. In a highly organized migration, 125 men, 100 women and at least 200 children sailed from Fort William in 1773. Although the area from which they had been recruited was solidly Jacobite, the reasons for their emigration were economic, as the owners of their lands commercialized their estates and sought to introduce new industries such as fishing and textile manufactures. The leaders of the emigration sought to continue to hold land on more traditional terms, and this may also have been why they gravitated to renting lands from Johnson by early 1774. Whether they thought that they would continue to rent lands indefinitely on Johnson's huge estates is not clear. Johnson's extraordinary mock baronial empire had developed after 1763 on the strength of his influence over the Iroquois nation as Superintendent for Indian Affairs in the Northern Department.[147] After his death in 1774, the Iroquois became associated with the political Loyalism of Johnson's son, Sir John. They left to join the British garrison in Canada in 1775, Sir John and most of the men among the Mohawk and Delaware Valley Highlanders followed in 1776. Their numbers were not large, but together with the Iroquois, the garrison in Canada and other New York Loyalists, they played a major role in the brutal frontier war that broke out in the region, punctuated by the unsuccessful invasion of New York by a British army led by General John Burgoyne. The result was that, even more than for Highland emigrants in the American South, there was no way back for Highland Loyalists from New York when it became part of the independent United States.

American works on Scottish emigration to America take as their point of completion the beginning or end of the American Revolution, whereas those written from a Scottish, British or Canadian perspective do not.[148] In part this is because a British North America came into existence in 1763 which survived in a very different form after the independence of the United States in 1783. The idea of the American Revolution is predicated against the idea of any continuity in 'American' history from the colonial period to the 'early national' or 'federal' period of American History, whereas the idea of British North America, not least because of the substantial legacy of the migration there in numbers of Loyalists from what became the United States after 1783, embodies continuity. Politically, there was no 'British North America' of course. There was the creation of an 'Upper Canada' populated by those, like the Iroquois and New York Highlanders, who had remained loyal to Britain, joining the predominantly French-speaking and Roman Catholic population of 'Lower Canada', who had demonstrated no desire to pledge loyalty to the Continental Congress. There were also four colonies that remained British after 1783 in North America: Newfoundland, Nova Scotia, New Brunswick and the Island of St John (later to be named Prince Edward Island). Nova Scotia and St John attracted significant numbers of Scottish emigrants after 1763 to what was for them sparsely settled colonies. They also, defended by a formidable garrison and naval base at Halifax, Nova Scotia, received an influx of Loyalist settlers from former British North American colonies after 1783, including slaves freed by the British as part of their southern campaigns in Georgia, the Carolinas and Virginia.

The small Scottish settlements established on St John and on the Nova Scotian mainland opposite in the 1770s would lead to significant additional 'chain migration' there from Scotland after 1783, expanding with the development of a successful timber trade between the maritime provinces and Britain that presented merchants with the opportunity of returning their ships from Britain, most frequently Scotland, with a paying cargo of emigrants rather than ballast only. In the nineteenth century, these settlements became the arena through which the Earl of Selkirk was drawn into the project of populating a significant area of Canada with Scottish Highland emigrants between 1803 and its tragic denouement at Red River in Western Canada in 1816. They also became part of the foundation myth of Confederation Canada, as significant numbers of emigrants from the Scottish Highlands continued to arrive in the maritime provinces in the early nineteenth century prior to confederation, strengthening the idea of a British Canada identifiable through continuous recruitment of immigrants from Scotland.[149]

This became possible because, in addition to the maritime Canadian connection with Scotland, the New York Scottish Highland migrants to Upper Canada during the American Revolution and its aftermath established 'a new Glengarry' at what became Glengarry County on the eastern border of Upper Canada, adjacent to the French-speaking but fellow Roman Catholic population of Lower Canada. It offered land to the Scottish Highland peasant population of Glengarry and other parts of the central Highlands of Scotland who were denied it by the revolutionary changes in estate management occurring there through the unrelenting commercialization of agriculture. This emigration continued into the nineteenth century, but 'most emigrated in the 17 years from 1785 to 1802 in at least seven large parties of emigrants leaving Scotland as a group with the intention of joining their fellow Highlanders and kin in Glengarry County'.[150] It involved thousands of people (about 3000) at a time when settlers were scarce in 'Upper' Canada. Governor Simcoe argued in 1792 that 'emigrations of hardy, industrious and virtuous men may be reasonably expected from the

Northern parts of Great Britain ... a great body of emigrants should be collected ... so as to become the very transcript and image of the British people ....'[151]

Different destinations

The great surge in Scottish emigration to North America between 1763 and 1775, and the controversy over what it represented, was seen 'as new, different, and extremely frightening.'[152] Emigration to North America became part of a radical critique of what Scotland was becoming that was obvious not just to Scottish ministers such as William Thom and John Witherspoon, who lamented the decline of spiritual purpose they associated with the Scottish Presbyterian tradition every bit as much as Cotton Mather and his fellow ministers in Puritan New England had lamented a similar decline there at the beginning of the century. The commerce and culture of the Enlightenment in Scotland were seen as the dynamic that would transform the country into a crucible of modernization, although for visitors such as Benjamin Franklin it was clear who would pay the price, and equally clear that emigration to America offered an alternative. His assessment of the achievements of the Scottish Enlightenment in its own country was far from positive. 'Had I never been in the American Colonies,' he wrote, 'but was to form my Judgement of Civil Society by what I have lately seen, I should never advise a Nation of Savages to admit of Civilisation: For I assure you, that in the Possession and Enjoyment of the various comforts of Life, compar'd to these People every Indian is a Gentleman.'[153]

The nature of Scottish emigration to America changed after the United States established its independence. Thereafter British emigrants to America had a choice; to emigrate to what remained of British North America or to reject everything that was British by choosing the United States.[154] One left Britain but continued to be British in Canada, and continued to be loyal to the Crown.[155] By contrast, emigration to the United States was to an extent a political act. No doubt this was not the case for every last emigrant to the US, but Charles Nisbet, a Presbyterian minister soon to emigrate there himself, wrote to John Witherspoon in 1784 in terms that presented emigration in such light, particularly as the British government took steps to try to discourage it.[156] Witherspoon had come to London to try to raise money for Princeton College in New Jersey, whose library had been destroyed by the British army in 1777. Nisbet wrote asking Witherspoon to try to persuade London merchants to send ships to Scotland to take on emigrants who could not pay their passage, but were willing to sign on as indentured servants for sale in America. 'Many hundreds, I might say many thousands on this coast would willingly emigrate to America,' Nisbet wrote, 'could they find any opportunity of getting a passage. But the avarice of the Glasgow merchants, and the terrors thrown out by the Crown lawyers in the Gazette, have deterred shipmasters from indenting poor people.'[157] It is true that Nisbet identified 'the deadness of trade and manufactures and the rise of rents and public burdens' as the reason for so much interest in emigration. Yet economic depression in Britain was presented as a political issue related to what had been contested during the American War. 'You may be surprised at my anxiety on this head, but I was known and persecuted as a friend of America during the war,' Nisbet wrote, and 'it was presumed at the peace that I had a correspondence with that country, and might be useful in recommending emigrants.' Nisbet did know that some ships were going from Aberdeen, 'but their terms are high and they go to Nova Scotia, a country unpopular among intended emigrants, who have a sort of notion of freedom, and are not ambitious of enjoying any more of the blessings of his Majesty's Government.' He wrote to Witherspoon that 'people of fashion' still insisted 'that America Might easily have been conquered' but he emphasized that popular opinion was of a very different order; 'the case is otherwise with the common people, who rejoice in that liberty which they are sensible they want, and which they hope to share.'[158]

Emigration from Britain, in other words, and its intended destination, had become associated with liberty and the idea that it had a geographical location. Witherspoon had responded to criticism from Scotland regarding his promotion of emigration to America by suggesting as much in his *Address to the Natives of Scotland Residing in America*, published in Philadelphia in 1776. He wrote that 'for a man to be a friend to his country' it was better to be concerned with 'the people that inhabit it' rather than 'the stones and the earth' of his native soil. Was he an enemy of his country if he wished to promote the welfare of the majority of the population over the privileges of the nobility and gentry who claimed to lead the nation?[159] Nisbet wrote to Witherspoon in 1784 that 'if you can give any help to the poor, disconsolate natives of this country, by giving them hopes of a passage to America on reasonable terms, I should be glad to hear from you,' as it was 'more necessary for the friends of mankind and of America to contrive some method for saving from starvation a great number of poor people in this eastern coast who are not able to transport themselves to Glasgow, tho' they were to get their passage free.'[160] Thus the issue of emigration from Scotland acquired a political context that would continue up to the aftermath of the American Civil War.

Preventing emigration

The revival of the emigration issue in Scotland after the American Revolution was demonstrated by the extraordinary report from the Collector of Customs at Campbeltown to the Commissioners of the Customs in Scotland regarding the arrival of an American ship, the *General Washington*, at the island of Colonsay in September 1791. The vessel had come to take 105 adults and 125 children to Wilmington, North Carolina, and the report emphasized government determination to ensure that no 'tools or utensils used in the woollen & Silk or made us of in the Iron & Steel Manufactures' were being exported with the emigrants and that no 'seducing of Artificers or Workmen imployed in those Manufactures to go into parts beyond the Seas' was to occur. The bewildered customs officer who had been ordered to Colonsay to inspect the vessel reported that the emigrants were 'poor labouring people that have been deprived of their Farms by their Landlords,' indicating that McNeill of Colonsay and neighbouring lairds had concluded that they should encourage the exportation of what was soon to be identified as 'a redundant population.' In 1803, in contrast, at the nearby island of Gigha, another McNeill laird wrote to the Lord President of the Court of Session that emigration to the United States should be made illegal and any men involved impressed into the navy.[161]

In 1791 David Dale, the former weaver who had opened what became the famous cotton manufactory at the falls of the river Clyde at New Lanark, attracted favourable publicity in the *Caledonian Mercury* for offering work in his textile manufactories to Highland emigrants from Skye whose ship had been driven in to Greenock through storm damage. The editorial praised Dale as 'a patriot who had saved them to their country' who desired 'to form them to habits of industry.' Yet the newspaper had to acknowledge that of the 400 emigrants only a quarter had accepted Dale's offer of employment, although it claimed that these were 'all, who were not indented.'[162] The account, published at a time of considerable political unrest in Scotland, concluded with a denunciation of the United States and a warning to those who might think of going there, as only the 'danger of the scalping-knife, or still more Barbarous cruelties' awaited them there.[163]

A year later, the same ship, the *Fortune*, of Greenock, was boarded by Malcolm Campbell the Customs Landwaiter at Bowmore in Islay, who reported 169 men, 112 women and 136 children were on board the vessel, and that they came from the islands of Coll, Islay, Jura, Luing (near Oban) and 'Wabdale' (Knapdale?). He wrote that 'the reasons they gave me for their Emigrating from their Native Country' were 'Poverty & oppression of Landlords and encouraging Letters from their Friends that is settled in the Country some time ago.'[164] Most landowners in Scotland were still in favour of retaining population. The Highland Society of Scotland compiled reports in 1802 on the abuses suffered by ignorant and unfortunate immigrants, which included an account of the misfortunes of the passengers of 'an Emigrant Ship that took on board Pasengers at Skye for Carolina in 1791.' It is clear that the ship was the *Fortune* of Greenock. The argument of the Highland Society was that conditions were so bad on emigrant ships that the government had to take action to protect those who might be tempted aboard them. Such was the 'disease, and filth' on this emigrant vessel that many children died, and the 'unfortunate people' who had taken passage on it 'completely cured of their passion for America', finding instead 'an asylum in the benevolence of Mr. David Dale who employed them in his extensive cotton manufactory in the vicinity of Glasgow.'[165]

The emigration issue drew attention in 1802 because a brief peace with Napoleonic France had meant that several large parties of emigrants had been able to leave the Scottish Highlands. The Highland Society of Scotland's reports were intended to promote government intervention. Henry Dundas, an opponent of emigration since the American Revolution, organized the parliamentary lobby that led to the first government legislation attempting to regulate the emigrant trade in the form of the Passenger Act of 1803.[166] This was passed, evidently without debate, by a parliament preoccupied with the threat of renewed war with France and reflected the perceived need to retain the population of the Highlands as a 'nursery' for the military. Related measures were to be funded by the government to strengthen the economy of the Highlands, notably the construction of the Caledonian Canal. The effect of the act was to raise the price of a passage to North America from under £5 in 1802 to more than £10.[167] The Highland Society had argued that the slave trade was better regulated than the Highland emigrant trade, which may have been a reason why William Wilberforce was made a member of the Select Committee on Emigration appointed by the House of Commons to consider legislation.[168] The intention was to make emigration more expensive, as well as to impose minimum standards for the health and safety of emigrants, but it also was intended to give British merchants carrying emigrants to British North America an advantage over vessels from the United States, who were required to allocate double the space per emigrant on their ships to that on British registered ships.[169]

There is only one recorded instance of the act being enforced, but it would have had an intimidating effect on people considering emigration.[170] It did not end emigration from Scotland, but was the last attempt to retain population in Scotland by a landed elite who would within decades conclude that emigration was a necessary option for displaced rural populations. The episode marked the beginning of the extraordinary career of the Earl of Selkirk as the advocate of Scottish Highland emigration to Canada as a means of avoiding the loss of emigrant population to the US. Selkirk organized his first emigration in 1802–1803, persuading a large group of emigrants from Skye to alter their choice of destination from North Carolina to Canada, although he had to take up lands on Prince Edward Island rather than Upper Canada partly because the government was reluctant to be seen as encouraging emigration.[171] In 1805 Selkirk published his influential *Observations on the Present State of the Highlands of Scotland, with a View of the Causes and probable Consequences of Emigration.* If the act didn't stop emigration, it did represent the end of the recruitment of emigrants by indenture by making it uneconomic for most merchants.[172] European 'unfree labour' was no longer of use in the agricultural economy of the United States or its infant manufactures. Scottish emigration to North America would develop in a very different way in the nineteenth century, but larger numbers of emigrants were drawn across the Atlantic because of the centuries of continued emigration from Scotland to America that had established it as their principal destination.

3

Sugar and Tobacco: 'Let Glasgow Flourish'

The Scottish West India trade

Trade with the West Indies had a major impact on the developing economy of Scotland in the eighteenth century. Some scholars have identified the Scots who went to the West Indies as indentured servants, soldiers, sailors, tradesmen, merchants, planters, doctors and administrators as a significant and distinctive element in the development of West Indian economic, social and political history.[173] Of course, the term 'West Indies' is the creation of British imperial discourse, denominating an area of trade. Recent work has preferred the regional term 'Caribbean'.[174] The British West Indies have been identified, in historical terms, as the British colonies in the region, separate and distinct from what some scholars have termed mainland 'British North America'. Yet it is clear that there were and are as many differences and distinctions among the peoples and places of the British West Indies as there are similarities. In the emerging 'Atlantic world' of early modern history the West Indies were 'the hub of empire', just as William Paterson had described Panama as 'the hub of the universe', occupying a sharply distinctive place between Europe and mainland North America that has not always been acknowledged in histories of either region.[175]

The Scots, like the Irish and Africans who were drawn into the region in the seventeenth century, helped make English possessions in the Caribbean in the seventeenth century British rather than English. Of course, the Scots and Irish who first came to the Caribbean in the seventeenth century were recruited as labourers once it became difficult if not impossible to persuade Englishmen to court almost certain death as indentured servants on the sugar plantations there. Having been drawn in as labour when sugar became so important to the region's economy in the second half of the seventeenth century, their role in the eighteenth century was sharply distinguished from that of the Africans who were brought into the region as slaves in ever greater numbers to work on the sugar plantations. By the nineteenth century, there was a black Britain in the Caribbean, almost forgotten in Britain itself once slavery was abolished in the British Empire and Britain was transformed by industrialization.

The first English colony to be established in the Caribbean was on the island of Barbados, initially with tobacco as its principal crop. Several prominent figures at the royal court in London sought to obtain charters from Charles I to give them authority to establish colonies in the Caribbean, and ultimately the Earl of Carlisle was successful.[176] Carlisle was one of the Scottish courtiers who had accompanied James VI from Scotland in 1603 when he accepted the throne of England as James I. Carlisle, then James Hay, almost immediately had himself naturalized as an Englishman in 1604, and returned to Scotland only on the two occasions upon which James VI and I visited his first kingdom. Of course Carlisle never went to Barbados, although his son would eventually secure substantial wealth through his father's charter. Those who did settle in Barbados were almost entirely English. When Civil War began in England it coincided with other conflicts associated with the Thirty Years War in Europe that disrupted the production of sugar in the Portuguese colonies on the South American mainland. With the considerable assistance of Dutch merchants, planters on Barbados shifted production from tobacco to sugar and benefited from a rising market. Their reward, despite establishing a right to participate in their government through a legislative assembly for the colonies, was the imposition of a series of Navigation Acts passed by the English Parliament (from 1651), intended to exclude the Dutch and anyone else (including the Scots) who might be inclined to try to benefit from trading in sugar with English planters.

Although other islands in what became known as the Leeward Islands, not far from Barbados, became English colonies at about the same time as Barbados (St Christopher/St Kitts, Nevis and Antigua), Barbados was unique in the rapidity with which the sugar trade developed there and the amount of wealth it generated. It became the first island to concentrate on the use of slaves brought from Africa as a labour force. For a time in the second half of the seventeenth century difficulties in recruiting indentured labour to Barbados from England led to an interest in taking Scottish and Irish servants as replacements, prompted by Cromwell's practice of sending captured Scottish and Irish prisoners there. Under the restored Stuart monarchy, merchants in Scotland and Ireland continued to seek cargoes of servants, including the 'thieves or robbers ... lusty beggars or gypsies' the Glasgow merchant William Gibson referred to when seeking a cargo of servants to take to Barbados and Carolina in the 1680s.[177] After the suspected involvement of Irish Catholic Jacobite indentured servants in a major slave rebellion on Barbados in 1692, the government there petitioned London to send Scottish indentured servants who were viewed as more reliable and as potential members of the island's militia. At the same time as the 'white' English population on Barbados was falling, the 'black' African population used as enslaved labour was becoming ever larger and, as demonstrated in 1692, ready to rebel if offered the prospect of success.[178] Scotland came to be seen as a source of emigrants to maintain 'white' population levels in Barbados.

Even before the end of the seventeenth century, the scale of the development of Barbados for sugar production meant that white labourers on the island became increasingly redundant.[179] Some did remain as smallholders or wage earners, providing a distinctive element in Barbadian society in comparison with other British Caribbean colonies. Increasing numbers left, however, migrating to other British colonies as they were established, including Jamaica (conquered from Spain in 1655), and contributing volunteers to oppose the French expeditions to the Leeward Islands from 1664–67. In 1670 the expedition sent from England by the proprietors of the new English mainland North American colony of Carolina stopped at Barbados to take on additional colonists because of the Barbadian interests of many of the original proprietors. The later Scottish colonists recruited to the Carolinas in 1684 were intended to reduce the influence of Barbadian interests in the colony.[180]

Darien formalized the Scottish presence in the West Indies. Why? Although the colony failed, its location had been chosen partly because Scots were already familiar with the Caribbean as opposed to alternatives in Africa and Asia. Scotland was already becoming an Atlantic nation. We know that in his early career William Paterson had travelled as a merchant to the West Indies and New England, although we do not have any detail of his experiences there.[181] New England, seemingly as distant from the West Indies as Scotland itself, nevertheless had established itself as a centre of English settlement in the western hemisphere in the seventeenth century largely because its crops and salted fish could be exported to Barbados and the Leeward Islands as the planters there concentrated on sugar production to the exclusion of crops that could be used for food. The English acquisition of Jamaica had strengthened this economic connection.[182] Although in theory excluded from trade with English plantations in America by the Navigation Acts, in practice Scottish contact with them increased over the course of the seventeenth century to the point that Scottish colonization in its own right had become accepted, in Scotland at least, as a realistic proposition.

When the two separate Scottish expeditions abandoned Darien, some vessels reached New York, choosing that port because New England was too distant and had fewer Scottish connections. More of the survivors went to (or could not get further than) Jamaica and Carolina. Those who remained in each colony reinforced the Scottish presence there and provided the basis for consolidating Scottish networks in the Caribbean once the parliamentary union with England legalized Scottish access to English colonies. After all, it had been the proclamation by the Governor of Jamaica that any assistance by residents of English colonies in America to the Scottish Darien expedition was illegal which led to the abandonment of New Caledonia by the first expedition. After it had capitulated to the Spaniards, the second expedition set sail for Jamaica, and many of its members remained there. Alexander Shields, the famous Presbyterian minister who accompanied the second expedition, survived the siege of Darien only to die in Jamaica, where his funeral expenses were paid by Scots already resident there.[183]

The *St Andrew* sailed to Jamaica with survivors from the first expedition, but by the time it reached the island so many men had been lost that the rest chose to remain on the island. One of their number was John Campbell, born in Inveraray in 1674, a former soldier who became the overseer of a plantation, later marrying a widow whose property included her own plantations in St Elizabeth's Parish in the west of Jamaica by the 'Scot's Cove' associated with the arrival of the *St Andrew*.[184] Campbell became a merchant as well as a planter, re-establishing contact with relations in Argyll by sending ships to the Clyde with cargoes of sugar. Although we do not know if these vessels returned to Jamaica with indentured servants from Argyll there is evidence that servants for Jamaica were being recruited in Argyll by 1740. We also know that relatives of Campbell went out to Jamaica as overseers and seamen both because Edward Long mentioned the substantial number of Campbells established in eighteenth-century Jamaica in his history of the island and because as late as 1754 a ship from 'Black River Jamaica' is recorded as taking indentured servants from the Isle of Jura to the Cape Fear Valley of North Carolina.[185] It was through connections with Campbell that the leaders of the 1738–39 emigration from Argyll to the Cape Fear Valley of North Carolina had identified Carolina as a destination and in subsequent years Campbells from Jamaica emigrated to mainland Carolina, just as some Loyalists after 1783 would leave the Carolinas to return to Jamaica.[186]

With negotiations for a parliamentary union underway after 1702 following the outbreak of war between England and both France and Spain, proposals that Scots be recruited to bolster the defence of English West Indian colonies were circulated even before the successful conclusion of negotiations for union. After all, the Darien expeditions had established that substantial numbers of Scots could be recruited to go there. In 1703 a proposal to recruit Scots at government expense to settle along the east coast of Jamaica was sent to the Privy Council in London.[187] The Governor of the Leeward Islands sent 'Lieutenant-Governor Walter Hamilton with some twenty vessels filled with troops from Antigua to St Kitts' in 1702 and forced the French forces there to surrender.[188] Previously divided between French and English authority, St Christopher's/St Kitt's was ceded to the British under the terms of the Treaty of Utrecht in 1713. Two Scots associated with the conquest of St Kitt's married into the plantocracy there, as John Campbell did in Jamaica, and as a result established direct links between St Kitts and Glasgow by going into trade.[189] As with most early Scottish involvement in West Indian society, details are obscure, partly because later generations enjoying landed property in Scotland were reluctant to acknowledge past Caribbean connections.[190] It appears that both men used their military rank in the St Kitts militia to support their status when they returned to Scotland as merchants, using wealth they had acquired through their Caribbean sugar plantations to capitalize their trade and to acquire land. James Milliken served as a member of the island council and later acted as business and legal agent for some of the island's absentee property-owners.[191] In about 1713 he married a widow from the neighbouring island of Nevis. He became associated with Colonel William McDowall when McDowall married Mrs Milliken's daughter by her previous marriage and acquired his wife's share of her grandmother's estate on Nevis. McDowall was a younger son of the McDowall of Garthland family in Wigtonshire.[192] Milliken's origins in Scotland are unknown, and it may be that they were invented when his son 'returned' to Glasgow to establish himself as a member of the merchant community there.

Milliken's son carried on his father's business. Like his father, he also became a member of the governing council for St Kitts. Both he and

McDowall expanded their landholdings on St Kitts and Nevis, providing the collateral which made it possible for them to enter trade. By about 1730 McDowall and Milliken had returned to Scotland, where McDowall obtained land in Renfrewshire.[193] They established James Milliken and Co. as a joint stock company, purchased one of the Glasgow sugar houses and became involved in shipping sugar to London as well as Glasgow. Members of the Milliken family continued to live in the Leeward Islands until the 1770s. In Scotland, James Milliken and Co. was wound up in the 1750s and its assets were transferred to a new company with partners from the family of Alexander Houston of Jordanhill, which was eventually renamed Houston and Co. The partners in the firm were involved in banking as well as the sugar trade, although some members of the Houston family purchased plantations in the West Indies and took up residence there.[194]

According to TM Devine's account of the Glasgow West India merchants, 'from c.1750 until 1815 about seventy-eight Glasgow merchants were members of firms which specialised in the importation of sugar, cotton and rum from the West Indies'.[195] Over that period they moved from participating in a trade which supplemented that of the burgeoning tobacco trade from the Clyde ports to providing connections and forming links which enabled Glasgow merchants to adjust to the impact of American independence on the tobacco trade. There was considerable continuity of participation in the tobacco and the 'West India' trades in the eighteenth century. The latter received less attention in Scotland because it was less specialized and involved fewer merchants, and because by the end of the eighteenth century increasing industrialization lowered the public profile of the colonial merchants in Glasgow as wealth began to be generated from manufacturing in Scotland itself rather than from trade in colonial goods.[196] In one sense the West Indian trade in Scotland differed essentially from its more famous trade in tobacco. The sugar and cotton which West Indian merchants brought to Scotland were not sold on to European merchants under the terms of the Navigation Acts, which after 1707 applied to Scotland as well as England and required that all colonial goods to be landed at British ports even if their ultimate market was continental Europe. Sugar was a commodity for the British domestic market, and while consumption was certainly increasing dramatically in Scotland by the end of the eighteenth century, Glasgow merchants would be supplying markets in England and Ireland as well.[197] It was also the Scottish West India merchants who brought cotton to the Clyde from Jamaica. Devine has argued that 'until c.1800 most raw cotton manufactured in Scottish mills was grown in the Caribbean islands, and imports of raw cotton rose from 627,648 lbs valued at £32,059 in 1785 to 2,254,932 lbs valued at £112,745 in 1800'.[198] During the same period the amount of sugar imported into Scotland increased by about 80 per cent.[199] Tobacco was an early modern colonial trade with limited but significant impact on a modernizing economy, in Scotland most noticeably by allowing a small number of merchants to generate significant amounts of capital, much of which found its way into the banking system.[200] Cotton and sugar related to industrialization and increasing rates of consumption in an expanding modern economy through textile manufacturing and to a lesser extent sugar refining.[201] Perhaps the influence of sugar was most significant as it entered the diet of an increasing number of people in Scotland, as it did of course across Europe in the eighteenth century.[202] Together, cotton and sugar were colonial commodities that linked colonial trade and Scottish industrialization in a way that tobacco did not.

Two developments fundamentally changed the status and import-ance of the West India trade in Scotland from 1793 to 1815. The first was the catastrophic impact of the wars with Republican France on the sugar economy of the West Indies and the impact this had on Scottish merchants and bankers with substantial investments in the West Indies.[203] The second was the growth of support for the abolition of slavery in Scotland and the effect this had of isolating those involved in colonial trade from broader developments in Scottish social and political modernization.[204] After the outbreak of war with Republican France following the execution of Louis XVI in 1793, the West Indies became a major centre of the British war effort. The British 'West Indian' interest had become increasingly important and influential in the expanding financial economy of Scotland in the 1790s, by which time the first Scottish politician to achieve significant power in British politics, Henry Dundas, had entered the cabinet, first as Secretary of State for Home Affairs and then as Secretary of State for War.[205] Dundas was Governor of the Bank of Scotland, he was an admirer of Adam Smith, whom he had introduced to Prime Minister William Pitt the younger, and he was convinced of the centrality of the £7,000,000 invested by British merchants and planters in the West Indies to the national interest.[206] War in the West Indies proved costly in terms of lives and treasure, but initial French successes were blocked by the expeditions Dundas sent there under the command of Scottish General Sir Ralph Abercromby. The example of the French Revolution and its ideology had encouraged slave rebellions which caused panic among the resident planter class and their agents, haunted by the spectre of what had happened to the French (Royalist) planters in Haiti before them. Dundas authorized the forced removal of native peoples from Jamaica and Saint Vincent to increase security, and responded to French use of liberated black troops by authorizing the establishment of equivalent 'British' regiments of freedmen and slaves.[207] By doing so, he incorporated the 'black' African labour force of the British Caribbean into the dynamic reinvention of what Britain represented which he promoted in the wars against Republican France. That expanding dynamic might be summarized as 'if the Scots could become British so could anyone else', provided those concerned accepted British laws and liberties.[208] The Carib and Maroon natives of St Vincent and Jamaica did not, which led to their removal to mainland Central America, an action that demonstrated that the British West Indies would become British as much through ethnic cleansing as through cultural integration.[209] Black 'West Indians' who enlisted in the new 'West India' regiments raised by the British army became British by doing so. Arguably, Dundas's decision to raise these regiments (and in the process make the British Army the largest owner of slaves in the Caribbean) ensured that British victories in the West Indies were consolidated and made the Caribbean a British sphere of influence despite the restoration of some colonies to other European countries after the end of the Napoleonic wars.[210]

Dundas also had much to do with the British government's attempts to rescue the finances of the sugar planters in the West Indies in the 1790s. In 1795, following the slave revolt in Grenada (during which the Scottish governor of the island was taken hostage and murdered) Dundas pushed through Parliament 'An Act for Enabling His Majesty to Direct the Issue of Exchequer Bills to a limited Amount, for the Purposes, and in the Manner mentioned therein', which made £1.5 million Sterling available as loans for merchants and planters in Grenada and Saint Vincent.[211] Dundas was thanked by one of its principal beneficiaries for 'the friendly interference' which ensured the Act's success. More money was made available in 1796, although this was not enough to prevent the largest and previously most successful of the Scottish West India mercantile companies, Houston and Co., from bankruptcy in 1800.[212] The assets of the partners in the firm amounted to £978,115 (including £413,834 in land held in Scotland, £110,000 held in estates on St Kitts and St Vincent and £454,280 in debts owed to the company by planters and other merchants), but were not enough to continue to meet liabilities, including unpaid loans of £554,378. The wealth held in land and loans could not be realized in a manner that could service the interest on such large debts.[213] Of course, not all Scottish West India firms suffered the fate of Houston and Co. The Glasgow West India Association was formed in 1807, the year the slave trade was abolished in the British Empire. Ironically, the Association was formed, not because the West India merchants of Glasgow were getting wealthier and more powerful, but because the campaign for abolition of the slave trade in Scotland had made it more difficult for them to defend their financial interests and social status in the changing political context of early nineteenth-century Scotland.[214]

The tobacco trade

Scottish impressions of contact with America and much American perception of colonial contacts with Scotland centre on the remarkable history of Scottish involvement in the great transatlantic trade in tobacco. At least an important part of that perception related to the fact that the distinctive Scottish domination of the transatlantic tobacco trade came to an end under the impact of the American war, although it is clear now that a significant Scottish involvement continued in the trade into the early nineteenth century. Building on the exhaustive research of the American economic historian JM Price, who had studied the transatlantic tobacco trade from the perspective of the site of the production of tobacco in the Chesapeake region of colonial America, TM Devine provided a major study of Scottish involvement in the tobacco trade which offered some explanation as to why a small, impoverished northern European country with a minimal record of success in transatlantic trade was able to dominate one of the major commodity trades of the eighteenth century Atlantic economy. With a negligible domestic market for tobacco, why did Scottish merchants come to monopolize so much of this lucrative trade? Arguably, if the ideas of the Scottish Enlightenment played a key role in the establishment and development of the United States, those ideas reached America via the ships of the Scottish tobacco merchants, in the form of the exported print culture of the Scottish Enlightenment, or in the ships taking Scots to American ports on outward voyages when there was plenty of room for passengers to take the place of the ballast necessary for an underfreighted ship.[215]

Scottish success in the tobacco trade is associated with the period of its greatest impact, in the third quarter of the eighteenth century, and the success of Scottish parliamentary union with England in allowing

Scottish merchants access to colonial markets denied to them prior to 1707. Yet the trade had its origins in early Scottish efforts to participate in Atlantic trade during the second half of the seventeenth century. The first recorded voyage to America by a ship owned by Glasgow merchants was in 1672. Some tobacco was imported from Barbados and Antigua, but most came from Virginia and Maryland 'though it was also the main item, and often the only item,' TC Smout has pointed out, 'in cargoes perhaps rather loosely described as coming from New England'.[216] Imports of tobacco from America declared to the Scottish customs averaged just under 200,000 lbs a year, which was, even at that early date, about 80 per cent of goods imported to the Clyde river ports during the 1680s. Much more tobacco was shipped coastwise via the English ports of Whitehaven, Bristol and Liverpool, in observation of the English Navigation Acts and their requirement that colonial commodities be landed at English ports before re-export. In 1701 alone over 2,000,000 lb of tobacco was imported into the Clyde from the English ports on the Irish Sea.

In 1675 George Hutchison sailed to Boston from Glasgow with store goods to trade for tobacco and found it hard to compete with English merchants, but did eventually sell his goods and bring a cargo of tobacco back to the Clyde. Glasgow merchants began to build on this early contact in the late seventeenth century. By the turn of the eighteenth century Swedish merchants were preferring Glasgow tobacco for price, if not for quality, and firms such as Bogle and Montgomerie had entered the trade.[217] Scottish merchants also bought tobacco in England both for domestic consumption and for trading on to continental markets. Although the English Navigation Acts were not frequently enforced against Scottish merchants, the possibility of seizure was a difficulty facing Scottish merchants that their competitors in England did not have to worry about. Trade in tobacco certainly did expand after union, but it took time for the Scots to build up volume. Trade in tobacco with the Chesapeake colonies of Virginia and Maryland grew at a greater rate than the West Indian trade. Smuggling was more significant than it would be later in the eighteenth century, even after the union. Although records are imperfect, Jacob Price has argued that while less than 200,000 lb of tobacco was imported annually to Scotland in the 1680s, this rose to 2,000,000 in 1715, doubled to 4,000,000 in 1725 and more than doubled again to 9,000,000 in 1744.[218] Over time, Glasgow merchants increasingly sourced goods they exported to the colonies (including indentured servants and free emigrants) from the Scottish Lowlands and the north of England. Just as Scottish salted herring and coarse linen to feed and clothe slaves were important in West Indian trade, so they found a market in the Chesapeake tobacco colonies as production there expanded.[219] The trade with the Chesapeake (and to a far less extent the West Indies) in tobacco may have grown slowly, but by the 1720s English merchants were putting pressure on Sir Robert Walpole's government to enforce the collection of customs duties on tobacco in Scotland more vigorously. Higher taxes at English rates had been introduced into Scotland after 1707. However, as jobs in the extended tax system were largely distributed in accordance with need for political patronage rather than collecting revenue, particularly in Glasgow, efficient collection of duties was not the most important attribute necessary for employment in the Scottish Customs. At first English ministers in search of Scottish support in Parliament were happy to accept recommendations for jobs on the basis of political necessity rather than the needs of the revenue, but this changed when English merchants began to lobby Parliament to enforce tax collection at Scottish ports.

The resentment of English tobacco merchants in Bristol, Liverpool and Whitehaven at what was viewed as unfair competition from Scotland after the union convinced Sir Robert Walpole as First Lord of the Treasury that he had to be seen to be doing something to solve the problem. 'Some sort of concerted action by English merchants seems to have been afoot as early as 1718', although it wasn't until the financial problems caused by the South Sea Bubble crisis were settled (and Walpole took office) in 1721 that provincial English tobacco merchants submitted statements of their complaints both to the Westminster Parliament and the Treasury.[220] The fact that Scottish tobacco merchants could undersell their English rivals was taken to mean that Customs fraud on a substantial scale existed in Scotland. For the English merchants, 'the only solution was to end the Union as far as the tobacco trade was concerned,' and reintroduce customs duties on that commodity in trade between Scotland and England.[221] Petitions were referred by Walpole to the English Board of Customs, who instructed their officers in Bristol, Liverpool and Whitehaven to comment on them. Bristol agreed with the allegation that there must be frauds in customs administration in Glasgow if Scottish merchants could ship tobacco to Bristol and undercut merchants there importing directly from America. Liverpool reported that the tobacco trade was in decline and 'near lost at Lancaster & Whitehaven' because of the competition from the Scots. They claimed that Scots paid higher prices in Virginia for tobacco, yet could undercut Liverpool merchants on price in the north of England, where Scottish merchants were dominating the market. It was even claimed that tobacco was sold at a lower price in Glasgow than it was in Virginia, and Scottish merchants could still afford to charter vessels from Whitehaven at higher rates than the Whitehaven merchants were accustomed to paying. Whitehaven merchants had to ship on the tobacco they imported to southern English ports to find a market for it because they could not compete with the Glasgow merchants. The Whitehaven seamen on a ship chartered by Scottish merchants reported that customs officers in the Clyde ports did not weigh tobacco when landed 'on the open quays but in walled enclosures' away from public scrutiny.[222]

These complaints about importation of tobacco in Scotland led to a full Treasury hearing in January 1721/22. Representatives of the English merchants argued that customs fraud in Glasgow meant that the union should be suspended and customs duties levied on imports of tobacco into England from Scotland. 'The entire defence of Scotland' fell on Daniel Campbell [of Shawfield], the Glasgow merchant and Member of Parliament for the Glasgow burghs, who himself dealt in tobacco as well as other commodities. He presented memorials signed by 44 Glasgow tobacco merchants. They denied that customs duty at Glasgow was not paid on the full weight of the tobacco imported. Hogsheads from planters in Maryland and the Eastern Shore of Virginia were lighter and the tobacco of poorer quality than the tobacco English merchants took on consignment from the more substantial Virginian planters on the western shore. If there was any tobacco being sold at prices that might indicate that customs duty had not been paid, it must have been put on the market by smugglers rather than the honest merchants of Glasgow. Tobacco was the only overseas trade of any significance from Glasgow, and although merchants exported some English goods, most of their exports to America were of Scottish manufacture. Was it not true that Bristol and Whitehaven merchants were not unknown in the illegal trade through the Isle of Man, and that sometimes Virginia planters sent consignments of tobacco to Bristol that were sold at less than the cost of duty and freight?[223]

Walpole and his colleagues at the Treasury responded to the hearing by sending additional customs officers to Scotland to check on fraud, and ordered one of the Customs Commissioners in Edinburgh to conduct a survey of current practice in Scottish ports regarding the importation of tobacco. The commissioner chosen, Humphrey Brent, was an Englishman. Customs officers at Port Glasgow told him that the weights of American hogsheads imported at Glasgow were lower than those imported at English ports because Scottish merchants in American bought 'light hogsheads that had received very little pressing', meaning that the tobacco in the hogshead had not been pressed to make it compact and allow a greater weight of tobacco to be packed into it.[224] There were also legal allowances for damaged tobacco. Smuggling was more of a problem than either of these reasons for claims that tobacco was being underweighed in Glasgow. Ships from Holland or the Isle of Man landed tobacco in the north of Scotland to avoid paying any duty, far from the reach of any customs officer.[225] This, however, failed to explain how tobacco landed so remotely could be transported to markets in the Lowlands of Scotland at costs that did not erode the advantage gained by the evasion of paying duty.

Brent investigated customs records at Port Glasgow thoroughly, sampling at random the accounts of nine vessels landing their cargo there. In every case he detected serious underweighing of tobacco being imported, costing the revenue £9,543 Sterling alone on three of the vessels sampled. Of course the Scottish tobacco merchants rejected Brent's claims. They insisted that much of the apparent discrepancy could be accounted for by tobacco paying no duty for reasons that were legal, such as allowances for damaged tobacco. The underweighing of tobacco by customs officers at Glasgow was not the problem, it was claimed, rather it was smuggled tobacco 'from Holland, Norway and the Isle of Man, which satisfied much of the Scottish demand and forced honest Scots traders to send their tobacco to England for sale.'[226] In England, however, tobacco merchants took Brent's report as vindication of their charges, and this time the big London tobacco merchants joined those from Bristol, Liverpool and Whitehaven in demanding parliamentary action. Parliament was under pressure to protect English commercial interest from depredation by the Scots. The Scots responded by reminding the Treasury of 'the sanctity of the commercial rights guaranteed to Scotland by the Union' and requesting that Parliament investigate evidence of English smuggling of tobacco as well. Even Brent in his report had found evidence of serious underweighing of tobacco entered at Kirkcudbright by one of the Whitehaven merchants in Cumberland. Modern research has established that systematic customs fraud through ensuring that imported tobacco was underweighed by customs officers was practised at Bristol and Liverpool as well as Whitehaven, sometimes by as much as 15 per cent.[227] Fraud only began to decline in both England and Scotland when domestic demand for tobacco began to fall after 1730. The Scots were not unique in cheating the British revenue, rather they had learned how to practise the same level of fraud in importing tobacco for domestic use as their fellow British (but English) tobacco merchants at Bristol, Liverpool, London and Whitehaven!

This, however, we know only in hindsight. In Parliament in 1722 righteous indignation at the scale of Scottish tobacco fraud was widespread. The House voted in committee that Parliament legislate to solve the problem. One of the leaders of attacks on Scottish tobacco frauds in the House of Commons was John Trenchard, 'the Whig libertarian', who introduced the motion that all tobacco imported into England from Scotland should be subject to customs duties, although he did accept that any tobacco exported from England to Scotland should pay duty as well. Walpole denounced this as 'an inflammatory speech to set people together by the ears, which some people had endeavoured at on other occasions and tended to break up the Union, the consequences whereof were dreadful'.[228] In fact, Walpole took the lead in deflecting the anti-Scots agitation of the petitioners and their supporters by proposing that there be a single British Board of Customs with some members sitting in Edinburgh and others in London, with the possibility of rotating membership. Two commissioners would concern themselves with customs collection at the outports to ensure that they were the same as at major ports. He also made substantial cuts in the level of customs duties on the importation of tobacco, thus deflecting the national animus of the parliamentary petitioners by reducing the tax burden on all legal trade in the United Kingdom. It was an example of Walpole's policy at the Treasury of cutting legal levels of tax to increase the possibility of improving levels of successful collection of it.[229] It did, however, mean a fall of revenue overall. Walpole evidently took the decision to do this to avoid encouraging national hostility between English and Scottish merchants.

Ironically, cuts in British customs duties on tobacco helped to encourage the reorganized French government monopoly on tobacco to look to Britain as its major source of supply. At first, however, Scottish merchants did not gain from this increase in the market for British plantation tobacco in Europe because they were buying tobacco at high prices whereas English merchants took commission selling tobacco by consignment, which lowered their risk of loss in a falling market. This meant that in an environment where customs duties on tobacco were reduced but efforts to collect it efficiently increased, particularly in Scotland, Scottish merchants found it more difficult to compete with their English competitors on price.[230] When the Scottish trade began to revive it was during a period of renewed war with France. Revival of the Scottish trade also coincided with the restoration of separate boards of Customs for England and Scotland in 1742 which came about because Walpole's political opponents wanted to undo all his works once he finally lost his grip on power. There is no evidence that tobacco fraud in Scotland increased after 1740, but the level of importation of tobacco to Clyde ports began its exponential growth during that period, and laid the foundation of 'the Golden Age of Tobacco'. It brought Scots more closely into contact with America after 1740, and increased their visibility and influence in the economy and society of colonial mainland British North America.

Jacob Price first drew attention to 'the rise of Glasgow in the Chesapeake tobacco trade' in 1954. Recorded imports of tobacco to Scottish ports in the years from the union to 1722 had risen from about 1,500,000 lb per year to 6,000,000. In the period of stagnation that followed from 1722 to 1741 imports rose more modestly to 8,000,000 lb, a 33 per cent growth over almost two decades, but then what Price called 'the heroic age' had begun. Despite the outbreak of war with France, imports grew to 10,000,000 in 1743, 13,000,000 in 1745, 21,000,000 in 1752, 32,000,000 in 1760 and peaked at 47,000,000 in 1771. During the same period the trade in England stagnated. According to Price, the Scots had about 10 per cent of the UK trade in tobacco in 1738. This doubled by 1744, just before the Jacobite rebellion of 1745. By 1758, when war had again broken out between France and Britain, Scotland had 30 per cent of the UK trade, and Scottish imports became more substantial than those for either the English outports or London itself. In 1765, two years after the end of the Seven Years War, Scottish merchants imported 40 per cent of all tobacco brought to Britain and in 1769 Scottish dominance of the British trade involved importation of almost 52 per cent of all tobacco imported into Britain.[231] This was the only year in which Scottish merchants imported more tobacco than merchants in the English outports and London combined.

Of course this commercial dominance belonged not so much to Scotland as to Glasgow. After more Westminster legislation relating to the tobacco trade in 1751, the small volume of tobacco imports to Scottish ports such as Ayr or Dumfries ceased completely. Why had this happened? What was the impact of this commercial success on both Scotland/Glasgow and Virginia/Maryland/America? The tobacco trade was a trade between the Chesapeake Bay colonies of Virginia and Maryland, and to an extent areas of North Carolina near the Virginia border, with northern Europe rather than Scotland per se. It was a British trade and although political union with England did not make Scottish success in Atlantic trade inevitable, the protection of the Royal Navy and the expanding markets available to British merchants did make it possible. Geographically, trade in tobacco gravitated to north-western ports because of the nature of transatlantic communication. Just as modern passenger aircraft fly north-west from Europe to America to reduce the distance of transatlantic travel, so shipping costs for a bulky commodity like tobacco were reduced by shipping it to a north-western British port. As the really profitable aspect of the trade was not selling to domestic markets in Britain but in re-exporting to continental markets in northern Europe, north-western British ports also derived advantage from their geographical position.[232]

In Scotland, it was a short distance, and therefore relatively inexpensive, to transport tobacco imported into the Clyde ports to east coast ports on the Forth estuary with well-established trading links to northern Europe. Without political union with Scotland, English ports such as Whitehaven would have drawn more benefit from the trade, hence the parliamentary attack on the Scots in 1721. However, with the defeat of the last Jacobite rebellion in Scotland in 1746, Scottish integration into the British state was secured, and the British government was committed to extending its authority there. The benefits of commerce were seen as central to this process. Scottish merchants also traded in tobacco on a different basis. English merchants almost always followed the practice of the sugar trade with the West Indies in importing cargoes of colonial goods on consignment, meaning that the tobacco remained the property of colonial planters until it found a buyer in Europe, with the merchant concerned taking a commission on sales. Scottish firms bought tobacco outright at the 'stores' and 'factories' they established in Maryland, North Carolina and, especially, Virginia. As tobacco cultivation had expanded in this area of America, so planters with smaller landholdings and fewer slaves became involved in the trade. The willingness of Scottish firms to advance them credit and to purchase crops outright gave them considerable advantages in attracting trade, and thus Scottish capital played a key role in the development of this major region of British North America and Scots became associated with British authority there.[233]

Scottish merchants were able to do this because the 'Farmers General of the French Customs', with a lucrative monopoly of the sale of tobacco in France, increasingly came to source their tobacco from Scottish merchants. Even when Britain and France were at war, as they were from 1742–48 and 1757–63, Glasgow merchants were re-exporting more than half of the tobacco purchased by French merchants. The

French bought more than a third of all tobacco re-exported from the Clyde ports to Europe.[234] The French also paid promptly through their Scottish agent, who for much of this period was the Edinburgh-based Scottish banker William Alexander. So, if Scottish merchants were taking risks in extending credit in the American tobacco market, they were expanding their supply of capital rapidly during the 'heroic age' of great success in the tobacco market because they were able to sell much of their tobacco rapidly for prompt payment in Europe. They kept their profit margins and prices down because they weren't selling on commission and because they didn't want to keep their capital locked up in their commodity for too long. Thus their great success lay in building up the volume of their sales of tobacco to European markets.

If the Glasgow tobacco trade played a key role in increasing Scottish contact with America and the importance of America in the process of the modernization of Scotland, so it was that Scottish access to European markets provided the key to Scottish success. This aspect of the trade received less attention until the American economic historian Jacob Price completed his exhaustive research on the sale of American tobacco to markets in France, and in the process found himself making a major contribution to Scottish history. There does not appear to have been a political motivation for the French focus on trading with Scottish merchants, but traditional Scottish links with continental Europe must have played some part. For example, the continental and London banking and mercantile interests of the Herries family of Dumfriesshire in the second half of the eighteenth century became enmeshed with those of the Edinburgh and London banking house of Coutts in the 1760s.[235] Thus by the middle of the eighteenth century, Scottish contact with financial markets in London as well as on the continent were central to the Scottish economy and encouraged the development of a precocious banking system that maximized the use of credit to fund economic activity in Scotland as well as the Chesapeake. It is important to keep in mind, however, that the 'heroic age' of Scottish success in the tobacco trade did not exceed three decades in duration. The trade changed as a result of the American War of Independence and renewed war between France and Britain from 1778 to 1783. The American War, however, did not bring Scottish involvement in the tobacco trade to an abrupt end. The Scottish tobacco merchants adjusted to the changing political and economic situation by diversifying their interests, but continued to trade in tobacco for as long as it remained profitable to do so. By the time of the French Revolution and the end of the monopoly situation in the French market, tobacco cultivation had declined in the Chesapeake as planters diversified their agricultural production by raising more grain.

Scottish imports of tobacco from North America decreased dramatically from 1775 to 1780.[236] Although this would seem catastrophic, the large firms who dominated the Glasgow tobacco trade by the 1770s had been able to stockpile large stores of tobacco, which enabled them to benefit from rising prices for tobacco in Europe as warfare in America disrupted supplies. Merchants also were able to obtain tobacco from neutral ports in the West Indies as the Netherlands did not enter the war against Britain until 1780, and Denmark remained neutral throughout the conflict. Tobacco was shipped from the Chesapeake to neutral West Indian ports in order to obtain badly needed funds for the American war effort. Glasgow merchants also diversified their interests. More of them began to explore the commercial possibilities of the West Indian trade. While some historians have questioned older assumptions that profits from the tobacco trade were used to fund the investment necessary for the industrialization of the west of Scotland, it is clear that those merchants in Scotland who profited from the tobacco trade invested some of those profits both in acquiring land and in industrial concerns that ranged from textile manufacturing to brewing and distilling. A good example of this is the tobacco merchant and banker George Murdoch. Even before the American war Murdoch and his fellow 'tobacco lord', William Cunninghame, established the Dalnotter Iron Company. By 1781 Murdoch extended his interests by investing in the Muirkirk Iron Company. Other investments included ropeworks, brewing and glass manufacturing. He also moved into salaried employment as Controller of Customs at Greenock and Port Glasgow from 1771 to 1784, an important post during the years of the American rebellion and consequent decline in the importation of tobacco into the Clyde ports.[237] Some merchants even toyed with the idea of growing tobacco on a commercial basis in Scotland![238]

The end of the war and British recognition of the independence of the new United States of America meant that British Navigation Acts no longer applied to trade with the United States and thus Scottish merchants with interests in the transatlantic tobacco trade no longer had to land tobacco at a British port before re-exporting it to European markets. There is evidence, however, that with the establishment of peace Scottish merchants renewed their trading with the Chesapeake, partly because there were many debts still due to them from American planters.[239] Vessels involved in the trade did not record this in British customs entries, as they would carry their cargo of tobacco direct to

European ports, even if they remained based in the Clyde, just as Scottish vessels involved in the slave trade can be identified only rarely because they left Scotland for Africa without slaves and sold their African cargo in the West Indies or mainland North America before returning to Europe with very different goods. As there was no indigenous merchant class in the Chesapeake, and little interest in the tobacco trade among American merchants in New England, there was still a role for Scottish merchants in the region and in the tobacco trade, and there was still a strong demand in the southern United States for goods of Scottish and British manufacture. It was the disruption caused by renewed war in Europe in the aftermath of the French Revolution that seriously affected the trade. More than two decades of war and the abolition of the French tobacco monopoly permanently altered the structure of the trade. Of course tobacco continued to be imported into Scotland, but it was the direct trade with Europe that had generated the substantial profits available through trading in tobacco in the eighteenth century. Moreover, many of those merchants who were owed substantial sums by American planters were able to pursue repayment as diplomatic relations between Great Britain and the United States improved in the 1790s. The introduction of US Federal Courts after the adoption of the US constitution in 1789 increased the chances of successful prosecution for debt.[240] In 1795 the 'Jay Treaty' between the United States and Great Britain recognized the issue of US debts owed to British creditors, while in 1796 the US Supreme Court ruled that state legislation contrary to the 1783 Treaty of Paris was illegal. The chief negotiator of that treaty, of course, was the Scottish merchant Richard Oswald, keen to ensure that commerce continued between the former colonies and Great Britain and that British merchants obtained payment of the debts due to them in America.[241] In 1802 a diplomatic convention between the United States and Britain 'provided that the United States should pay Britain £600,000 in compensation to be distributed among those who still had outstanding claims.'[242]

Despite the fact that there were complaints that payment was late and was not made in full, a considerable amount of the large debt owed to Scottish mercantile firms by their clients in what became the United States was eventually repaid. By the time it was received, the capital concerned could be invested in a far larger number of ways than had been available during 'the Golden Age' of Scottish trade in tobacco, and the tobacco trade itself had been transformed. The renewed outbreak of hostilities between Britain and the United States from 1812 to 1815 disrupted trade, although the vast expansion of US cotton exports to

Britain in the decades after 1815 indicate that demand had moved from catering to a pan-European market for consumption of tobacco to a new commodity directly required for a manufacturing industry at that time unique to Britain. Most of this manufacturing activity was situated in the areas of the north-west of England and the west of Scotland that had been so important in the American trade in the previous century.[243]

The slave trade

One reason slavery was never really associated with the tobacco trade in Scotland was that those Scots who did own tobacco plantations lost their links with Scotland while Scottish merchants in the Chesapeake were involved in buying tobacco, not slaves, and in providing British goods for American planters. We know little about Scottish planters owning slaves in the Chesapeake, but in Prince George's County, Maryland, in the 1720s 'George Murdock', parish minister and owner of 150 acres and two slaves, and 'George Buchanan', a merchant who held 1200 acres and four slaves, were identified as 'outsiders' (rather than Scots) who had become successful tobacco planters there.[244] The salted herring and coarse linen exported from Scotland to feed and clothe slaves in the West Indies were also exported to the Chesapeake.[245] Tobacco production did not have to involve large numbers of slaves, and the lower mortality rate among slaves in the Chesapeake meant that the slave population increased as much through natural reproduction as by continued importation of slaves from Africa and the West Indies. As payment for slaves usually involved cash rather than credit, the credit supplied by Glasgow tobacco firms was not directly linked to the acquisition of slaves by planters in the Chesapeake, but by increasing the purchasing power of the planters, it did indirectly free up capital for the purchase of slaves to expand tobacco production. Scottish firms dealt disproportionately with tobacco planters producing small amounts of tobacco on land that had only recently been cleared. For a small planter, even modest investment in the purchase of a small number of slaves could lead to the ability to substantially increase production. There were few American merchants active in the region who could compete with the Scots in offering credit, partly because capital accumulation was shunned in favour of the acquisition of land.[246]

Although most slaves brought to Scotland in the eighteenth century were brought from the West Indies, some had come from the Chesapeake. One of the earlier cases involving a slave of African descent in

Scotland that came before the Scottish courts involved a Scottish merchant named Robert Sheddan and a slave who in Scotland became known as James Montgomery. He had been purchased by Robert Sheddan, a merchant from Beith in Ayrshire, from Captain Joseph Hawkins in Virginia in 1750. Sheddan brought him to Scotland, where he was apprenticed to Robert Morrice, a joiner in Beith west of Glasgow for 18 months.[247] By the spring of 1756 Sheddan had arranged to sell the boy back to Hawkins in Virginia 'for the original price of £56 plus 1,000 lb of tobacco', the tobacco to be paid in recognition of the increased value Montgomery's apprenticeship in Beith had given him. He refused to go. Sheddan, with the help of Morrice, forcibly took him to Port Glasgow but Montgomery escaped. We know about his case because Sheddan offered a reward for the return of his 'property' that resulted in Montgomery's apprehension in Edinburgh and incarceration in the tollbooth there. There was enough interest in Montgomery's case to lead to an action for his release being raised in the Bailie Court of Edinburgh and later before the Court of Session in Edinburgh. Robert Gray, Procurator Fiscal of the Bailie Court of Edinburgh, argued that Montgomery was a servant who left his master when he realized that he was going to be sent to Virginia 'to make a penny of him, reducing him again to slavery.' Sheddan's lawyer argued that his slave had been well treated and that the effort and expense to train him as a joiner demonstrated that he 'by no means intended to put him to the common and usual employment of a slave', although one of the actions before the Court of Session to recover his slave was presented baldly as 'Sheddan v[ersus] a Negro.'[248] It emerged in the pleadings before the Edinburgh courts that James Montgomery had been baptized as a communicant member of the Church of Scotland and hoped that this would support his efforts to obtain his freedom.

On 19 April 1756, the day before Montgomery was going to be taken to Glasgow, he obtained a certificate from John Witherspoon, minister of Beith, native of East Lothian, opponent of the Moderate Party of the Church of Scotland and later President of the college at Princeton, New Jersey. Witherspoon had instructed Sheddan's boy in the teachings of the Church of Scotland as a Christian church, and arranged for his public baptism before the congregation of Beith under the name James Montgomery-Sheddan, although he had been brought to Scotland under the name 'Shanker'.[249] In the course of the legal dispute Sheddan's lawyers insisted on referring to his slave as Sheddan or Montgomery-Sheddan. Nothing in the certificate of baptism claimed that its possessor was a free man, but Witherspoon's support was important.

Robert Gray's efforts to represent Montgomery-Sheddan included the assertion that 'there is no such thing as slavery in this country', and cited in support of it the work of the great seventeenth-century Scottish lawyers Sir George Mackenzie and Viscount Stair, as well as of Lord Bankton, who was the judge hearing the case in the Outer House of the Court of Session. Sheddan's lawyers in reply referred to Andrew Fletcher of Saltoun, the great Scottish patriot in the last Scottish Parliament of 1703–1707, who had proposed enslaving the poor of Scotland to keep them alive during the terrible famines suffered in Scotland during the last decade of the seventeenth century, in justification of Sheddan's right to Montgomery as his property. Lord Bankton set a date in January 1757 for the case to be heard before the full bench of the Court of Session, but unfortunately James Montgomery died before that date and the case was dropped.[250]

We can document how one Glasgow tobacco firm became drawn into direct trading in slaves, although this in turn drew it into the West Indian trade, thus illustrating their connection. It was unusual for Glasgow firms to trade in slaves as well as tobacco, and the firm of Buchanan and Simson initially contacted merchants with more extensive connections with the slave trade in Liverpool in an effort to secure slaves for their correspondents at St Kitts in the West Indies and Maryland in the Chesapeake.[251] In 1759 the firm became more directly involved in the trade, purchasing 25 slaves in Barbados who were sold at a profit at slave markets in Maryland. By the autumn of 1761, Buchanan and Simson had formed a separate partnership devoted to trading in slaves under the name 'The Snow Pitt and Maxwell's African Company', in which it took a half interest including a share for their correspondent George Maxwell in Maryland. Other shares were held by Captain James Buchanan and the chief clerk, William Buchanan, with the wealthy Glasgow bankers and merchants Colin Dunlop and Alexander Houston holding more than a quarter of the shares (the latter of whom also had West Indian trading interests of course).

Two Glasgow ships ('snows'), the *Patriot Pitt* and the *Maxwell*, were the vessels of the trade. The ships were sent from Glasgow to take on Liverpool captains experienced in the slave trade, but the firm tried to recruit another Buchanan, Colin, to sail with the *Patriot Pitt* as 'Second Captain' on the grounds that 'when you Return we shall give you the Command of a Ship in that Trade ... & if it succeed you will then be in a way to make a Fortune.' The ships were freighted with brandy purchased from the Isle of Man, 'East India goods' (calicoes?) from London and Halifax woollens from Yorkshire. One of the Liverpool captains was asked to arrange for the purchase of additional textiles in Manchester suitable for the West African market. The outward cargo thus contained no Scottish goods, indicating one reason that Liverpool rather than Glasgow dominated the slave trade. The *Patriot Pitt* could hold 300 slaves and the *Maxwell* 200, and the intention was that slaves would be sold in the Chesapeake through Maxwell in Maryland and the tobacco merchant Neil Buchanan in Virginia. Final accounts for these voyages do not appear in the surviving records relating to the trade of this firm, but it also was involved in investing in Liverpool slaving voyages in 1762 and 1763. The firm was wound up in 1763 after the sudden death of its major partner, George Buchanan, Jr, at the age of 34. Its successor firm was Buchanan, Hastie and Co., the majority of whose shareholders were members of the Buchanan family, which played a major part in the Glasgow tobacco trade until the disruption caused by the American War of Independence forced it to declare bankruptcy in 1777.

The great Glasgow tobacco firm of William Cunninghame and Co. was one of the major success stories of the Glasgow tobacco trade during its 'Golden Age', concentrating on the Virginia trade. Its principal partners by the early 1770s were the prominent Glasgow merchants Andrew Cochrane, Robert Bogle, John Murdoch and Peter Murdoch with William Cunninghame as managing partner. Cunninghame's grandiose Glasgow townhouse later became the Royal Exchange in Glasgow, and today forms part of the Gallery of Modern Art in Glasgow. Most of the surviving correspondence relates to the organization and operation of the firm's extensive network of stores in Virginia. This did involve the use of slave labour, not as field hands on tobacco plantations but as manual labourers essential for the successful operation of a store such as that at Falmouth in Virginia. There were 14 slaves living there in 1774: five house servants, a carpenter, a longshoreman and seven crew for the sloop and schooner which presumably were necessary to distribute goods to planters and to transport hogsheads of tobacco back to the store in readiness for dispatch to Glasgow and the Clyde.[252]

In 1774 the factor at the Falmouth store, James Robinson, reported on this establishment to the partners, who had queried the necessity for the number of slaves employed there. In Robinson's letter the slaves are referred to by their names or as 'negroes' or 'servants', but never as slaves.[253] The five house servants were Cuffy, Martin, Lucy 'and her two children, Patty and Sarah'. 'Jonathan' stowed ships. Of the seven men employed on the store's sloop and schooner, 'Adam, Jack, Frame [sic] and Jack [sic]' worked the sloop *Lark*, while 'Primus', 'James' and 'Mark' worked with 'a white servant' on the unnamed schooner. 'Phill a carpenter' was described in a manner that demonstrated just how valuable a slave with a craft skill could be. He was 'extremely useful on many occasions', which included building a stable at Culpepper store. In addition, because of his skills, 'when we have no employment for him he can readily be hired at 50s. per month'. Whether this sum represented Virginia currency or Sterling is not apparent in the text, but clearly Phill's work commanded a premium. Robinson conceded that 'probably there may be one too many servants for the houses' but argued that 'four are as few as can be done with' because he and others at the store were 'frequently abroad' on business and 'that all our clothes are washed at home', presumably by Lucy, Patty and Sarah. The Scots, however, cut all the firewood and brought it to the store. 'Jonathan, Lucy and her children are a family of negroes purchased by Mr Alexander Cuninghame' (by then back in Glasgow), Robinson added. He then continued by writing a sentence of rather different import: 'the children have since grown up, and I propose selling one of them when an opportunity offers.'[254]

Thus while it is clear that Glasgow tobacco firms seldom took possession of tobacco plantations, the trade did involve some of them taking possession of slaves and sometimes selling them as they would livestock or indeed a hogshead of tobacco. With the disruption to the tobacco trade caused by the American Revolution, however, slavery became more obviously an issue in Scotland because of existing links with the West India trade. When the famous tobacco lord William Cunninghame retired from the tobacco trade in the 1780s to pursue his interests in land in Scotland, he invested (and eventually lost) much of his capital in a firm engaged in the West India trade that in time brought with it ownership of three plantations in Jamaica. Even before the American Revolution, slaves brought from the West Indies to Britain had raised the legal issue of whether they remained slaves once in Britain. In 1772 Lord Chief Justice Mansfield, the Scottish judge who presided over the Court of King's Bench in London, ruled that James Somerset could not be taken from England against his will, even though he had been brought there from the West Indies as a slave.[255] Similar cases involving the status of black slaves/servants in Scotland came before the Court of Session. In 1769 'Black Tom', a slave brought to Scotland from Grenada by Dr David Dalrymple to his house at Lindifferen in Fife, was baptized as a member of the Church of Scotland by Dr Harry Spens, at that time minister of the Parish of Wemyss in Fife.

'Black Tom' took the name of David Spens after his baptism. Dalrymple had intended to send David Spens back to Grenada, not as a field hand, but as a carpenter. Instead Spens, with the support of the minister and elders at Wemyss, declared his liberty as a Christian: 'I am now by the Christian Religion Liberate and set at freedom from my old yoke, bondage, and slavery and by the laws of this Christian land there is no slavery or vestige of slavery allowed.' Spens's declaration went on to denounce Dalrymple's 'tyrannical power'. He intended, it was asserted in the declaration, to use this power to 'dispose of me arbitrally at your despotic will and pleasure and for that end you threaten to send me abroad out of this country to the West Indies.'[256] Dalrymple went to law to protect his property, but before the resulting action could be decided by the Court of Session, he died, leaving David Spens a free man as well as a member of the Church of Scotland.

In 1773 Joseph 'Knight', a black man who had been brought from Jamaica to Scotland by Sir John Wedderburn of Ballandean in Perthshire some years previously, read about the Somerset case in England in the Scottish press and on that basis claimed the right to leave Wedderburn's household in Perthshire. Wedderburn did not want to send Knight back to Jamaica; this is what made the Knight case in Scotland different from the Somerset case. When Knight gave evidence to local magistrates in 1773 as evidence for an action before Perth Sheriff Court, he testified that Sir John had responded to his request for his freedom by telling him 'that he would not give him his freedom here because he would starve as no body would employ him but that he would give him his freedom in Jamaica and a house and some ground'.[257] But Wedderburn had dismissed Knight's wife, Annie Thomson, from his service, even though he had met the costs of their marriage, her care when she gave birth to their son, the latter's baptism and his burial after his death. Local Justices of the Peace in Perthshire ruled that Knight was a slave, but when Joseph's supporters helped him appeal to the Perthshire Sheriff Court, it ruled that 'the regulations in Jamaica concerning slaves do not extend to this Kingdom.' Wedderburn appealed to the Court of Session in Edinburgh as Scotland's supreme court, and in 1778 they confirmed by an eight to four majority that Joseph was a free man, and with that judgement, our record of he and Annie Thomson ceases.

The report on the judgement in the *Caledonian Mercury* declared that 'it must give a very high satisfaction to the inhabitants of the United Kingdom, that the freedom of Negroes has obtained its first *general determination* in the Supreme Civil Court of Scotland.'[258] Part of the changes that took place were indicated by the very different history of another runaway Virginia slave in Scotland, Peter Burnett, who became a weaver in Paisley in the 1780s and was a friend of the poet Robert Tannahill's family.[259] By 1778, in the midst of the British war to retain its colonies in America, there was a debate over whether, as Samuel Johnson put it, 'the loudest yelps for liberty' came from 'the drivers of negroes,' but this did not change the legal basis of slavery in the British West Indies.[260] There was not a wholesale movement of firms formerly specializing in tobacco into trade with the West Indies, but the trade recruited merchants who had the capital to invest in existing networks to which they were related through kinship or business. Robert Lang, a manufacturer in Paisley, entered into trade in partnership with two planters in Grenada; Lang exported Scottish and English goods to Grenada while his partners sent sugar, cotton and other goods from Grenada to Britain.[261] Some successful West Indian planters returned to Scotland to set up as merchants once they reached the financial position of being able to become absentee proprietors on their home islands, just as McDowall, Milliken and others had before them. The successor firm to James Milliken and Co., Alexander Houston and Co., expanded its mercantile interests in the West Indies after the American war by adopting the 'store system' developed by Scottish tobacco firms to the sugar trade in the Leeward and Windward Islands, enabling them to secure a regular supply of hogsheads of sugar in a manner that allowed their ships to be promptly filled with cargo when they reached the West Indies and thus able to return to Scotland quickly.[262]

As British involvement in the slave trade attracted more criticism in the United Kingdom in the years following the American Wars of Independence, so it was that the West Indian planters and the merchants who traded with them became associated with justifying their business. Tobacco production now was identifieded with the United States, although some was grown in the West Indies. It was slavery in the West Indies that formed the focus of the debate that grew in intensity in Britain with the beginning of the campaign to abolish the slave trade in the British Empire launched by William Wilberforce in 1787.[263] After abolition, the West Indies were pushed to the periphery of British public concerns and became a backwater of empire. Memory of just how important the 'small islands' of the Caribbean had been to Britain's economy and society became obscured by the great political issues of the nineteenth century such as constitutional and land reform, relations between church and state and empire in India.[264] There is no doubt, however, of 'the pervasive and enduring influence of the Caribbean on

Scotland, and of Caribbean Scots on Britain'.[265] Of course, during this time, what was British (and thus what could be Scottish) in the West Indies was changing, as the older British colonial possessions were joined by Dominica, St Vincent, Grenada and Tobago after the conclusion of the Seven Years War in 1763, and received a considerable influx of Scottish investment and immigrants. At the turn of the nineteenth century the British presence in the Caribbean expanded further by the acquisition of St Lucia, Trinidad and British Guiana. Although the islands of the West Indies remained slave societies after the abolition of legal trading in slaves after 1807, Westminster's intervention marked a turning point in the history of the region. With the end of the Napoleonic Wars, a slump in the market for sugar led to a major economic downturn and increasing cotton production in the southern states of the United States affected the market for another major West Indian commodity.[266]

After European peace was finally achieved in 1815 the campaign to abolish slavery itself in the British Empire gathered strength. This led to colonial resistance to the campaign, fuelled by the outbreak of several major slave rebellions such as those in Barbados (1816), Demerara (1823) and Jamaica (1831). Some West Indian planters were in favour of independence as a means of preventing abolition. The eventual solution to increasing confrontation between native elites and British colonial administration was the parliamentary grant of £20 million compensation to slave owners for the emancipation of their slaves in 1833. At least some Scottish landowners with West Indian interests used income received as compensation for the loss of their slaves to extend their landholdings in Scotland and to invest in improving their estates there.[267] The British Colonial Office plan for an apprenticeship system that would require slaves to work for their former masters for a period of four to six years did not operate well and final liberation of 750,000 former slaves in the British West Indies took place in 1838. The effect varied from colony to colony, as a 'rent-wage' system developed that bound former slaves to the plantations where they had lived and worked before securing their freedom. In addition, in 1846 the Westminster parliament which had itself been transformed by the Reform Acts of 1832 and 1833 moved to withdraw the tariffs on the importation of sugar which was not 'British'. British planters had to produce sugar at a price that would not be undercut by planters able to use slave labour in Brazil and Cuba. Values of West Indian estates fell dramatically. In Jamaica, for example, an estate valued at £80,000 before abolition was sold for £625 in 1849.[268] Of course, this was not the end of Scotland's connection with the West Indies, but after the abolition of slavery it was a fragmented and episodic connection that had nothing like the impact on Scotland of the booming sugar trade of the eighteenth century and the campaigns against slavery of the late eighteenth and early nineteenth centuries. The mercantile connection came increasingly to be focused on Glasgow, although there are examples of legacies from wealthy Scots in the West Indies being received for public projects in other parts of Scotland.[269] The importance of the West Indies in the campaign to end slavery in 'Britain' also created a distinctive debate in Scotland that impacted on the changing political and social culture of the country in a manner that we do not yet fully understand. It is clear that the tobacco and the sugar trades enmeshed Scottish merchants and Scotland itself in the institution of chattel slavery in the British Empire. The issue that increasingly came to public attention in Britain after 1776 was one that asked how a nation whose unwritten constitution enshrined the liberties of its citizens could participate in a trade involving the sale of fellow humans and in an economic system whose profits were generated by a labour force who were enslaved? Very few slaves came to Scotland from America, but their presence raised issues that would link their own condition dramatically to the future of British liberty and the British constitution.

Part II

Transatlantic Scotland: Cultural Exchange between Scotland and America

4
Slavery and Scotland

Scottish involvement with British colonial trade to the West Indies and North America brought it into contact with the developing system of transatlantic chattel slavery. Slavery provided the labour necessary for the production of the commodities such as sugar, tobacco, cotton and coffee, as well as rice and indigo, that began to generate rich profits for European planters. By the late eighteenth century, however, the rise of opposition to 'British' slavery in Scotland influenced the changing nature of Scottish society as Enlightenment ideas became less focused on 'improvement' and more about equality. By the nineteenth century, Scottish participation in the campaigns to end the slave trade and eventually slavery itself in the British Empire came to play a key role in the reinvention of the country as a modern society. Scotland was no longer a politically independent state or kingdom, but national identity instead became associated with an idea of moral mission. This was one reason why Scotland was so important in the development of the Liberal Party in the United Kingdom during the nineteenth century.

The first parliamentary act to permit serfs in Scotland more freedom was passed at Westminster in 1775, thus making it more difficult to justify the ownership of slaves of African descent in Scotland as being compatible with the traditional law of Scotland relating to colliery serfdom. It is clear that the conditions under which colliery serfs were employed in the coal mines of Fife and the Lothians in Scotland were far from being the same as those endured by slaves in the western hemisphere.[270] Adam Smith had argued in the first edition of the *Wealth of Nations*, published in 1776, that slavery was uneconomic.[271] Free labourers would support themselves on a cheaper and more efficient basis than overseers could maintain slaves. 'The experience of all ages and nations, I believe,' wrote Smith, 'demonstrates that the work done by slaves, though it appears to cost only their maintenance, is in the end the dearest of any.' Smith argued that anyone who could not acquire property 'can have no other interest but to eat as much, and to labour as little as possible.'[272] Only violence would obtain work beyond this from a slave, as illustrated by the ferocious slave codes of the British plantation colonies in the West Indies.

Slavery and race in Enlightenment thought

Yet the other leading light of what we think of as the Scottish Enlightenment, David Hume, took a racist perspective on British slavery. Slavery in the British sugar colonies was not unique in its dependence on African slaves as its labour force by the eighteenth century, but the post-union kingdom of Great Britain was unique in adopting this system while it concurrently defined itself in terms of the constitutional liberty of the subject. How British were British colonies if only those who owned slaves could be free? Although Hume asserted 'that slavery is in general disadvantageous both to the happiness and populousness of mankind and that its place is much better supplied by the practice of hired servants', in the 1754 edition of his essays he added an essay on 'national character' that contained the statement:

> not to mention our colonies, there are NEGROE slaves dispersed all over EUROPE, of whom none ever discovered any symptoms of ingenuity; though low people, without education, will start up amongst us, and distinguish themselves in every profession. In JAMAICA, indeed, they talk of one negroe as a man of parts and learning; but it is likely he is admired for slender accomplishments, like a parrot, who speaks a few words plainly.[273]

Thomas Jefferson was to write in similar terms about the young Boston slave Phyllis Wheatley in his *Notes on the State of Virginia*.[274] The attitudes of both men demonstrate the contradictions that undermined the ideals at the heart of Enlightenment culture.

Leading figures of the Scottish Enlightenment who became identified with the British campaign to end the slave trade in the empire included the academic clergymen James Beattie and William Robertson. Robertson published a sermon in 1755, The Situation of the World at the Time of Christ's Appearance, reprinted several times in subsequent decades, that associated the rise of Christianity with the advent of modern civilization and part of the abolition of 'the practice of slavery through the world', which was, as Iain Whyte has pointed out, a remarkably positive statement to make in 1755 given the state of the British Empire at that time.[275] It may be that Robertson's knowledge of the existence of slavery in British colonies was minimal in 1755. By the time he published his *History of America* in 1777, he included criticism of Spanish enslavement of Native Americans and, in Book VIII, a promise that the introduction of 'negroes' as slaves in America would be 'fully explained in another place', although this ambition was never to be realized. In the brief unfinished chapter on Virginia included in posthumous editions of the *History of America*, he noted the introduction of negro slaves but did not discuss this in any depth, commenting that 'their aid seems now to be essential to the existence of the colony, and the greater part of field-labour in Virginia is performed by servile hands.'[276] William Wilberforce wrote to Robertson in 1788 to express his appreciation that Robertson's portrayal of slavery in his *History of America* provided evidence that could be used to support the British campaign for the abolition of the slave trade.[277]

The campaign against the slave trade

James Beattie's career developed later than Robertson's, and part of his attacks on David Hume's work related to the latter's racism. Beattie's teaching at Marischal College, Aberdeen, included significant attention to the evils of slavery. Beattie drafted the Marischal College petition to Parliament in support of the campaign to abolish the slave trade in 1788 and helped to organize the petition from the town council of Aberdeen in the same cause in 1792. British defeat in the American Revolution had led to controversy in Britain and the colonies over the resettlement of the slaves freed by the British during their campaigns in America, and ultimately prompted the British campaign for the abolition of the slave trade in that part of the British Empire in America that remained to it after US independence.[278] How could the British free the slaves of rebels while tolerating slavery in their own West Indian colonies? Could the trade in slaves taken from Africa to those colonies at least be abolished? As a result of the debate that ensued, the Society for the Abolition of the Slave Trade was founded in London in May 1787. By 1787 the movement to reform the British constitution in the aftermath of the failure to retain the American colonies was underway, along with contemporary agitation in England and Scotland for reform of the Church. The Westminster Parliament already had agreed to allow unprecedented autonomy for the Irish Parliament in Dublin. Reform was in the air.

A desire for fundamental change in politics and society was gaining ground in Britain. The campaign to abolish the slave trade (but not slavery itself) drew on expanding support for reform in Britain and its empire. In many ways the campaign to petition Parliament to abolish the slave trade in Britain would provide a model for the subsequent campaign to reform the British constitution itself. Earlier in the same decade, the Church of Scotland had been divided by a last great effort by the so-called 'Popular Party' of the church to end the legal right of 'patronage,' whereby the Crown or private landowners exercised predominant influence as a property right in the appointment of Church of Scotland ministers.[279] In many ways, the Church's participation in the campaign to abolish the slave trade would reunite the Church and give it a sense of moral mission during a period of increasing social and political tension in Scotland itself.[280]

Although petitions were sent to Parliament from Scotland in favour of the abolition of the slave trade, it was the tour of Scotland in 1792 to raise support for the campaign by William Dickson, a Scot who had returned from the West Indies to live in London, that involved the Church of Scotland in the campaign. Dickson had left Moffat as a young man to take up a desirable situation as secretary to the Governor of Barbados in 1772. He returned to London in 1785, and in 1789 published *Letters on Slavery* there, addressed to the prominent Scottish landowner Sir James Johnstone of Westerhall, whose family had invested in sugar plantations on Grenada in the Windward Islands after they had been ceded by the French to the British in 1763. The great campaigner in 1792 on behalf of the Society for the Abolition of the Slave Trade was Thomas Clarkson, a veteran who had been touring Britain in pursuit of its aims since 1788, and had visited Scotland in 1791. He found his encounter with Scotland 'vexatious', however, and declined the honour of returning there. Dickson had offered his services to the committee on its formation, but had not previously taken an active role in its campaign. Clarkson probably had chosen Dickson because he was familiar with the structure and doctrine of the Church of Scotland, as well as the distinctive features of Scottish law and local government. In a predominantly Quaker organization, this marked Dickson out for the mission. He chose, in effect, to become something like a missionary to the country he had left in very different circumstances 20 years previously. The Society for the Abolition of the Slave Trade had succeeded in persuading the Westminster Parliament to establish a Select Committee 'to take the examination of witnesses respecting the African Slave Trade', and promoted the publication of a booklet presenting an abstract of the testimony heard by the committee. This was reprinted in Scotland by the societies already established in Edinburgh and Glasgow to work for the abolition of the slave trade in support of Dickson's tour. Most of those Dickson contacted to solicit support were ministers or members of the Church of Scotland rather than of the 'secession' Presbyterian churches who were recruiting ever greater numbers of members disturbed by the close association of the Church of Scotland and the British government.[281]

If all members of the Church did not respond to Dickson's requests for aid, a substantial number did. William Robertson's son (his father had just died) joined the Society for the Abolition of the Slave Trade and promised Dickson that 'Scotland will not be outdone by England in this glorious rivalry.'[282] At Aberdeen Dickson received an honorary degree from Marischal College, almost certainly as a result of the efforts of James Beattie. It would be misleading to imply that the prominence of the issue in Scotland in 1792 was down to Dickson completely, but his return visit to the country he had left as a much younger man must have helped to ensure that there was a marked Scottish element to the parliamentary petitioning campaign of 1792, at a time when almost all Scottish Members of Parliament were elected in the conservative interest. According to Iain Whyte, 185 petitions in favour of the abolition of the slave trade were received by Parliament from Scotland in 1792 out of a total of 519.[283] In addition, 67 statements and resolutions were published in the Scottish press, such as that by the Gaelic Congregation of Edinburgh which expressed its 'detestation of the oppressions of every kind by which the coasts of Africa have been harassed and desolated ...' In January 1792 the *Glasgow Courier* published a letter that argued that eating West Indian sugar was equivalent to whipping a slave![284] By 1792 there were five societies for the abolition of the slave trade in Scotland. On 5 March 1792 the Edinburgh society obtained more than 3500 signatures to a petition to abolish the slave trade at a public meeting attended by Dickson and addressed by the prominent Scottish Whig lawyer and politician, Henry Erskine. There were 10,885 signatures to the Edinburgh petition when it was forwarded to Parliament, more than that from any other city in Britain save London and Manchester.[285]

The great fear of those behind the 1792 campaign to end the slave trade, of course, was that it would be associated with contemporary agitation for reform of the British constitution, or more seriously, with the political revolution unfolding in the kingdom of France. In addition, the astounding rebellion of the slaves in the French sugar colony of St Domingue in 1791 had preceded Dickson's campaign in Scotland and raised the spectre of race war in the Caribbean. In part, Clarkson and other leaders of the Society for the Abolition of the Slave Trade may have been convinced that a second bloodbath awaited in the British sugar colonies if the system of slavery there was allowed to continue as it had during the eighteenth century.[286] By 1793 what had become the French Republic would emancipate all the slaves in St Domingue, although subsequent French involvement with its former colony would be less glorious. Wedgwood's famous medallion of 1787 with its legend 'am I not a man and a brother', added a powerful visual symbol to the impact of French revolutionary emancipation. The cocktail of wide-spread agitation for universal adult male suffrage in Britain, the success of republicanism in France and growing impatience with sectarian and racist bigotry created an explosive chemistry that the men behind the petitioning campaign were determined to exploit. Their own aims were far from revolutionary, given that it was the slave trade rather than slavery itself that they wished to abolish.[287] There was an anxiety to demonstrate that their efforts would always be carried out within the framework of the constitution. Dickson, for example, was horrified when he realized that women and boys had signed the Abolition peti-tion at Dundee.[288]

The petitioning campaign certainly had an effect on the House of Commons at Westminster, where Henry Dundas introduced a bill to abolish the slave trade to the West Indies through 'gradual abolition.' It passed in the Commons, only to fail in the House of Lords. How far did Dundas really favour abolition? The Pitt ministry's strength was in the Lords, whereas in the Commons, Dundas, Grenville and Pitt himself had to take the burden of defending government policy. The ministry could concede abolition in the Commons knowing that it would fail in the Lords, and thus could keep Wilberforce and other independent MPs who favoured abolition inclined to support the government. Dundas was convinced that the wealth of the West Indian sugar trade was essen-tial for the future of the British Empire in the aftermath of the loss of its former mainland colonies, and in less than a year would begin the war against revolutionary and republican France by sending a British fleet and army to the West Indies in an attempt to gain control of the region. If mainland American colonies had been lost by exerting Westminster's parliamentary authority over their assemblies before the America War of Independence, did not abolition involve the same risk of conflict and loss given that most of the colonies had their own assemblies? 'The co-operation of the legislators of the West Indian islands will be absolutely necessary to give effect to that mode of abolition which I conceive to be most eligible', Dundas told the House.[289] Yet the West Indian assemblies represented no one but those whites who served the interests of the planters there, while the planters themselves, almost to a man, had left their plantations to enjoy the profits of the sugar trade on the estates and the town houses they were able to purchase in Britain with the wealth they brought from the colonies. This was the empire striking back. Dundas was focused on imperial expansion in the West Indies. Convinced that access to imperial markets through the Treaty of Union had brought about the transformation of Scotland, Dundas would bring about parliamentary union with Ireland to ensure a sufficient pool of emigrants, soldiers and administrators for the overseas empire.[290]

Apologists for British slavery and increasing support for abolition

One influential contribution to the debate over the abolition of the slave trade was the *History of Dahomy* published by Archibald Dalzel in 1793. Dalziel (as he spelled his surname before he was forced to declare bankruptcy in 1778) had trained in medicine and become involved in the slave trade as a surgeon. He had enjoyed some initial success trading on his own account as a slaver, but lost his capital when American privateers captured the slaving ships in which he had invested in 1778. He continued to be involved in the trade through employment with Liverpool and London merchants, and testified before the Privy Council in 1788 to the effect that the slave trade was in general humane. From 1791 to 1802 he returned to Africa as governor of the principal trading station of the Company of Merchants Trading to Africa, many of whose members as subscribers supported the publication of his *History of Dahomy*. Dalzel sought to defend the slave trade by portraying Africa as a dark and savage continent and the slave trade as the instrument of deliverance for many of its inhabitants, who by its agency were able to escape a state of savagery through their exportation to America. His history did not dwell on their lives as slaves in the western hemisphere but on their probable fate should they remain in Africa.[291]

'Whatever evils the slave trade may be attended with (and there is no good without some mixture of evil)', Dalzel wrote, 'this we are sure of, it is mercy to the unfortunate brave; and not less to poor wretches, who, for a small degree of guilt, would otherwise suffer from the butcher's knife ....' He rejected the idea that it was the slave trade itself that provoked intertribal violence in Africa. 'If it were advanced,' he wrote, 'that the desire of gain tempts one nation in Africa, or any where else, to make deprivations on another; we might justly answer, that should this desire be obviated, some other would excite to the same violence.'[292] At another point in the book he wrote that 'Asiatic pomp and European necessity for labourers inured to a tropical sun, appears to have been the only effectual instruments of mercy, the only means whereby the lives of many of these unfortunate people have been saved.'[293] For Dalzel, the British slave trade was an aspect of the beneficial effect of expanding European contact with the non-European world characteristic of the spread of Enlightenment civilization in the eighteenth century.

In 1807, the centenary year of parliamentary union with Scotland, Parliament abolished the slave trade in the British Empire. One reason was that Dundas's West Indian campaign of the 1790s had come at a ferocious cost in lost lives among the thousands of British sailors and soldiers sent there. Union with Ireland in 1801 would eventually alter the balance of power in the new House of Commons, although it is not possible to attribute abolition solely to this. The spectacular loans voted by Parliament in the 1790s to sustain the sugar merchants trading to the West Indies had also provoked as much of a reaction against the region in Britain as did the losses among the British troops. By 1807 Dundas had been impeached and Pitt was dead, but the case for delay by 'gradualists' in regard to the slave trade was well and truly over.[294] The slave republic in St Domingue had fallen, the French Republic had become a Napoleonic European empire and the political radicalism that had appeared such a threat to conservative interests in the 1790s had abated. This was partly because France no longer represented the alternative of republicanism to British limited monarchy, and partly because many radicals had fled abroad, turned their attention to trade unionism or become focused on reaping the rewards of a wartime economy.[295] Abolition did not stop the Atlantic slave trade, however, although the US abolished slave trading in 1808. Would successful abolition lead to eventual emancipation, or was a less brutal and authoritarian slave regime possible in British colonies, allowing Britain to continue to receive the economic benefit of the wealth generated by West Indian plantations?

The campaign to abolish slavery, more than the campaign to abolish the slave trade, became part of the moral culture of unionist Scotland in the nineteenth century. It provided for Scottish participation in a wider cause that offered moral redemption in a changing world.[296] Yet the West Indian trading interest in Scotland grew more assertive after the abolition of the slave trade, particularly with the formation of the Glasgow West India Association in 1807 and the emergence of the *Glasgow Courier* and its editor, James McQueen, as defenders, not as they saw it, of slavery, but of the benefits the West Indies brought to the modernization and expanding economy of what they conceived as Britain and its empire.[297] Thus the debate over the future of slavery in the British West Indies became something of a vehicle for debate in Scotland over what modern Scotland would come to be in the nineteenth century. The abolition campaign, it has been argued, 'was a classic example of the way in which Scotland used' American issues (particularly democracy, republicanism and slavery) 'to bring into focus its own situation ....'[298]

After 1815 the debate was over whether slavery in the West Indies could be 'ameliorated' to avoid the cruelties of the past. The point was generally conceded that if Africa was a savage and dark continent, the West Indies had witnessed extraordinary cruelties inflicted on the Africans who had been brought there. The claim was that this had changed with the abolition of the slave trade, and that it was wrong to campaign for freedom for West Indian slaves when so many agricultural labourers, factory workers and Highland peasants laboured under such distress in Scotland and elsewhere in Britain.[299] The West India interest in Scotland took up many of these themes more aggressively in 1823 and after as the prospect of abolition loomed. How could Britain free its slaves when rival European interests in the West Indies and mainland South America retained them? Was it not enough that Britain had taken the lead in abjuring the trade in slaves from Africa, ensuring that planters had to invest heavily in the health and happiness of their existing slaves, when so many European interests continued to participate in trading, despite the efforts of the Royal Navy?[300]

As petitioning to Parliament regarding the issue increased in the 1820s, not all of those from Scotland were in favour of abolition. The West India lobby in Scotland wanted to remind Parliament of the great wealth that had been generated for all of Britain, including Scotland, through this trade. The petition submitted to Parliament from Cromarty and Tain in 1824 supported amelioration, but warned against exciting slaves to rebellion 'by delusive hopes'. Of course the core of the West India interest in Scotland was in Glasgow. The petition from the planters and merchants of Glasgow and Greenock in 1826 drew attention to their concern to protect their slaves not only in terms of 'Well-being', but also as property which was now threatened by the interference of those who did not understand the value of 'one of the brightest gems in the crown' of Britain. The Glasgow West India Association supported the proposal to establish a government inquiry into conditions of slaves and their welfare, but argued that it was essential that members of this commission be 'practically acquainted with tropical agriculture and the control of agricultural labour in the colonies.'[301] Those who had no experience of plantation agriculture, it was argued, had no right to assume a posture of moral superiority over those who had. While most Scottish newspapers were sympathetic to gradualist emancipation, the *Glasgow Courier* emerged as a leading opponent of it. Its editor, James McQueen, who had been the overseer of a sugar plantation in Grenada, had returned to Scotland and became editor of the *Glasgow Courier* sometime in the early 1820s. He argued that calls for the emancipation of slaves in the West Indies increased the dangers of slave rebellion and violence there. If emancipation came, it would have to be introduced gradually among a population unsuited for 'that rational freedom which is established in civilised states.' McQueen emphasized 'the volatile state of Haiti and the failure of Sierra Leone to measure up to the ideals of its founders' as a cautionary tale for uncritical proponents of abolition. [302]

By the 1820s, with an increase in interest in reform issues, paradoxically there were fewer petitions from Scotland urging abolition of slavery itself in contrast to the campaign of 30 years previously to abolish the slave trade. Perhaps the issue was perceived as a metaphor for the social tensions in Scotland regarding reform of the British constitution and the consequent changes in Scottish society that many expected or feared as a consequence of this. Gordon Pentland has argued that 'while the Whig government hedged its bets over slavery' there was no doubt that the experience of parliamentary reform shaped the responses of both the West India interest and the abolitionists in their own campaigns.[303] Those who sought to defend the existence of slavery in the British Caribbean associated their campaign with that to maintain what its defenders considered as the integrity of the British constitution.[304] Pentland discusses an extraordinary example of anti-abolitionist propaganda in Edinburgh, which appears to make an explicit link between the campaign to reform the constitution and that to abolish slavery in the British Empire. It took the form of a mock printed election handbill entitled *Caesaa Thompson to de black electors of Eboro*. 'Caesaa Thompson' is presented as a 'free Nigaa' come to Scotland to seek a seat in Parliament, or, as the text expressed it, 'dat little house', through 'Po-lickit-all Union' and concessions from the king.[305] The example of slaves rising above themselves appears to have been used as a way to fan fears over the repercussions of expanding the electoral franchise. On the other hand, abolitionists and political reformers shared an agenda for dramatic change. The slave interest was presented as part of the Old Regime, a corrupt elite defending its interests in a particularly despicable form of private property, and thus part and parcel of all that the radical reform movement sought to destroy. Once reform was achieved, abolition must surely follow, The Scotsman believed, with an article in 1833 presenting abolition as an issue in which there were 'the planters arranged on one side, and the British people on the other.'[306]

Whereas in 1792 the Scottish campaign in favour of the abolition of the slave trade was led by the synods, presbyteries and parishes of the Church of Scotland, the campaign for the emancipation of British slaves in the 1820s demonstrated the changes brought by a new generation in Scottish society. Scotland was still a Protestant and Presbyterian nation, but the national Church represented and included a much smaller proportion of its population than it had previously. In the campaign against slavery, societies dedicated to the issue allowed Scots of all Christian denominations to come together in support of this one cause. As in 1792, however, there was an anxiety to present the slavery issue as separate from, and in a sense of greater priority than, political reform of the British constitution. Church organizations remained important, but the United Associate Secession Church took a leading role in a campaign that accelerated in intensity as the separate issues of Roman Catholic emancipation and reform of the constitution also came to dominate public attention. It was an age when public meetings and popular petitions as media of protest against the status quo were reported in considerable detail in an expanding newspaper print culture, but also in other published forms of communication in print. The Earl of Rosebery presented a petition for the end of British slavery from Glasgow in 1826 that had 39,000 signatures. The petition from Dundee 'measured 63 feet in length' and the signatures were 5 column inches deep. Over the autumn of 1830 and winter of 1831, 338 petitions for the abolition of British slavery were sent to Parliament from Scotland, including almost 100 from congregations of the United Associate Secession Church.[307]

While many churches and trades guilds in Scotland that called for abolition of slavery also petitioned *against* Roman Catholic emancipation, there does seem to be more evidence of links between those campaigning for reform of the British constitution and those calling for the abolition of slavery in the form of concurrent petitioning campaigns. There were also contrasts, however. Petitions to Parliament advocating parliamentary reform came mostly from civic sources, whether on behalf of magistrates, burgesses or trades guilds. In Scotland, certainly, the idea that clergymen should not become involved in politics appears to have limited engagement with the issue of political reform by secession churches, as well as by the Church of Scotland, which many expected to act as a defender of the established political order. Anti-slavery petitions, however, were mostly from secessionist and dissenting church congregations, as well as from political unions and more generally from the inhabitants of cities and towns.[308] Whether this indicates that the abolition issue engaged a broader section of the Scottish population than the political reform movement led by the middle class is difficult to establish. Conservatives were against both, but in an age of religious evangelical revival political issues did not always map directly on to broader changes in Scottish society. One characteristic of the Liberal political culture emerging in Scotland at this time was that it could accommodate considerable diversity under the broad banner of opposition to the conservative landed interest.[309]

With the abolition of British slavery in 1833 and the end of the 'apprenticeship' scheme to retain the labour of former slaves in 1838 the Scottish Abolitionist movement fundamentally changed. It was no longer focused on the West Indies, although emancipation marked not the end of Scottish involvement there but its decline. Scottish Presbyterian missions became significant in the Caribbean only after abolition. Individual Scots continued to emigrate there, although its reputation for having an unhealthy climate and the increasing availability of alternative destinations for emigration meant that the connection declined to the point that the street names of West Indian origin in Glasgow and Edinburgh, and the gravestones in some of their older kirkyards, were all that remained of what had once been so central a commercial connection in the Scottish economy.[310] 'It's a not so delicious irony', the Scottish write Jackie Kay wrote in 2007, 'that the anniversary of the bicentenary [of the abolition of the slave trade] is also the tercentenary of the union between Scotland and England, which allowed Scotland to profit from the slave trade in a big way, and changed the face of Glasgow in particular.'[311]

Attention moved from the West Indies to the issue of the continuing legality of slavery in parts of the United States. Why? Slavery in the Spanish and Portuguese Empires, and in Africa in general, was larger in scale as an expression of the evil and affected more individuals, but the legacy of the previous colonial connection with the US created a powerful bond.[312] Since American independence, communication across the Atlantic had become easier and Scottish churches, educational institutions and merchants all continued to have links with the United States that in some ways strengthened rather than diminished.[313] In the years from 1833 until the aftermath of the American Civil War the issue of slavery in the United States attracted a great deal of attention and comment in Scotland and in the process engendered a fundamental change in the relationship between Scotland and America. In the middle decades of the nineteenth century, the great issue of the future of slavery in the United States assumed a major presence in Scottish public life. It was not the only presence, of course, in the era of clearances in the Highlands and the complete disruption of the national church, but in a nation that increasingly came to define itself in terms of moral and educational issues, the continuing existence of slavery in the expanding United States was a crime against humanity that demanded worldwide attention, including that of the world's largest empire.[314]

5
Scotland and Native Peoples in the Americas

Did the interaction of Gaelic and Scots cultures in early modern Scotland create a culture with acute sensitivity to the issues implicit in the European debate over conditions of barbarism and civility in human society? Or were the Scots, as subalterns of empire, consigned to deal with native peoples while its profits and the power went elsewhere? Particularly in the eighteenth century, Scots were at the centre of the debate over the future of native peoples in America. This was partly because there had already been a debate in Scotland during the sixteenth and seventeenth centuries relating to this issue but focused on the people of Scotland rather than America. The great Scottish classicist, George Buchanan, was a critic of the impact of early European colonization in America, particularly in his poem, *In colonias brasilienses.* Buchanan denounced European barbarity in America, particularly that of the Portuguese colonists in Brazil. For Buchanan, 'the empire was an inherently unstable and vulnerable commercial world' which excluded the possibility of a virtuous life.[315] Although familiar with Gaelic, Buchanan believed that the classical languages were the languages of civilization. He was, after all, to become the greatest Latinist in Europe in his lifetime. In his *History of Scotland*, he wrote that 'the gradual extinction of the ancient Scottish language' was something that he could 'perceive without regret'. 'Let us pass from rusticity and barbarism,' he wrote, 'to culture and civilization, let our choice and judgement repair the infelicity of our birth.'[316] Buchanan had been subject to trial by the Inquisition while teaching in Portugal, an experience which appears to have affected his views on rusticity and culture. For Buchanan, no reports of American savagery, even cannibalism, could equal the depravity of what the Portuguese colonists did to the native peoples of Brazil.

Early contact

Buchanan's pupil, James VI of Scotland, equated Spanish conquest of native peoples in the Americas with the Roman conquest of the ancient Britons (including the Scots). Both Native American and ancient British societies were founded on tribal social organization and strong bonds of real or imagined kinship. Both lacked, or rather James imagined them to lack, what might be called the civic humanism of the Roman Republic and Empire. The lack of a broader sense of shared civic responsibilities in these societies defined them to James as savage. Indians were 'beastly', and this was the reason they had been enslaved and suffered subjection to the Spanish.[317] James was hardly alone in Europe in considering the natives of America to be savages in contrast to the civility of the European Renaissance, but he also considered many of his fellow Scots to be 'savage'. The disputed lands of the border country with England remained difficult for the Scottish monarchy to control even after James became king of England in 1603. The Scottish Highlands of the west and north posed even greater challenges, and James responded to these by promoting a policy of 'plantation'.[318] The language used in the records of Scottish government tells its own tale, referring to 'the barbarous and desteastable form of living of the present inhabitants', which was 'lascivious' and even imagined to include cannibalism. Scottish Privy Council minutes record an aspiration to carry out 'the full extermination of sic a vermine' and their replacement by 'civile people'.[319]

After James VI of Scotland became James I of England his major project was to make a single kingdom of Britain, and in this he failed. There ensued more than a century of an unsatisfactory halfway 'union of the crowns' without any corresponding parliamentary union. This had an impact on Scottish contact with America, which initially took the form of charters granted under the authority of the Scottish Crown by James VI to one of the Scottish courtiers who followed him to England, Sir William Alexander of Menstrie, whose lands were near the birthplace of George Buchanan in central Scotland.[320] By the end of the sixteenth century Scots fishing vessels were going to Newfoundland and, of course, Scots almost certainly had made contact with America before 1603.[321] However, the royal charters were more about contact with the idea of America and a transatlantic 'New World' than the physical movement of Scots there. After James as king of England granted charters that led to English attempts to establish settlements in the Chesapeake Bay, he encouraged Scots to join the colony. The

Spanish ambassador reported that more than 100 of them had left London on ships bound for the Jamestown settlement.[322] It was contact with the governor of Newfoundland that encouraged Sir William Alexander to seek a charter from James VI as king of Scotland to allow him to try to plant a colony between the lands granted to the Plymouth Colony and those claimed by the French in the St Lawrence River Valley.[323] He published his *An Encouragement to Colonies* in London in 1624, in the aftermath of voyages, made by vessels that he had funded, to look for possible sites for a colony on the mainland opposite Newfoundland. In his pamphlet Alexander in effect took James VI's ideas of colonizing the Highlands and transferred them to what he called 'Nova Scotia'. One of the justifications Alexander gave for Scottish colonization was that the Indians would 'by our meanes ... learne lawfull Trades and industries,' which as Arthur Williamson has commented, was ironic given that in 1629 Alexander attempted to revive his scheme to establish 'New Scotland', by negotiating with Highland chiefs near his own lands in central Scotland to 'transport themselves and their followers to settle themselves into New Scotland.'[324]

A brief record of the efforts of Alexander's son, also named William, to establish a settlement at Port Royal on the Bay of Fundy justified its establishment as 'for the benefit of Grate Britain', but also discussed contact with native peoples there, already familiar with European settlers from previous French expeditions. The settlers were not all Scots, indeed the majority may have been English, including Protestant dissenters. The report on the natives differs little from other early encounters between European colonists and the people who were living in the lands they chose for settlement, but it does record that amicable relations were established to a degree. It is clear, however, that in this the Scots were following the precedent established by the Basque fishermen and French traders who had made earlier contact with the people they encountered. Yet the language of savagery and civility is present in the midst of an irenic account of peaceful coexistence. These were people who feasted 'when they meet, till all there store be gone so every day serves it selfe'. While they were 'subtill in their truckings, and nimble fingered, ... a people among whom people may live verry weel', they were also 'continuall eaters and drinkers of the best if they have it.' Another party of native people who came with hides, 'asking of us if we wer a friend' were noted as 'a more civil and sober company'.[325] Civility and sobriety were obviously the measure of civilization, and many Native American peoples would fall short of this in Scottish and other European settlers' estimation.

When groups of Scots did come to America as part of private mercantile projects to plant colonies in East Jersey and Carolina in the second half of the seventeenth century, of course contact with native peoples was an issue. This was implicit in the contrast between the East Jersey settlement of the 1680s and that at Stuart's Town in South Carolina. The former had previously been settled by colonists from New England and, while not populous, in effect was an agrarian colony near enough to the port of New York to benefit from trading there. In the Carolinas, European settlement had been recent and closer to the Spanish garrison at St Augustine than to the tobacco colony of Virginia. The tribes in the region were numerous and warlike if provoked and after the first colonists in the Carolinas, from Barbados, provided the provocation war with native peoples became characteristic of the early history of the colony. East Jersey, in contrast, was a proprietorial colony associated with the Society of Friends, who had been concerned to promote good relations with the people they found there when they took up their lands. Some of the indentured servants recruited in the Borders of Scotland wrote to relations after their arrival that 'for the Indians Natives, they are not troublesome any way to any of us, if we do them no harm, but are a very kind and loving people.' Another colonist made the brief observation that 'the Indians are a harmless People, and very kind to us, they are not a hairie People as was said to us in Scotland.'[326]

There are consistent references in the letters of Scottish settlers in America back to Scotland of the possibility of living in peace with native peoples. No doubt other colonists did so as well, but Scots were different from the English, French and Dutch in having an element of their own population that could be seen as savage. What recent research has made clear is that Scotland was not so different from Sweden and Denmark in the seventeenth century, in that all were kingdoms with northern clans that could be perceived as savage and barbarous. The Scots, were different, however, in that increasing numbers of them were coming into contact with American peoples who would be perceived as uncivilized.[327] By the end of the century and the dispatch of the Darien expeditions, more than 200 years after first European encounters with the Americas, this may have been part of Scottish confidence that their colony at Darien would be something different from other European plantations. It would achieve better relations with native peoples than the Spanish with their black legacy of atrocities, but also better than those the English had experienced in the Caribbean and mainland North America during the seventeenth century. Most, if not all, of the Scottish pamphlet literature claiming that native peoples in Panama had the natural right to trade with the Scots without Spanish interference did not refer explicitly to the Scottish experience of negotiating Highland and Lowland cultural differences within a single polity, but it has been argued that this was a significant factor in Scottish concepts of the nature of American colonization.[328] While the majority of the investors in the Company of Scotland were landowners in the Lowlands or were from burghs there, a substantial number of the colonists were Highlanders, particularly in the second expedition. There were native auxiliaries on both sides when Spaniards confronted Scots at Darien in 1700. The Scots' belief in their ability to negotiate satisfactorily with native peoples did make their contribution to British colonization in North America distinctive. Robert Wodrow, minister of the Church of Scotland parish at Eastwood outside Glasgow and an indefatigable antiquarian, recorded an acute interest in the native peoples of the Caribbean at the time when the Darien expeditions were being dispatched from Britain. The questions he sent with one of the surgeons accompanying the second Scottish expedition to Darien were about whether 'the natives' believed in one God. He had read John Eliott's speculations that Indians in New England were descended from the ten lost tribes and wanted to know 'if they have any tradition of any strangers coming among them, before the Spaniards' and 'if there has been observed any agreement between their language and our Irish or Highlands', the latter point having been suggested to him by Lionel Wafer's book on the isthmus of Darien.[329] Alternatively, as David Armitage has pointed out, English colonization became British once the English began to draw on Scottish manpower in their colonization projects in the eighteenth century.[330] Governor Daniel Parke of the Leeward Islands wrote to London in 1707 requesting 'tenn thousand Scotch with oatmeal enough to keep them for 3 or 4 months' for an attack on Puerto Rico on the grounds that they would be more expendable than an alternative force.[331]

The Society in Scotland for the Propagation of Christian Knowledge

This aspect of Scottish colonization in America after the union appears most clearly in the history of Scottish participation in the early colonization of Georgia, south of Carolina, in the 1730s. In Georgia the trustees' representative, James Oglethorpe, was successful in forging good relations with the Cherokee, Creek, Chickasaw and other Indian 'nations', although it should be noted how problematic European names for Indian 'nations' and their 'kings' and 'princes' could be. There is evidence that Oglethorpe played on the distinctive and striking culture of the Highland colonists he had recruited for Georgia in some of his negotiations with Indian tribes on the borders of Georgia. As war threatened between Spain and Britain in 1739, Oglethorpe took a party of Highlanders with him to a meeting of the 'Creek nation' at their 'town' of Coweta, 500 miles north-east of Frederica in Georgia.[332] The Creek 'king' present at the meeting held a British flag as a sign of friendship, although it was neutrality that was promised in the event of conflict with the Spanish, not an alliance. The Highlanders wore their plaids and carried targes and broadswords. They were presented as a martial people, apparently to encourage Creek warriors to assist the British.[333]

In the Cape Fear Valley a group of more than 300 Gaelic-speaking Highlanders arrived from Gigha, Kintyre and Knapdale in Argyll in 1739. One of their leaders was Duncan Campbell of Kilduskland in Knapdale, who had sold his estate in Scotland and emigrated to Jamaica before returning to Argyll to recruit colonists to help take up lands in North Carolina. He left the Cape Fear Valley in the late 1740s to return to Scotland, and in 1748 a petition for a Gaelic-speaking minister to serve the 'Argyll Colony' was noted by the Presbytery of Kintyre. It claimed that the party had settled 90 miles up the Cape Fear River at a place remote from other settlements, 'not far from the *Indians*.'[334] This is the only reference to native peoples in the surviving documentation relating to Scottish immigrants from the Highlands in the Cape Fear Valley, which may be related to the catastrophic smallpox epidemic that cut a swathe through native peoples in North Carolina before 1738. The largest 'nation' in the region, the Cherokee, may have lost half of its people in this epidemic. Modern estimates, always problematic, suggest a population decline for the Cherokee from 20,000 in 1719 to 8500 in 1755.[335]

There is a striking reference to the Maroon Indians of the Blue Mountains on Jamaica in a letter written in 1771 by Alexander Morison, a tacksman from Skye, to justify his decision to give up his lands there in favour of emigration to North Carolina: 'I can say as the Indian to Governour Trelawny that I grew out of this ground and have as strong an attachment to my native soil as any man, but the low price of cattle and kelp has put it out of my power as well as many of my neighbours to pay our rents.'

Morison presented himself as being similar to the Maroons, but the extensive claim for compensation as a British Loyalist that he made on his return to Britain after the American War of Independence demonstrated that he had been a man of considerable wealth. However in his letter to the management of the Macleod estate on Skye in 1771 he compares himself to one of the Maroon Indians in Jamaica with whom Governor Edward Trelawny, a Cornishman, agreed a treaty in 1739 to secure peace with the native population on terms that discouraged their continued assistance to runaway slaves. Was Morison familiar with this exchange between Indian and Trelawny from a literary source? We know from his Loyalist claim that he possessed an extensive library. Or had he become familiar with this reported exchange through contact with some of the Scottish tacksmen, wadsetters and small landowners who had emigrated to Jamaica in the 1730s? What is certain is that this Highland tacksman was comparing his situation as a tacksman/lease-holder of rented lands faced with the prospect of steeply rising rents with that of the Maroon Indians on Jamaica in 1739. As a Gaelic-speaker and a practitioner of traditional medicine, Morison compared the pressures he faced in keeping his land to those experienced by Indians in America.[336]

The Highlanders recruited for settlement in Georgia had been accompanied by a Gaelic-speaking minister named John Macleod, who was sponsored by the Society in Scotland for the Propagation of Christian Knowledge (SSPCK) to serve the spiritual needs of the Presbyterian Gaelic-speaking colonists, just as the leaders of the Argyll colony in North Carolina had petitioned the SSPCK in 1748 for a Gaelic-speaking Presbyterian minister. Although Macleod left Darien in Georgia for the presbytery of Charleston in South Carolina, the SSPCK did retain an interest in a Presbyterian mission to America. Their efforts, however, turned to New York and New England, rather than the American South, and to encouraging Presbyterian missions to American Indians, rather than providing Gaelic-speaking Presbyterian ministers for Highland emigrants.[337] Why? Donald Meek has argued that the society's activities reflect the changing priorities of religious culture in eighteenth-century Scotland, which might be summarized succinctly as shifting 'from civilization to salvation as the first priority' under the influence of the Protestant evangelical culture of the time. The SSPCK was drawn into American activity by the Georgia Trustees, who were looking to the Scottish Highlands for colonists, and by existing cultural links between Scottish Presbyterians and the Congregationalists of New England, as the society supported the work of three missionaries to the Indians on the frontier in New York and Massachusetts through correspondents in Boston. In a change of policy that reflected its changing priorities in both America and Scotland, the society ceased to support missionaries who would not live as well as work with Native American communities. Instead, it responded to an appeal from America to do something about 'the deplorable, perishing state of the Indians on the border of New York, New Jersey and Pensilvania', and began to support missionaries who lived in Indian communities in Long Island and outside Albany in New York. The best known of these was David Brainard, whose journal was published posthumously, edited by the famous American clergyman Jonathan Edwards. When Brainard initially arrived in 1743 at Kaunaumeek, New York, to begin his mission, he stayed 'with a Gaelic-speaking Highland family who had come to the area about two years previously and who lived some two miles from his station among the Indians. Brainard commented that he had 'but one single person to converse with that can speak English. Most of the talk I hear is either Highland Scotch or Indian.'[338]

Brainard's aim was to 'civilize' the Indians as well as to serve them spiritually, and he had no doubt about the necessity of this. 'They are in general unspeakably indolent and slothful,' he wrote, 'they have been bred up in idleness and know little about cultivating the land, or indeed of engaging vigourously in any other business.'[339] Yet there is a case that Brainard's sponsors in Scotland were drawn to support of the Christian mission to native peoples in North America by their experience of the problems of promoting it in the Scottish Highlands. One of the SSPCK's reports on the conditions it faced in the Scottish Highlands declared that 'when a people are idle or slothful we can hardly expect that any principles will render them virtuous or useful members of the state.' The difference between Scottish Highlanders and North American Indians was that Highlanders spoke a single Scottish Gaelic language, albeit a language with appreciably different regional dialects. North American Indians spoke languages of considerably more cultural complexity and variation which Europeans found difficult to learn. While a translation of the Bible for Native American use was completed by John Eliot in 1663, it was translated into a particular dialect of Algonquian and consequently was accessible only to a small minority of Native Americans even after they were introduced to the culture of print. In Scotland there was a translation into Gaelic of John Knox's *Book of Common Order* in 1567, although one of the New Testament was not published until 1767 and that of the Old Testament was not completed until 1801.[340] By the second half of the eighteenth century Gaelic was becoming the language of evangelical Protestant revival in the Scottish Highlands, with a consequent increase in the number of ordained and lay preachers who brought this religious movement into the centre of the indigenous culture of the region rather than perpetuate the use of English as the language of 'civilization'.

The SSPCK expanded its links with native peoples in the northern colonies because there were more Presbyterian and Congregationalist clergy there sympathetic to the Church of Scotland. From 1764, the SSPCK began to support Eleazar Wheelock's schools to train Native Americans as Protestant Christian missionaries in New York and New England. It was this connection that led to the appearance in Edinburgh in 1767 of Samson Occom, an ordained Presbyterian Native American minister, who appeared before the General Assembly of the Church of Scotland to appeal for financial support for Wheelock's schools. Occom spent more than two years touring England, Ireland and Scotland appealing for funds. Wheelock's emphasis on the importance of learning native languages in the pursuit of successful missionary work chimed with the move in Scotland to recognize that promoting the English language would not work in the interest of evangelical missionary work in the Scottish Highlands. Assisting Wheelock appealed to Scots who believed that they shared Wheelock's goals in promoting Christian salvation of peoples who might once have been viewed as savages, but were now seen to be fellow souls entitled to Christian salvation. In contrast, on his return to New England, Occom quarrelled with Wheelock when he learned that the latter planned a merger of his schools that would ensure that most of his future students would be of European creole descent whose birth language was English.[341]

Scots in the Indian trade

To the south, new lands opened up for European settlement in the early eighteenth century as native peoples declined in numbers under the impact of exposure to European diseases. Yet the Indian trade had quickly become a principal feature of early colonization in Carolina in the late seventeenth century, and while coastal areas around Charleston had developed a plantation economy producing rice and indigo using slave labour by the early eighteenth century, the Indian trade with the populous (by Native American standards of the time) tribes in the region remained lucrative. Scottish involvement in this trade first arose after Scottish Highland Jacobite prisoners taken at the surrender of Preston in 1715 were sentenced to transportation to Charleston by English courts.[342] At the time the colony had just survived (barely) a

major war with the Tuscarora and Yamasee Indians and was in desper-
ate need of manpower. One of the 15 McGillivrays thus transported,
Archibald, later became an important Indian trader. Later one of
the young men who had been recruited to Georgia in 1736, Lachlan
McGillivray, left Darien for Charleston and with the help of Archibald
McGillivray entered the Indian trade at the age of 21.[343] He became a
prominent trader, planter and merchant in Carolina, based on his skill
in learning native languages, particularly Creek, and he married a
woman of the Wind Clan in the Creek Nation, Sehoy Marchand. Loyal
to Britain, he returned to Inverness after the American Revolution.
Another record of links between the Scottish Highland Jacobite prisoners sent to Charleston in 1716 is the testament of Myles MacIntosh in
the South Carolina Probate Records from 1729. There is no record of
him as a Jacobite transportee, but the original transportation would
have established a 'chain' for further migration, which presumably
included him. In a later assignation of MacIntosh's will recorded in
December 1734, his widow identified him as 'sometime tenant in
Kellochie [Inverness-shire], thereafter Indian trader in Charleston'. The
Jacobite connection has been identified by David Dobson through two
of MacIntosh's executors (William MacKenzie and Duncan McQueen),
who were Jacobite transportees to Charleston in 1716, while another
named executor, Andrew Allen, 'was a burgess and guilds brother
of Glasgow, a merchant and member of the St Andrew's Society
of Charleston.'[344]

In 1743 the Scotsman James Glen arrived in Charleston as governor
of South Carolina. He was not a Highlander, but like William Alexander
in the early seventeenth century, he held land in the central Lowlands
of Scotland not far from the Highland line. Glen soon became involved
in the Charleston Indian trade as an investor as well as Royal Governor,
which attracted criticism about conflict of interest both from
contemporaries who were aware of his financial involvement and from
historians of the Carolinas for his less than comprehensive acknowledgement of his commercial interests.[345] Glen's association with the
prominent Scottish role in expanding British imperial authority in the
region before the American Revolution did not enhance his reputation
after American independence. From another perspective, however,
Glen became part of a distinctive Scottish influence on the development of British imperial policy toward native peoples in the region,
which privileged the interest of those peoples over that of the European
creole settler and planter community. The degree to which this policy
was based on empathy for native peoples as opposed to a desire to retain

the economic benefit in trading with them is open to debate, but there were similarities in the economic and social pressures accelerating in the Scottish Highlands in the eighteenth century and the situation Scots like James Glen encountered in the Carolinas when they arrived there.[346] This judgement could be applied to the history of contact between people in the Scottish Highlands and government in Scotland as much as to native/settler relations in North America.

As governor in South Carolina Glen became a proactive advocate of diplomacy with tribes and native confederations in the region to ensure that they accepted their principal source of European trade goods as Charleston and other centres of British trade, rather than the Spanish or French trading posts. In writing to the French governor of Louisiana in 1749 about the return of prisoners of war, Glen discussed 'the Indian Nations' in terms very like those employed by Scottish pamphleteers at the time of the Darien expeditions, arguing that native peoples, according to the Law of Nature, were sovereign if they remained independent.[347] Of course Glen, like the Scots favouring colonization of Darien, harboured commercial ambitions that could only be fulfilled if 'Indians' were recognized as members of 'Nations' that could be conceptualized as something like the kingdoms and nations of Europe. If European kingdoms were transcending religious conflict and feudalism through an increase of commerce, so should their equivalents elsewhere in the world.[348] One might doubt the civilizing power of commerce, however, when reading Glen's account to the government in London of his success in persuading the Cherokee to punish 'a man of note a great hunter and Warriour' who had shot and murdered 'an Englishman' who 'was but a Worthless drunken fellow a Packhorseman'. Glen reported that he was gratified that contrary to his expectations 'the affair was managed by the Indians with great circumspection procedure and Justice', executing the guilty party and beheading his corpse. Glen reported with satisfaction that 'when his [the murderer's] relations desired leave to bury him, they were told by the headmen that he must lye & rot above ground, that all the English that passed might see their Justice and how punctually they fulfilled their Engagements'. He concluded by stating, drawing on Scottish Enlightenment ideas of stadial history, that it was 'a great step towards civilizing savage and barbarous Nations when they can be brought to do public Acts of Justice upon their Criminals.'[349]

It would take more extended discussion to disentangle the feudal and barbarous aspects of the satisfaction Glen displayed in demonstrating the sacrosanct status of 'the English traders', from the confident statement that these together demonstrate the 'civilizing' quality of 'public Acts of Justice'. Was the 'Worthless drunken fellow a Packhorse-man' who was the object of this public Act of Justice avenged because he was an Englishman or because he was a trader? Glen was confident that 'savage and barbarous Nations' could be civilized, although his words hardly justified his actions. In the Scottish Highlands three years later, in a process that Allan Macinnes has described as 'exemplary civilising', the man accused of the murder of a government factor on a forfeited Jacobite estate was executed after conviction by the Scottish Court of Justiciary, who insisted that after execution his body remain on the gibbet specially constructed for it for an unspecified period of time.[350] Glen's last actions as governor in 1756 related to his project to build a British/South Carolinian fort among the 'overhill' (trans-Appalachian) villages of the Cherokee. Glen left South Carolina in 1758 to join his cousin John Forbes at his base in Philadelphia, with the regiment of Montgomery's Highlanders sent to South Carolina in 1757 after it had been raised in Scotland. The Duke of Cumberland as British Commander-in-Chief was reluctant to employ Highland regiments in Europe, and as a consequence the existing Highland Regiment (the Black Watch) and two additional regiments raised in the Highlands after the outbreak of the War (Montgomery's 77th Foot and Fraser's 78th Foot) were all sent to North America, where it was thought that their qualities were more suited to the 'savage' nature of warfare there, as had been demonstrated in the defeat of the first British expedition against Fort Duquesne led by General Braddock in 1755.[351]

Glen agreed with Cumberland, writing to Forbes: 'the great superior-ity that the French have in Indians can hardly be compensated But by Colonel Montgomery's Scots Highlanders and Colonel Washington's American Highlanders.'[352] The implication was that Washington's soldiers, recruited from the western Virginia frontier along the Appa-lachian mountains, even if they were not dressed in what a Scot would define as 'Highland dress', were not only dressed in a manner distinctive from other British soldiers but in their quality represented something Glen perceived as 'Highland'.[353] Developing the analogy he wished to make further, Glen continued his letter to Forbes by criticizing Virgin-ian efforts to recruit Cherokee auxiliaries for the campaign, and joking that 'a thousand or two of Croatts or pandowrs' would be 'cheaper and more under command than as many hundred Indians'. 'Pandowrs' are defined in the *Oxford English Dictionary* as a military force raised originally in Croatia in 1741 for service with the Austrian army against the Turks who 'became renowned for their ferocity and brutality'.[354]

Thus Glen added Croatian Pandours and American Cherokee to his account, describing 'pandowrs' as 'cheaper and more under command' than Indians, yet vouching for the 'behaviour' of Indians from the Cherokee 'Nation' provided that 'Leaders' and 'persons of authority' from the Cherokee came with their 'young men'. Previously Forbes had written to one of his officers that he would urge Glen 'not to turn Indian', while he was in western Virginia at Fort Cumberland with Washington.[355] Clearly, for Glen and Forbes, Montgomery's Highlanders had more in common with Virginia 'highlanders' (or mountain men, as the Americans would have called them), Croatian Pandours and the Cherokee than they did with Lowland Scots such as themselves.

Fort Duquesne fell partly because Forbes persuaded many Indian tribes in the Ohio River Valley to maintain neutrality rather than help the French to defend the post. In the meantime Glen's successor as governor of South Carolina, William Lyttelton, had embarked on an aggressive policy of negotiation with the Cherokee which led to open war and the need to request British military protection for the colony. Jeffrey Amherst, the British commander preparing for an attack on French Canada, reluctantly accepted that he had to respond and chose Scottish troops for the task, the majority of them drawn from Montgomery's Highland Regiment. Amherst gave strict instructions that the troops were to rejoin the army in time for the planned advance on Canada in 1759. In the meantime, Lyttelton received promotion to the governorship of Jamaica, leaving a native South Carolinian, William Bull, as lieutenant governor with responsibility for civil affairs. When Montgomery's detachment arrived, he proceeded to attack some of the Cherokee towns before withdrawing and returning north. The next year, with hostilities still unresolved, another detachment of British solders returned to Carolina, this time under the command of Montgomery's Lieutenant Colonel, James Grant, and after another campaign peace with the Cherokee was finally achieved.[356]

Several thorough accounts of this conflict exist, but the point here is not to dwell on a narrative of the war, but to consider some of the principal points to emerge from this encounter between Scottish Highland soldiers and the Cherokee. We know much about the dislike shared by the Scottish commanders Montgomery and Grant toward William Bull as governor of South Carolina. Regrettably, we know much less about the reactions of the rank and file of Montgomery's Highlanders to the Cherokee.[357] Fighting in the mountainous country in the northwest of what is now South Carolina, the Cherokee were not defeated in battle, but by the systematic destruction of many of their principal settlements and crops. Matthew Dziennik has suggested that many Highland soldiers saw themselves as able to conquer lands from native peoples by their swords, drawing on traditional Highland ideas of the right to secure lands by conquest. This contributed to the idea that British success in North America from 1757 to 1760 and after had been secured by the Highland regiments, giving Scottish Highlanders privileged rights to the benefits of taking up land in America at a time when all Scots were coming under increasing criticism in Britain.[358]

First Archibald Montgomery, and later James Grant, concluded that the Cherokee were very far from being at fault for their war with the southern American colonists. Colonial governors and soldiers had not kept faith with the Cherokee and were more concerned with taking their land than establishing a lasting peace. Both officers, along with John Stuart (see below), became associated with the Indian policy of limiting settler encroachment on native lands that would characterize British policy in North America for the rest of the eighteenth century. Montgomery and Grant felt that the British Army was being used by dishonest colonists who were unwilling to do their own fighting in an unjust cause. Montgomery wrote to his commander Amherst in New York on 24 May 1760 that 'those Indians are Rogues as they all are, but I fancy they have sometimes been hardly dealt by, and if they could tell their own story I doubt Much if they are so much to blame as has been Represented by the People of this Province' [South Carolina]. Many of the Cherokee regretted attacks against British soldiers and settlers, despite their grievances against the South Carolinians. Montgomery and Grant took the lead in arguing that the purpose of the British military presence was to bring about negotiations for peace, not exact vengeance on native tribesmen on behalf of colonists eager for more of their lands. Grant, particularly, was aware that South Carolina was unable to raise its own troops because the colony was dominated by slave-owners terrified that sending too many poor whites as soldiers against the Indians would make coastal South Carolina vulnerable to renewed slave rebellion similar to that experienced in the Stono rebellion of 1739.[359]

The immediate beneficiary of the refusal of Scottish officers to follow South Carolinian orders was John Stuart, originally from Inverness, who was appointed Superintendent for Indian Affairs in the Southern British colonies (including Virginia) from 1763. The post had been established along with its equivalent for the north in 1756 as part of British efforts to make a more coordinated response across all of its colonies to the accelerating conflict with France and the rivalry this engendered over relations with native peoples. The original incumbent for the Southern Department, Edmund Atkin, had not been considered effective. An English immigrant to Charleston who entered the Indian trade, he had returned to England in the 1750s while remaining a member of the South Carolina council, and after Braddock's defeat had been called upon to advise the Board of Trade in London on Indian affairs, which led to his appointment. After his return to South Carolina, he married Lady Anne Mackenzie in 1760, a daughter of the Jacobite third earl of Cromartie whose estate had been confiscated after the 1745 rebellion, but that was the limit of any connection he had with Scotland.[360]

John Stuart, Alexander McGillivray and the Southern Frontier

John Stuart was the son of an Inverness merchant who had supported the Jacobite rebellion of 1745 in Scotland. Stuart himself was not involved in the rebellion, as he had been sent by his father to train as a merchant in London and then Spain, before becoming a member of Commodore George Anson's expedition which circumnavigated the world between 1740 and 1744 after the outbreak of war with Spain in 1739. He was one of 145 survivors who returned to England with the sole ship to complete the circumnavigation in an expedition which had cost 1300 lives, but did receive prize money from the sale of the Spanish galleon that he and his colleagues had captured before their return to England. With this modest amount of capital, Stuart left London in 1748 to emigrate to Charleston in order to trade in partnership with a fellow Scot, Patrick Reid. After Reid's death in 1754 Stuart was unable to keep trading, demitting his office as Secretary of the St Andrew's Society of Charleston as a consequence in 1755.[361] Around the same time he was commissioned in the South Carolina Provincial forces and was sent to the garrison maintained by South Carolina at Fort Loudoun in what is now eastern Tennessee. James Glen had established the fort to prevent French incursions into that region. Prior to that there is no direct evidence of Stuart's involvement in the Carolinian Indian trade, but from 1756 established himself as a diplomat rather than an Indian fighter, particularly with the Cherokee whose lands surrounded Fort Loudoun. He was a notable survivor of the Cherokee assault on the fort that precipitated the British expeditions against the Cherokee.

Stuart's success in 1761 in persuading James Grant that it was wrong to attempt to subjugate the Cherokee completely to South Carolinian colonial authority, and instead to make peace with them on more favourable terms, marked him out to Grant as the man to direct British policy toward native peoples in the American South. He was successful in persuading both Jeffrey Amherst as British Commander-in-Chief and the Board of Trade in London of the wisdom of this. From 1763 to 1779 Stuart took the lead in formulating British policy in the south-east of mainland British America, and that policy was predicated on the idea of preventing the local creole white settler population from exploit-ing native peoples. In the process Stuart recovered a fortune, only to lose it later through his determination to preserve British authority in North America through an alliance with the native confederations of the south-east. In pursuing this agenda he relied disproportionately on fellow Scots such as Alexander Cameron, Lachlan McGillivray and David Taitt, as well as James Grant (who had become governor of East Florida in 1763) and George Johnstone (the Scottish governor of West Florida after the British took possession of the Spanish Florida colonies under the terms of the Peace of Paris in 1763). Johnstone by 1765 was writing to the Secretary of State in London that native peoples in the region 'are a much more moral & virtuous people than ourselves & ... most of their Vices are of Importing: Every Evil Seems to Spring Cheifly from the corrupt Conduct of the Traders & the little Power which Gov-ernment has over them.'[362] This illustrates how the 'stadial' view of history that was so influential in the Scottish Enlightenment affected the views adopted by many Scots who came into contact with the native peoples in the region as representatives of British authority. Human societies at different stages of social development were to be accommodated rather than eliminated, and had their own virtues as well as vices.

Johnstone's secretary was James Macpherson, 'the sublime savage', as James Boswell rendered him, 'translator' of what he claimed was the ancient Gaelic poet Ossian, the Homer of Scotland. *Fingal, an Ancient Epic Poem in Six Books: together with several other poems composed by Ossian, the son of Fingal* had been published in London and become an international sensation, as well as a classic of Georgian English literature. The First Lord of the Treasury, the (Scottish) third earl of Bute, had arranged for Macpherson to accompany Johnstone to Florida as a mark of royal patronage. David Hume was unimpressed. He wrote to Hugh Blair that he hoped that Macpherson would 'travel among the 'Chick-isaws or Cherokees, in order to tame him and civilise him.'[363] Hume originally accepted that Macpherson's poetry was genuinely translated from the work of an ancient poet rather than adapted from examples of oral tradition Macpherson had collected in the Highlands, but he had changed his mind. He told Boswell in 1775 that 'if fifty bare-arsed highlanders should say that Fingal was an ancient Poem, he would not believe them, ... it was not to be believed that a people who were continually concerned to keep themselves from starving or being hanged, should preserve in their memories a Poem in six books.'[364]

Russell Snapp has written that 'perhaps Scottish contemporary historical theory about the virtues of primitive peoples and the relative corruptness of "civilised" peoples had an influence on John Stuart', although Hume's comments to Boswell indicate that there was not universal acceptance of ideas of 'stadial' history in Scotland at the time.[365] One example of a Scot who did make the comparison between Scottish Highlanders and Indians was William Lorimer, tenant of Moulinearn near Dunkeld and a tutor in the family of Sir James Grant of Grant. He wrote in his commonplace book that the 'Scots Highlander' was 'more warlike, & like the modern Indians who will apply to no cultivation of lands, no trade but to sit idel at home, sleeping, dosing & drinking, when they are not abroad hunting or fighting – The latter look on labour of any other kind as the work of slaves, ...'[366] The impact of Scottish political economy, or 'the science of man' at the centre of the phenomenon we define as the Scottish Enlightenment was a significant factor in the advancement of agrarian change in south-eastern North America both before and after American independence. What can most often be defined as 'stadial history', the idea that all human societies develop through similar and progressive stages of organization, was associated with the Scottish Enlightenment, but Scots were not its only exponents in the Lower South. Governor James Wright of Georgia had written that 'the Cherokees I think are half a Century before the Creeks, they are much more civilized and I believe better disposed yet still they are Savages,' while David Ramsay, the historian of South Carolina, wrote in a later work (1804) that economic change would 'transform savage warriors to peaceful farmer,' and Thomas Fitch of Georgia in 1810 believed that the Creeks had 'advance[d] from the Hunting to the Shepherds to the agricultural and manufacturing life, and are becoming Commercial.'[367] All of these writers were American rather than Scottish, although it must be conceded that Ramsay's parents were Irish Presbyterians.

Stuart and his agents, however, wanted to give the native peoples they were responsible for more time to pass through additional stages of social development. Stuart and agents such as David Taitt (who like Lachlan McGillivray had taken a Creek wife) argued that only an expanding transcolonial British imperial authority could protect native interests from traders who promoted the consumption of alcohol in native communities and the sale of land to clear trading debts. The Indian trade had changed. The early British and Irish immigrants, such as Lachlan McGillivray or George Galphin, who had entered the trade in the 1740s, when James Glen was still governor of South Carolina, were succeeded by the type of traders the Indians often called 'Virginians', who had much less respect for native traditions and laws. In 1768 a Creek identified as 'Captain Aleck' contrasted earlier times when 'the White Men and Red Men lived like brothers', defining 'White Men' in 'earlier times' as 'English Men and Scotch Men', with whom he had 'been long acquainted, and always found them to be good men'. 'But these Virginians', he continued, 'are very bad people, they pay no regard to your laws.' Writing to James Grant in 1770, John Stuart reported that the 'Virginians are insatiable .... In short they want all the Cherokee hunting ground.'[368]

Stuart and David Taitt were like James Grant in preferring native societies to the thrusting commercialism that developed after 1763 on the American frontier, as land speculation accelerated and the settler population 'increased at a rapid rate unrestrained by fears of Indian attack'. Stuart became President of the St Andrew's Society of Charleston in 1772 and made his old Cherokee foe Ouconnastotah, the conqueror of Fort Loudoun, a member of the society in 1773. That same year Stuart moved to limit land cessions demanded by self-interested colonial authorities. By 1773 war was threatening, and to many Carolinians and Georgians, defence of native peoples amounted to denial of colonists' rights to self-government. It also, as British troops were redeployed from the Indian frontier to American towns on the coast in dispute with British administrators, raised the fear that native peoples might form a force that would work with British authorities to undermine colonial liberties. It meant that British agents such as Stuart (and Grant before him), were not willing to defend colonists from native attacks, but indeed might one day encourage them to carry them out.[369]

That proved to be the case when General Gage in Boston ordered Stuart to encourage the Cherokee to attack rebellious colonial frontier settlements, trusting Stuart's agent Alexander Cameron, their 'Brother Scotche' (pronounced 'Scotchy') that their 'Father' the king would send them ammunition to help them fight as soon as it could be done. [370] Stuart had already been forced to abandon his wife and household in Charleston for refusing to support resistance to British authority. A Creek embassy in later years would travel to Charleston to demand that Stuart's wife be released from house arrest as the price of peace with them. By the time Stuart died in 1779, he was in exile in Pensacola, and the Florida colonies taken from Spain in 1763 had become both the centre of Indian and British resistance to the American rebellion in the region and the basis of the 'southern strategy' which the British pursued from 1779 to 1781 in order to retain at least this portion of their mainland North American colonial empire. With Spain declaring war on Britain in 1779, Pensacola was lost to the British, and in the aftermath of further British failures in the South by 1781 the Cherokees, Creeks and smaller tribes were destitute. When the British announced that they were to cede Florida back to the Spanish as part of the peace of 1783, some headmen asked that the Indian allies of the British be allowed to go as well. Instead, Loyalist merchants involved in the Indian trade left Savannah and Charleston when they were surrendered to the American Congress and were able to establish themselves under Spanish protection at Pensacola to guarantee continued access to British trade goods for the native confederations. This allowed them to continue to resist the westward expansion of settlement on their hunting grounds. This explains the act passed by Georgia's patriot legislature in 1782 forbidding Scots from entering Georgia (with some exceptions), and characterizing them as possessing 'a decided inimicality to the Civil Liberties of America' which had been expressed 'through their promotion of a Ruinous War, for the Purpose of Subjugating this and other confederated states.'[371]

Before his death Stuart had encouraged the British authorities to back the young Scottish merchant William Panton, who before the American Revolution had emigrated from the north-east of Scotland to become a clerk in the firm of his fellow Scot, John Gordon, in Charleston. He became a prominent support of the Loyalist cause in South Carolina and Georgia, as Gordon had been before he left for London to pursue claims for lands in Florida. Lachlan McGillivray had introduced Panton to his son Alexander when he brought the lad to Savannah and Charleston to learn about the Indian trade. After Lachlan left Georgia because of his Loyalism, returning to Inverness rather than going to London, Alexander McGillivray returned to the Creek nation and through his mother's clan assumed a position of leadership there that during the post-war period would involve him in close collaboration with William Panton in Florida.[372] From 1783 until his death in 1801 Panton worked to tie the native peoples of the south-east into trade with his firm and the interests of Britain, providing them with the guns, gunpowder and ammunition that enabled them to resist demands from the United States for their land. The distress experienced by the Indians in 1781 was alleviated once Panton could guarantee supplies, and the Spanish authorities agreed to continue Panton's privileges after they took possession of Florida, as it offered them a means of limiting American encroachment in the region. Florida would remain Spanish until 1819, when Andrew Jackson followed up earlier US conflict with the Creeks by attacking the colony, executing some British Indian traders, and forcing the US Federal Government into countenancing annexation. Panton's partnership with Alexander McGillivray ended with the latter's death in 1793 at the age of 43. Together they had convinced the Creeks and the Spanish that only vigorous opposition would prevent the US from not only taking Creek lands, but Florida as well. The result was war on the frontier.[373]

By McGillivray's death, however, the Indian trade no longer paid as well as it had before the American Revolution. Even from 1763 to 1776, the scale of John Stuart's expenditure on gifts to native peoples provoked a Parliamentary enquiry in London. There was an ideological edge to Panton and his partners' support of trading with the native peoples of the region that gave way increasingly in the years after his death in 1801 to the realization by his heirs and successors that the only way they would be able to achieve payment of the substantial debts run up by the Indian confederations over more than a generation would be to persuade their clients to sell their lands. That route became inevitable after Jackson's victory over the British in the attack on New Orleans in 1815.[374] After that victory the Spanish were unable to sustain their position in Florida and with this went any chance of native peoples avoiding total reliance on the United States for their welfare. Indian removal to the lands purchased by the United States west of the Mississippi equally became inevitable as any pretence of acknowledging native peoples and their political confederations as sovereign under the natural law acknowledged in Enlightenment discourse collapsed in the face of the harsh imperatives of US westward expansion. It was a history in which the Scottish element could be traced back to Darien and beyond, but also one in which the interests of Scottish imperialists and native peoples were equally doomed when pitted against a creole elite. Something like this history would be repeated in Canada during the nineteenth century in a manner in which Scots would again play a key role, but in a very different larger dynamic affected by what happened to the native peoples of the United States during the nineteenth century.[375]

6

The Spiritual Connection

From the first conception of a 'New Scotland' in America in the early seventeenth century, the idea was associated with those who subscribed to a distinctively Scottish Protestant Reformed religious tradition. Of course, their missionary statements of purpose were always allied with, and arguably in reality subordinated to, the economic priorities of trade and colonization. However, one distinguishing feature of early Scottish contact with America was the fact that the Protestant Reformation in Scotland developed in a manner that was distinctive in Europe and the British Isles. By the end of the seventeenth century the failure in Panama at Darien could be interpreted in terms of a covenanted nation failing to meet the demands of its special relationship with God. Implicit in European colonization of America was the idea that one day the 'old world' would be superseded by the new. In a Scottish context, in the century following the failure at Darien in America, the idea that God had chosen America rather than Scotland as the site of the spiritual renewal of a corrupt human race grew in influence in Scotland.[376]

This can first be traced in some detail in the relatively little that we know about Scotland's (and the re-established Church of Scotland's) relationship with Puritan New England after the British Revolution of 1688. The revolution gave rise to the development of a British state that tolerated Protestant dissent without embracing it, as part of a complex polity originally founded on a special relationship with the United Provinces of the Netherlands and a significant portion of the Holy Roman Empire in Central Europe. Out of this came a dynamic of popular religious revival that, as WR Ward has shrewdly commented, 'began in resistance to a real or perceived threat of assimilation by the state in its modern shape.'[377]

The revival was linked to religious tension in central Europe between Protestant German-speaking states and Roman Catholic Habsburg Austria which contributed to the creation of a major stream of German-speaking emigration to what by 1707 had become British North America. It is clear that the evangelical revival in colonial British North America was related to the growing threat from French Canada and Louisiana in the mid-eighteenth century. Presbyterian Scotland shared with Puritan New England a sense of being Protestant election that was reinforced by struggles against agents of the pre-1688 Stuart monarchy as they sought to extend royal authority over both 'provinces'. However, the contrasting experiences of two 'provinces' in the eighteenth century resulted in New England taking a leading role in achieving American political independence while increasing Scottish participation within a broader British Empire.[378]

Scotland and New England

Even if restricted to a more sharply defined period of the late seventeenth and early eighteenth centuries, there are problems in using New England as a model of British provincial culture for the purposes of analysing what happened to Scotland after 1688. Scotland was an ancient kingdom whose king had assumed the throne of England in 1603. The authority of the Crown was rejected by the Church of Scotland in 1641 on the issue of assimilation, if not integration, with the Church of England and this was followed by involvement in wars in England, Scotland and Ireland that for Scotland ended with comprehensive military defeat and conquest by Oliver Cromwell's New Model Army in 1651. This was followed by restoration of the Stuart monarchy in 1660, then by the acceptance of the crown of Scotland by William of Orange in 1689 following his invasion of England with a Dutch army in 1688. The population of Scotland, at above 1,000,000 in 1700, was more than ten times that of 'New England', however it is defined, and the leading urban centre in New England, Boston, was much smaller than the capital of Scotland, Edinburgh. New England had resisted the policies of the restored Stuart monarchy, perhaps more effectively than a Scotland which was increasingly divided between those who accepted an episcopalian Church of Scotland and those who adhered to the Covenanting Scottish Presbyterian tradition of the middle of the seventeenth century.[379]

However, for a Church of Scotland restored to Presbyterianism by the Scottish Parliament in 1690 the Puritan churches of New England offered the possibility of a shared mission in a changing and challenging wider military conflict in Europe against Roman Catholic France after the Revocation of the Edict of Nantes in 1685. In Scotland the Presbyterian church was faced with the formidable challenge of asserting its authority over both a divided aristocracy and large areas of northern Scotland where few were sympathetic to Presbyterianism. Military conflict with France began with the accession of William of Orange (as William III in New England but William II in Scotland) in 1688 and would last until the Treaty of Utrecht in 1713 (and in Scotland the defeat of a major 'Jacobite' rebellion in favour of the exiled Roman Catholic Stuart dynasty in 1716). By that time the ancient kingdoms of England and Scotland had finally been united in the United Kingdom of Great Britain in 1707 under the English-born, episcopalian Queen Anne. Massachusetts and the other New England colonies were affected by the union of 1707, in that Scottish merchants and immigrants were given legal status there, but as a colony Massachusetts, with a new royal charter, was increasingly subject to intervention from London. To a degree, that intervention was welcomed, as French-inspired attacks on the Massachusetts and New England frontier increased between 1688 and 1713, but it also represented a threat to Puritan churches in the colony. In Scotland the union with England in 1707 presented new challenges, despite the guarantees given as part of it. After 1707, the Church of Scotland was, legally, subject to a parliament which was overwhelmingly made up of episcopalian members of the Church of England. The dangers were obvious to its clergy, and unacceptable to many of its members. The church remained a uniquely Scottish national institution after 1707, but not a sovereign one. After 1776 the separation of church and state in the United States became an increasingly attractive model to more and more Scots within and without the Church of Scotland as a means of preserving Scottish national identity and a distinctively Scottish Christian mission.

By the end of the seventeenth century Scottish ships and merchants, especially from Glasgow, were trading with Boston and New England, making regular correspondence between Scotland and New England possible. The great Scottish Presbyterian minister and historian, Robert Wodrow, exchanged letters regularly with ministers in Boston including the famous Cotton Mather.[380] If Wodrow was of limited prominence in Scotland during his career, his correspondence was wide, like that of many clergymen of the European protestant movements of the time. His vast manuscript collection was later preserved in the Advocates Library in Edinburgh. Many of Wodrow's manuscripts were published in the nineteenth century as a means of asserting the continuity of the Scottish Presbyterian tradition from the seventeenth century as the Free Church of Scotland from 1843 sought to establish itself as its custodian.[381]

Wodrow's correspondents in Boston shared with him a sense of a reformed and Godly church in danger in modern times, one that had lost sight of the virtues and sacrifices of those who had established the independence and mission of the reformed churches in New England and Scotland. In 1702 Cotton Mather published in London a work he entitled *Magnalia Christi Americana, or, The Ecclesiastical History of New England*, which envisaged 'the movement of Christian civilization from Europe to America.'[382] Ned Landsman has described *Magnalia Christi Americana* and similar histories published by New England Puritans as intended 'to persuade New Englanders of their role as a special people' who had to take note that 'whatever calamities befell them signified God's displeasure.'[383] As early as 1706 Robert Wodrow wrote from the manse of his parish of Eastwood near Glasgow to his correspondent Lachlan Campbell, minister of the Church of Scotland at Campbeltown on the Kintyre peninsula in Argyll, 'I have frequently thought it a pity that noe endeavour have been used to preserve and retrieve many remarkable passages of Providence which might make Magnalia Christi Scoticana, to equall Mathers Americana.'[384]

In 1712 Mather wrote to Wodrow enclosing 'two or three late American treatises,' and praising the Church of Scotland.[385] Wodrow in reply declared his intellectual debt to Mather and his family; 'from a child almost I have loved the Mathers, though I never proposed to myself the happiness and honour of writing to any of them.' The *Magnalia* was the subject of special praise. 'I shall say nothing of [it] to yourself,' Wodrow wrote, 'but I bless the Lord ever I had it …. This part of your labours did let me into a new world of this I was formerly stranger to.'[386] Mather later became a subscriber to Wodrow's *History of the Sufferings of the Church of Scotland* (published in two volumes in 1721 and 1722), and wrote to Wodrow that Scottish ministers had accepted congregations in New England who had, 'joyfully flourished under their holy ministry.'[387] Wodrow and Mather also corresponded about the Irish Protestants who were emigrating to New England, with Wodrow relating that the Scots were vexed 'to hear that the wild Irishes are coming down, and taking the leases our countrymen had, and swarming out in such numbers, as very much threatens the British interest in that kingdom.'[388] For both men, Irish Presbyterians were 'brethren' from 'the North of Ireland' or 'Ireland' rather than 'Scotch-Irish'. As William Ferguson observed many years ago, 'many of the so-called "Scotch-Irish" who migrated to the American colonies were natives of Scotland taking advantage of organised means of emigration which existed in Ulster earlier than in Scotland.'[389] It was no mistake that in the eighteenth century, emigration from Scotland to British North America first became a noticeable phenomenon in the south-west of Scotland and Glasgow, and that in the Highlands the first emigrants left from Argyll on ships largely chartered in Belfast and Larne. For Mather and Wodrow, 'brethren' from Ireland were Presbyterians who shared much with the Congregational traditions of New England and the Presbyterianism of the restored Church of Scotland. Although they represented 'the British interest' in Ireland, they were religious dissenters from the established episcopalian Church of Ireland, unlike those who had become members of the established Presbyterian Church of Scotland after 1690.

'The Great Awakening'

WR Ward has written that when Irish Presbyterians began to arrive in America, they 'brought with them different notions of Presbyterianism' that were 'in unstable combination'. The result was a divided clergy which responded in different ways to English, Irish and Scottish traditions of Presbyterianism. It also meant that Presbyterianism in America, like Congregationalism in New England, did not gain strength from the phenomenon that in America has been termed 'the Great Awakening', a popular religious revival that some historians have argued represented the first social and cultural movement that united mainland British North America. One of its legacies was that after the American Revolution older Presbyterian and episcopalian traditions in America gave way to the Methodist and Baptist movements that became associated with the revival. It meant that both Scots and Irish Presbyterians in America eventually became assimilated into an evangelical Protestant Christianity very different from the national religious traditions in their countries of origin. What was the Great Awakening? The term originates in discussion of localized religious 'revivals' in Britain, Ireland and America that were associated with resistance to attempts to establish religious uniformity under the Stuart monarchy.[390] Local revivals were usually focused on a charismatic clergyman able to attract numbers of people to large open-air meetings where the message of awareness of sin and the possibility of spiritual rebirth was propagated, and criticism of religious orthodoxy implied. Recent work has argued that the Protestant religious revivals of the eighteenth century were much more fluid than a confrontation between traditional clergy-led orthodoxy and popular evangelicalism, arguing that there was a middle ground held by those who supported religious revival at the outset, 'but [who] became concerned about the chaotic, levelling extremes that the awakenings produced.'[391] Radical evangelicals ignored social conventions in an eagerness to proselytize in an inclusive manner that broke down previous social divisions.[392]

Part of what created a protonational Protestant religious evangelical phenomenon was the tour of British North America from 1739 of George Whitefield. He travelled from south to north, deliberately flouting denominational boundaries while using the culture of print and the expanding commercialization of public life in greater Britain (whether America, Ireland or Britain itself) to make religious revival central to public life first in America, but also in Britain after his return there following his American success. Whitefield had arrived in Georgia in 1738 aged 24. Intent on the foundation of an orphanage there based on the famous orphanage at Halle in Germany, he returned to London to raise funds to support the enterprise. Although he was ordained as an Anglican clergyman, Whitefield's preaching bore a Calvinistic stamp that brought crowds in their thousands to hear him in England. He added to his campaigning by publishing 46 sermons before he was 25. The tour was supported by a wealthy layman, William Seward, who also acted as publicist for the venture with great success. Although wishing to remain an Anglican, Whitefield ironically became identified with religious dissent, particularly in America. His tour of America lasted from 1739 to 1741 and almost defined the term 'barnstorming', although he spoke to crowds that far exceeded in number those who could be accommodated in normal venues for religious services. From 1739 to 1745 American printers and publishers issued more titles annually that were written by Whitefield 'than by any other writer on any subject.'[393]

There had been revivals in America before the arrival of Whitefield, notably in New England and the so-called 'Middle Colonies'. In particular, Jonathan Edwards of Massachusetts already had published *A Faithful Narrative of the Surprising Work of God ... in Northampton* in 1737. Its publication is often regarded as the beginning of 'the Great Awakening' in America, but 'the significance of the pamphlet lay less in the importance of what it reported, than in the way it corresponded to hopes and fears much more widely held', as its publication in England and in German translation demonstrated. In the Middle Colonies, the sons of the Scottish Presbyterian William Tennent and others were educated by their father at his 'Log College' at Neshaminy in Pennsylvania, which acted as the template for the establishment of further seminaries at Fogg's Manor, Nottingham, Pequea in Pennsylvania and in Hanover and Louisa counties in Virginia.[394] Tennent's eldest son, Gilbert, became an associate of Whitefield after the latter's arrival in the Middle Colonies. The Tennents and their associates had promoted revival in a number of communities in New Jersey and Pennsylvania before the arrival of Whitefield, and the attention he drew gave them an opportunity to expand their campaign.[395] Although Tennent drew on the traditions of Ulster and Scottish Presbyterianism, he also drew on 'a rhetoric and programme derived largely from Dutch and Lower Rhine sources', through the agency of the Dutch Reformed preacher Theodorus Frelinghuysen in New Jersey. Frelinghuysen's efforts to convert new members to his faith had, in turn, had been influenced by the Congregational traditions of the Lower Rhine.[396] Thus Whitefield came into contact with the traditions of part of the European evangelical revival while he was in America through the American Presbyterian Tennent, and he brought aspects of this to Britain with him in 1741. It also led to Tennent's famous declaration of war on the 'unawakened' clergy, *The Danger of an Unconverted Ministry*, which divided American Presbyterianism for a generation, from 1741–58. It influenced Whitefield's attacks on rival clergymen, and declared opposition to the authority of a clerical hierarchy, whether episcopalian or Presbyterian.[397]

Whitefield returned to England, still only 27 years of age, and from July to October 1741 made the first of 14 visits to Scotland before his death in 1770.[398] He brought the transatlantic 'Great Awakening' with him. Although the Church of Scotland was an established church, it still, particularly in the west of Scotland, looked back to 'the vivid and living memory of mass revival in the seventeenth century in Ulster and in parishes in the West of Scotland.' Orthodox ministers of Protestant established churches in the early eighteenth century often proclaimed that religious piety was in decline, but Scottish ministers such as Robert Wodrow were unique in their identification of the fall in numbers attending outdoor communion ceremonies as evidence of a decline in the influence of religion in Scottish society.[399] In Scotland orthodox Calvinist ministers had protested at government intervention in the church aimed at establishing the right of the Crown, the nobility and the gentry to appoint the ministers of the kirk. Led by the brothers Ralph and Ebenezer Erskine, a group of ministers had rejected the authority of the General Assembly of the Church of Scotland on this issue, which led finally to their expulsion from the church in 1740, when they wrote to Whitefield to urge him to come to Scotland.[400] Their secession from the Church of Scotland received the 'approbation' of Gilbert Tennent and his followers in America and their works were translated into Welsh as the revival reached Wales. In 1739 John Wesley had written to Ralph Erskine 'for advice on the strange psychic phenomena which accompanied his preaching in Bristol', and both he and Whitefield, at least in the initial days of the 'Secession Church' in Scotland, sympathized with its difficulties in dealing with the ecclesiastical authorities in Scotland.[401] Once the final break with the established Church of Scotland came for the Erskines and their followers in 1740, however, any chance for cooperation with English Methodists through the newly established Secessionist 'Associate Presbytery' disappeared.

Whitefield returned to Scotland in 1742 to participate in a sensational revival in the old Covenanting Presbyterian parish of Cambuslang in Lanarkshire, south-east of Glasgow. The minister there, William McCulloch, had intended to emigrate to South Carolina as a young man to find a calling in the presbytery there, but applied too late to the Church of Scotland scheme which would have made it possible for him to go. Instead, he found a place as chaplain to the Hamilton of Aitkenhead family, and in 1731, at the age of 40, became minister at Cambuslang, where he immediately had to deal with the problems caused by the formation of the Secessionist Associate Presbytery. By 1741 he had become editor of an evangelical newspaper published in Glasgow, *The Weekly History*, and followed news of the revival in New England and Whitefield's role in it with intense interest, presenting in his writing and preaching 'a synoptic, even cosmic, view of the revival as a whole.'[402] Although McCulloch was not a charismatic preacher, he was asked by a substantial number of families in his parish to hold weekday meetings which evoked 'strange spiritual signs', which led to parishioners seeking his counsel.[403] McCulloch began to preach daily to ever larger crowds in mid-February 1742. In the summer Whitefield arrived, seeking now to work within the established church in Scotland. His first sermon at Cambuslang that year drew an estimated 20,000 people, with communion celebrated outdoors in the tradition of seventeenth-century Scottish Presbyterianism. A month later, he appeared in support of another communion in the parish which drew even larger crowds. The success of both the revival at Cambuslang and Whitefield's support of it was reported widely in America through his supporters there.[404]

Kilsyth, also in Lanarkshire, had a more established network of Covenanting 'Praying Societies' than was the case in Cambuslang, but it followed Cambuslang's example in the use of the Scottish tradition of outdoor communion as a vehicle for evangelical revival once the parish session (and the praying societies) agreed to hold several communion days rather than the customary annual event. Another Scottish parish, at Muthill in Perthshire, experienced a revival, although there the social background was tension between episcopalian and Presbyterian sympathizers rather than competing traditions within the latter. John Erskine, who had not yet risen to prominence as minister of Greyfriars Kirk in Edinburgh and a leader of the 'Popular Party' of the Church of Scotland, 'thought that events in New England and Scotland together were a prelude to the end-time.'[405] There was a willingness among many Scots clergymen to look beyond Scotland and seek for meaning in the broader experience of transatlantic Protestant evangelical awakening. Erskine promoted the work of the American Jonathan Edwards in Scotland for the rest of his life, arranging for the publication of British editions of many of his works creating an impact on dissenting culture in England as well as Scotland. The issue of church patronage remained deeply divisive in Scotland, however, and 'the Lowland church could neither sublimate its policy disagreements in revival, nor sustain revival itself.' As a result the seed of non-Presbyterian dissenting Protestantism was planted in Scotland, which was to have far-reaching repercussions during the second half of the eighteenth century and to lead to a revolution in religion and linguistic culture in the Scottish Highlands.[406] Thus the suspicions of the Associate Presbytery about Whitefield were quite correct. In many ways the Scottish revivals of 1742 marked a turning point in Scottish contact with America far more important than the defeat of Scottish Jacobitism in 1746 which has attracted so much more attention in Scottish History.

Methodism became a movement rather than a denomination. It sought to cross atavistic boundaries and barriers and opened up communication from German-speaking eastern Europe to the American frontier. Wesley attended the Church of Scotland General Assembly for four successive years from 1763 to 1766 and Whitefield worked within the Church of Scotland establishment during each of his 14 visits to Scotland. They were both English, but their movement in effect ended the dream 'that religious societies would generate a revival on [a] community basis.'[407] The career of John Erskine of Edinburgh personified this trend. He never emigrated to America, but from his youth he was drawn into an intense interest in religious revival in America and the question of what that meant for the future of Scotland. As a 20-year old Divinity student, Erskine burst into print under the inspiration of George Whitefield's first visits to Scotland, publishing *The Law of Nature Sufficiently Promulgated to the Heathen World* in 1741 and *The Signs of the Times Consider'd* in 1742. In the latter, he argued that transatlantic evangelical revival in America and Scotland possibly marked the approach of the millennium. Soon he was corresponding with prominent clergymen in America, notably Jonathan Edwards.[408] Erskine edited and arranged the publication of many of Jonathan Edwards's sermons in Scotland, as well as those of other American clergymen. At the end of his life he edited *Select Discourses from the American Preacher* (1796–1801) and *New Religious Intelligence, Chiefly from the American States* (1802), although he was also interested in European Protestant discourse. He was not the only Scottish admirer of Edwards. There are Gaelic language editions of Edwards's *Sinners in the Hand of an Angry God* published in 1863, 1876 and 1889 in the National Library of Scotland.

Erskine was a strong opponent, like most evangelical Presbyterians, of interference in the affairs of the Church of Scotland by the British government, and this also led him to oppose British policy toward the government of its American colonies after 1763. He published three pamphlets on the subject, including one that appeared anonymously in 1769 under the title *Shall I Go to War with my American Brethren?* (reissued in Edinburgh in 1776 under his name). Erskine developed the idea that transatlantic revival in New England and Scotland heralded the Second Coming and the end of the world by arguing that conflict between America and Britain was a portent of this. He did not state the idea outright, but implicit in his pamphlet was an idea he shared with other ministers of the Church of Scotland, that Scotland's place as the Lord's anointed nation of the Presbyterian Covenant was to be passed on to a new nation led by the Congregationalist 'New Englanders'. 'Though some may pronounce it enthusiasm', he wrote, 'I must add, that as the first planters of New England honoured God, by leaving their estates, their friends and their native country, that they might worship him, though in a wilderness ... God has honoured them and their posterity, with distinguishing instances of his favour and protection.' Puritan New England was thus presented as superior to the Covenanting and Presbyterian Scotland of the seventeenth century, which of course through military defeat by Cromwell had failed to demonstrate that it enjoyed the favour and protection of the Deity. By contrast God had 'reproved the numbrous tribes of Indians' for the sake of Puritan New England. 'By unusual sickness and mortality,' Erskine wrote, 'he drove out the heathen, and planted them, increased his people greatly, and made them stronger than their enemies.'[409] What had happened to Scotland during the same period? Erskine did not write about this, but the Scottish Revolution of 1689 had led to state violence against fellow Scots (would Erskine have seen them as heathen?) at Glencoe and failure to plant at Darien in Panama in 1700, leading soon after to a Union of the Scottish Parliament with an English Parliament dominated by members of the episcopalian and manifestly uncovenanted Church of England.

Erskine did write about an increase of the influence of Roman Catholicism in Britain, and related this to the American crisis.[410] The Church of Scotland's investigations in the Highlands, Erskine wrote, demonstrated that in many places there 'Popery has also increased'. The British government had not 'erected churches and schools in the places where they were most needed' after the Jacobite rebellions, and 'ministers and schoolmasters, well acquainted with the Popish controversy' were not present in sufficient numbers in the Highlands to prevent the spread of Roman Catholicism there.[411] In contrast, Erskine wrote, 'pardon my also observing the laudable zeal of the Massachusetts Bay colony, to testify Her gratitude to God for the conquest of Canada, by forming plans, and subscribing large sums of money for Christianizing the Indians.' In 'North Britain', these plans 'found not the encouragement they deserved, ... which from a narrow bigoted spirit in South Britain, were altogether blasted.' Why? In Scotland there was concern at sending money out of the country, no matter how noble the purpose, as 'a national loss'. Erskine also pointedly quoted 'a late dignatory of the Church of England' who was said to have advised, 'that heathens should rather be permitted to remain heathens, than be converted by Presbyterians or Congregationalists.'[412] Warming to his theme, Erskine warned about the possible price of victory over the Americans. 'If they were reduced to subordination by military means, is it impossible that a King should arise, intoxicated with the sweetness, and puffed up with the pride of ruling, with uncontrouled sway so populous and extensive a continent; and ambitious that his will might give law in Britain, as well as in North America?' Might the Americans, Erskine wrote, be then employed to reduce 'us to the same state as themselves?' In the Stuart Restoration reigns of the later seventeenth century, similar points were made about the uses to which the Stuart monarchy could put the manpower of its kingdom of Ireland against England, or that of the Highlands of Scotland against the covenanted Presbyterians of the

Lowlands. Now Erskine interpreted the battle for the future of North America after the defeat of France as posing a similar threat in a broader British context.[413]

Erskine's friend and former colleague in the 'Popular Party' of the Church of Scotland, John Witherspoon, had just emigrated to New Jersey to take up the post of President (Principal) of the Presbyterian College of New Jersey at Princeton when Erskine published the first edition of *Shall I go to War with my American Brethren?* The appointment had been brokered by a Princeton graduate studying medicine in Edinburgh, Benjamin Rush, who convinced the trustees of the college that Witherspoon was a good orthodox Calvinist. They were also convinced that his appointment 'could help heal the breach that had plagued the American [Presbyterian] church since its division in 1741 during the American Great Awakening.'[414] In America Witherspoon found the absence of a state church, given the weakness of the Anglican Church in the Middle Colonies and New England, to his advantage, and he soon became involved in American politics. He is remembered in America as the most successful President of Princeton in the eighteenth century, but also as a signatory of the Declaration of Independence. In Scotland, Witherspoon was one of many devout Presbyterians who felt marginalized in their own church as it became ever more closely associated with the British state.[415] In America he both played an important role in the creation of a new nation and ensured that the religion of its people was liberated from the influence of the state. In America the ideas of the Scottish Enlightenment became part of a political agenda that drew on the dynamic of the separation of church and state, and religious pluralism.[416] It was an example that would make a profound impact on the changing public culture of Scotland in the nineteenth century.

The motif of fundamental revolutionary change in mainland British North America as a result of the American Revolution is so strong, at least in American historiography, that it can be difficult to follow threads of continuity in the spiritual connections between American and Scottish Protestantism.[417] These weren't exclusive, of course. It was the Englishmen Whitefield (who died in Massachusetts in 1770) and Wesley who made the greater impact in creating an expanding culture of interdenominational evangelical Christianity than either the Tennent family of America or the Erskine brothers in Scotland. Perhaps that was what was revolutionary at the time. The religious culture of Scotland and America became less nationally specific even as American public culture increasingly became dominated by a nationally distinct political discourse. In Scotland the religious culture changed but until 1843 it changed mostly within the national framework of more than 900 Church of Scotland parishes, as the church bore the brunt of the struggle to accommodate rapid social change within the national public culture that predated the union. This is one reason why some writers have asserted that the General Assembly of the Church of Scotland acted as a national forum for the Scottish nation in the eighteenth and early nineteenth centuries in the absence of any secular parliamentary equivalent.[418] American historians of religious revival sometimes attempt to distinguish between a mid-eighteenth century 'Great Awakening' and a 'Great Revival' or 'Second Great Awakening' at the end of the century, while others have argued that the movement was the vehicle for the continual growth of evangelical Protestant culture as a central part of America public culture as a whole.[419] Witherspoon and Erskine continued to be part of this movement on either side of the Atlantic until their deaths (in 1794 and 1804 respectively). If it is misleading to claim a privileged position for Congregationalism and Presbyterianism in the movement for American independence, it is true that the British army targeted the churches of both during the Revolution.[420] Perhaps it is on account of this that both flourished in the US after independence.[421]

By the 1780s, and continuing into the 1790s, another series of revivals had occurred in western Pennsylvania, Virginia and North Carolina, which spread later to the Kentucky and Tennessee frontier. A striking characteristic of American frontier revivals before and after the American Revolution was the incorporation of large-scale outdoor meetings which featured both outdoor communion and preaching that clearly drew on Protestant Irish and Scottish traditions of communion as an annual 'communal' ceremony for congregations. The revivals were spread over a large geographical area and denominational involvement was not restricted to Presbyterians. Evangelists such as Elisha Macurdy, who became known as the preacher 'who knocked the people down', presided over outdoor communion sessions 'that attracted as many as ten thousand people on the Pennsylvania frontier.' The outdoor communion ceremonies that featured in the evangelical culture of western Pennsylvania from the end of the Revolution until the nineteenth century used traditional Scots psalmody, communion tokens and a structured schedule that lasted several days rather than just the Sabbath. Nor was this practice limited to Pennsylvania. By the 1790s revival had spread to North Carolina and as late as 1866 a series of articles appeared in the *North Carolina Presbyterian* urging restraint during the outdoor 'communion season' to avoid excessive impropriety.[422] Embedded in this phenomenon were the first published sermons in Scots Gaelic (anywhere), which appeared in Fayetteville, North Carolina, in 1791 as part of the 'Great Revival' there. Both 'were preached in the Raft Swamp district of North Carolina, inland from Cape Fear', in what was identified in the resulting publication as the first month of autumn 1790 by the Rev. Dougal Crawford, who was from the island of Arran between Kintyre and the Scottish mainland in the west of Scotland.[423] As emigrants from Argyll in particular continued to arrive in the Cape Fear Valley of North Carolina in the 1790s, it is no surprise that there should have been some demand for a publication in Scots Gaelic that 'was evidently intended to provide a set of useful materials for both private devotion and (when necessary) public worship.'[424] Although linguistically specific, the sermons and the prayers published with them clearly reflected the context of revival in North Carolina, but also the expanding evangelical networks in Scotland. Donald Meek has argued that the sermons were intended to be read in both Arran and North Carolina, on the basis that the prefaces to the publication are dedicated both to Crawford's home parish of birth at Kilmorie in Arran (he became an assistant there in 1795) and to 'the congregation in Raft Swamp and the congregations in Robeson County' (North Carolina). The pamphlet, then, is a perfect artefact of the transatlantic nature of the evangelical Protestant Christianity that was making such an impact on both American and Scottish culture in the second half of the eighteenth century.[425]

The evangelical inheritance

In the nineteenth century changes in transatlantic travel and improvements in communication increased opportunities for cultural exchange between Scotland and America. The issue of the slave trade and slavery itself in the Americas provided a powerful moral issue that drew attention to the western hemisphere. Little research has been carried out on how this affected Scotland, but it is apparent that America became an increasingly important influence on the changing religious culture of Scotland as it became a more ethnically diverse and pluralistic society. The influence of the results of Irish contact with America were also important in a manner that is yet to be researched thoroughly, but they are clear in the development of a 'Scotch-Irish' American ethnic identity that was predicated on systematically associating Irish

Protestants with Scotland and with Scots in America.[426] Because of the importance of religion in the educational systems of the United States, Canada and Scotland, these complex and variegated transatlantic exchanges came to have significant consequences on education, particularly higher education, on both sides of the Atlantic.

We have to be wary of allowing the survival of sources relating to the experience of Scottish emigrants to America who became famous to shape a simplistic view of the emigrant that valorizes their act of emigration uncritically. However, there are aspects of the biography of that most famous nineteenth-century emigrant from Scotland to America, Andrew Carnegie, that can tell us something about the traumatic changes and conflict that wracked Scottish religious and spiritual culture in the 1840s, when the great Disruption of the Church of Scotland broke the most powerful institution in Scottish public life. Carnegie was a child emigrant to the USA in the hard years of the 1840s, but these were also years full of glowing images of America as a land of wealth generated by the discovery of gold in California. He cherished the family story of his father's rejection of Church of Scotland Calvinism during the decade of crisis for the church from 1833–43. 'If that be your religion and that your God', his son recorded his father as declaiming in his *Autobiography*, 'I seek a better religion and a nobler God.'[427] Yet many of his biographers sought to explain his material success in terms of the religious culture of his country of birth and its influence on his family. Years later, during the height of his career as a philanthropist, when asked why he donated only organs (rather than money) to churches, he joked that it was 'to lessen the pain of the sermons.' Carnegie had the money to return to Scotland and set himself up in mock Scottish baronial splendour at Skibo Castle in Sutherland, but he never attended the Church of Scotland. When he was elected Lord Rector of the University of St Andrews in 1902, after establishing the Carnegie Trust for the Universities of Scotland, he intended to deliver an address under the title 'A Confession of Religious Faith',' which proposed replacing traditional Christianity with a new system of beliefs drawing on the writings of Charles Darwin and Herbert Spencer. Persuaded by the Principal of St Andrews that this would be too controversial, Carnegie spoke instead on 'The Industrial Ascendency of the World' and the need for Britain and Europe to follow the American model to peace and prosperity. It was a fitting introduction to the vision that the twentieth century would be American.[428]

Carnegie had also been a patron of the American evangelists Dwight Moody and Ira Sankey, who turned evangelical Christian mission into showbiz. They eschewed 'the hysterical enthusiasm associated with the American camp meeting' and promoted ecumenical cooperation between all churches.[429] One reason that it has been asserted that Moody and Sankey's great barnstorming evangelical roadshow in Britain and Ireland from 1873–75 made the most significant impact in Scotland was that they sold nondenominational Protestant Evangelicalism to the nation and in the process sowed the seeds of the reunification of the Scottish Presbyterian churches in 1900 and 1929.[430] They brought music and song to Presbyterian Scotland. Ira Sankey's *Sacred Songs and Solos* made a fortune in royalties for charitable causes in Britain from part of its worldwide sales in the tens of millions, but it was particularly well received in Scotland.[431] In one Edinburgh meeting (Moody and Sankey used public halls and auditoriums for their services rather than churches) a choir of black American singers was concealed in the gallery, and at a signal from Sankey they stood to their feet chorusing 'there are angels watching over you.'[432] Scotland had never experienced anything like it.

Although the United Presbyterian Church, under pressure from their English congregations, had removed the ban on organs in its churches in 1872, it was as much Sankey's rousing virtuosity with the harmonium that brought the church organ to Scotland as Carnegie's philanthropy.[433] In *Sankey's Story of the Gospel Hymns* published in Philadelphia in 1906, Sankey claimed that one woman in Edinburgh rushed out of one of their meetings crying 'Let me oot! Let me oot! What would John Knox think of the like of you,' although perhaps the anecdote tells us as much about Sankey's ideas of Scottish religious culture as it does of loyalty to the memory of Knox in late nineteenth-century Scotland.[434] It has been argued that 'part of the reason for the decline in sectarian animosity' [in Scotland] was to be found in the evangelicalism of Moody and Sankey and its impact on the country.[435] This helped to promote interdenominational Presbyterian efforts to agree a shared Psalmody for use by all their congregations. Drummond and Bulloch have argued that it was the 'Free' Church of Scotland formed as a result of the catastrophic Disruption of the Church of Scotland in 1843 that changed most profoundly as a result of Moody and Sankey's mission, as church life in Scotland became 'less doctrinal and more emotional' under the influence of the Americans.[436] 'Those who have met surviving converts,' they wrote, 'can have no doubt that a permanent change was made in many lives.'[437] John Coffey has argued that an anticlerical influence was evident in the reception given to Moody and Sankey in Scotland because of the contrast with 'the labyrinthine complexity of Calvinist orthodoxy', and 'the clerical domination of the Presbyterian establishment.'[438] Moody and Sankey communicated directly with the lay Christians who came to their services. *The Scotsman* published a letter from 'An Onlooker' in December 1873 which observed:

> it may appear to many a *very remarkable and unaccountable circumstance* that a city so amply provided with a superior class of clergy, as regards education and ability, should, by the advent of two American preachers of no very remarkable learning or eloquence, be so profoundly stirred; and that our clergy should be found attending the meetings and looking on in wonder and amazement.[439]

To this observer, the contrast between the complex doctrinal sermons and the manner in which Moody and Sankey 'sing and recite the declaration of God's goodness and forgiveness' provided an explanatio-nas to why '*thousands*' were flocking to attend the meetings held by the Americans. They spent months in Scotland in late 1873 and early 1874. Their meetings at the Corn Exchange west of the centre of Edinburgh drew regular crowds that filled it to its capacity of nearly 6000 people. From February to April 1874 in Glasgow Moody regularly spoke four times a day and claimed to have made 3000 converts.[440] Prayer sessions were held in the city over a nine-month period, which resulted in the formation of the Glasgow United Evangelistic Association as a 'means of begetting throughout the Christian community a new sense of responsibility and deeper compassion in relation to the spiritual and temporal needs of the city's poor and its social outcasts.'[441] This was done through the provision of meals for the homeless and day refuges for destitute children, as well as prayer meetings and Bible fellowship classes.

Although they went on to make an enormous impact in Ireland and preached to millions in London in 1875, Moody and Sankey returned to Scotland to perpetuate the influence of their first mission, in 1881–83 and in 1891–92. They came to personify an American evangelicalism that over the course of the nineteenth century led to a reinvention of Scottish Presbyterianism and public life in Scotland. It has been argued that this re-energized sense of mission influenced Moody and Sankey's British admirers Lord Shaftesbury and WE Gladstone as well, and increased evangelical commitment to the Liberal Party, characterized by its moral campaigns on the issues of Temperance and Public Health.

In this way the spiritual connection that had characterized the distinctive cultural exchange between Scotland and America in the seventeenth and eighteenth centuries came in the nineteenth century to reflect distinctive American contributions to British and Scottish public culture as the British constitution was changed by Reform Acts extending access to the constitution to an ever-growing proportion of the British and Irish male population. The survival of the United States after its Civil War, and the successful confederation of Canada, meant that constitutional monarchy in Britain and Ireland increasingly absorbed democratic influences from North America by the time the Third UK Reform Act became law in 1884. The advent of mass secular socialism would change this irrevocably after the end of the First World War, but it was an important part of the lost world of Victorian Scotland that is now so often forgotten.

Epilogue: 'The Scottish Invention of the USA'

In 1996, more than 20 years after the appearance of his pioneering book *Scotland and America 1750–1835*, Andrew Hook published an essay under the title 'The Scottish Invention of the USA'. He argued that the importance of America to the transformation of the Scottish economy in the eighteenth century was not as significant as 'the Scottish invention of the USA'. For Hook, 'what Scotland imported from the American colonies was tobacco; what she exported to the American colonies was ideas.'[442] From the perspective of early American history, Ned Landsman has also written in an important essay that it was Scottish influence that was crucial in creating 'that particular optimistic vision of unlimited American potential, which was, in origin, British, liberal and provincial'. Ironically, Landsman argued, this 'has often been reinterpreted as uniquely American, New English and exceptional.'[443] Hook's essay was a shrewd analysis of the reception of a study the American author Garry Wills published in 1978 on the American Declaration of Independence under the title *Inventing America*, which met with a reception that was initially quite positive, but later tempered by a reluctance by many reviewers to concede that a political journalist and professional writer could write a work of importance to our understanding of early American history.[444] This meant that the emphasis that Wills gave to Jefferson's debt to leading thinkers of the Scottish Enlightenment in the composition of the declaration became obscured by a shifting argument between other American scholars on the exceptional nature of Jefferson's use of his intellectual sources in creating a text of extraordinary historical importance.[445] Thus the exceptional originality of the document was highlighted by American commentators rather than the importance of the Scottish Enlightenment as a source for many of the ideas that gave it such historical importance.

David Armitage has written in *The Declaration of Independence: A Global History* that the 'global vision' of the American 'generation of 1776', 'was enshrined in the comprehensive histories of European commerce and settlement that burgeoned in the years around 1776', identifying examples such as the Abbé Raynal's *Philosophical and Political History of the Settlements and Trade of the Europeans in the East and West Indies* of 1770, Adam Smith's *Wealth of Nations* of 1776 and William Robertson's *History of America* of 1777.[446] For the purposes of this study, the important point is that Smith and Robertson were both leading lights of the Scottish Enlightenment. Only Raynal represented the much more populous and wealthy nation of France that arguably was at the centre of the European Enlightenment tradition, but the important point is that the Declaration of Independence reflected an awareness of broader global issues rather than a claim that the American Congress was unique in its declaration. In relation to the Scottish Enlightenment, the point would be that what was Scottish about the Enlightenment in Scotland was the awareness that it was a former kingdom that had to work out its future in the wider world via a route other than political independence. What is striking about this is that this agenda was the opposite of the political independence pursued (and achieved) as an important part of the Enlightenment in America that created the independent United States.

Of course, as Hook had pointed out in his earlier essay, there was nothing new in claiming that Scottish merchants, emigrants and culture made a significant impact in North America during the eighteenth century, but why has this attracted so much attention in recent decades? There was still tension between ethnic celebration and the idea of cultural transfer in both American and Scottish interest in the historical connection between the two countries. One manner in which this has been expressed has been through recent suggestions that the Scots associated with the adoption of the American Declaration of Independence were influenced by the Scottish so-called 'Declaration of Arbroath' of 1320, more properly referred to as 'A letter from the Scottish Magnates to John XXII Arbroath Abbey, 6 April 1320.'[447] The Declaration of Arbroath began to be presented as a Scottish 'Declaration of Independence' during the medieval Scottish 'wars of independence' that by 1328 established the independence of the kingdom of Scotland from any claim of English feudal superiority. In Canada, from 1991, individual provincial legislatures began to adopt 6 April as a day appropriate to celebrate the contribution of Scots to the development of Canada, and in 1998 the Senate in Washington approved the designation of 6 April as 'National Tartan Day' on similar grounds. Senate Resolution 155 stated that the date had 'a special significance for all Americans, and especially those of Scottish descent' because the Scottish Declaration of Arbroath/Independence served as a model for the American Declaration of Independence.[448] It is here that genuine difficulties emerge for Scots in accepting the US resolution as having any validity, or as being based on anything other than dubious ethnic chauvinism. Given that citizenship in the United States is based either on a) birth or b) a conscious decision to apply for US citizenship, it is difficult to accept that 'ancestry' can make a person Scottish, although the fact that at the time of writing it is impossible to become a citizen of Scotland, as one can become a citizen of the United States or the Republic of Ireland or other countries, makes comparisons difficult.[449] It has been pointed out that of the 56 men who signed the American Declaration of Independence, all but eight were born in the American colonies.[450] It has also been pointed out that the idea of a 'Tartan Day' is Canadian and American, 'not, in a crucial sense, a Scottish event at all.'[451] Other parts of the world may adopt the idea, but it is not a Scottish national day in Scotland on the model of Canada Day, the Fourth of July or Bastille Day in Canada, the United States and France, respectively.

Although there is no direct evidence for any link between Scotland and the US Declaration of Independence other than the fact that two Scots signed it, as Neal Ascherson has commented, the fact that neither James Wilson or John Witherspoon 'is known to have spoken or written a word about Arbroath in their lives ... is not to say that the 1776 Declaration owes nothing to Scottish political ideas.'[452] Although the 'Declaration of Arbroath' is a medieval document, it was rediscovered in the muniment room of the Earl of Haddington at Tyninghame House in East Lothian in the 1670s, just as the debate over the status of the Stuart dynasty as kings of Scotland came under increasing scrutiny there. The first published English translation of the text of the Declaration of Arbroath was issued in Edinburgh in 1689, the year that the 'Claim of Right' adopted by the Scottish Parliament declared that James VII of Scotland (James II of England) had 'forfaulted' the throne of Scotland as an absentee king.[453] In that the English Declaration of Rights passed by the Westminster Parliament in 1689 is thought to have been a source for Jefferson's Declaration of Independence, this marks the limit of any possible connection between the two declarations. Jefferson's declaration clearly had the British parliament's Declaratory Act of 1766 in its sights, an act which asserted the authority of the Westminster Parliament 'to make laws and statutes of sufficient force and validity to bind the colonies and people of *America* subjects of the crown of *Great Britain*, in all cases whatsoever.'[454] This related to the issues raised in 1688/89 over the relationships of the parliaments of Scotland and Ireland to the English

Parliament at Westminster.[455] The fortunes of the Irish and Scottish parliaments diverged after 1689. The Declaration of Arbroath was reprinted a further four times in Edinburgh in 1700, 1703, 1705 and 1706 but not anywhere else.[456] Civil War in Ireland meant that its parliament became an assembly limited to Protestants that enacted the infamous Irish penal laws, was excluded from the negotiations for parliamentary union between England and Scotland between 1702 and 1707 and suffered the indignity of its subordinate status to the Westminster Parliament being reaffirmed by the latter's Declaratory Act of 1720.[457] In contrast, the Scottish Parliament began to develop independent policies that brought it into conflict with the priorities being set by the executive and legislative government in London and the Netherlands.

Scottish and American unionism

The Company of Scotland chartered by the Parliament of Scotland in 1695 failed to establish a Scottish plantation in the Americas but in the process established Scotland as an Atlantic nation. Almost immediately following the failure of the Panamanian expeditions, efforts began to try to convince the English Parliament to take up the idea and to bring about a parliamentary union between England and Scotland that would be founded upon generous compensation to the shareholders of the Company of Scotland for the losses incurred by the American expeditions. One of the negotiating tactics adopted by the Scottish commissioners was that if the English Parliament refused to accept the terms of the treaty, the Scottish claim to Panama could be revived and the Company of Scotland could continue to trade if it was able to raise further capital allowing it to do so. Allan Macinnes has argued that 'Scotland was dependent on overseas trade, commercial networks and an entrepreneurial willingness to circumvent international regulations for its very survival as a distinctive European nation in the later seventeenth century', and that much of the activity of Scottish merchants in Atlantic trade involved participation in Dutch, Swedish and Danish colonial ventures as much as those that brought about contact with the English.[458] For the Scots, union had to carry with it secure entry into transatlantic trading networks.

This still did not save the Company of Scotland's presence in America at the end of the seventeenth century. Neither did it save the Scottish Parliament, the majority of whose members voted for parliamentary union with England because they believed it was the only way to save

a Scottish economy that had suffered large-scale losses through speculation in overseas trade or the only way to save the distinctive Presbyterian Church of Scotland from an episcopalian counter-revolution.[459]
The majority of members of the Scottish Parliament had concluded that
Scotland needed a union politically.[460] This did not mean that there
was majority opinion in Scotland in favour of union, but those in
Scotland against the union were so distrustful of each other that they
were unable to unite in opposition.[461] Jacobite supporters of the Stuart
monarchy and Presbyterian supporters of the new Church of Scotland
would do anything to deny their opponents victory and in the latter
case, that meant accepting parliamentary union with England as the
lesser of two very great evils. Ultimately, it led to the de facto separation
of church and state in eighteenth-century Scotland that provided the
essential basis for the triumph of the Scottish Enlightenment and the
reinvention of the nation as a cultural space where 'extremes could
meet'.[462] How did this affect Scottish contact with America? In the most
obvious sense, Scottish contact with America and American contact
with Scotland grew after Scotland's parliamentary union with the
English parliament at Westminster was agreed and implemented in
1707. Until 1754 that meant that British union had made it easier for
the Scots to participate in, and grow, Atlantic networks. After 1754 this
context changed when the British Board of Trade in London became
interested in promoting a union of British North American colonies as
a means of improving their ability to defend themselves against attacks
by the French in Canada and their Indian allies. Unionism thus had
acquired a transatlantic context by the middle of the eighteenth century
as Scotland nationally became defined by union with England.

   In 1760 Adam Smith wrote from Glasgow to his London publisher
about additions and corrections for the planned second edition of *The
Theory of Moral Sentiments*. As part of that letter he included, as one Scot
to another (his publisher was the Scottish-born London publisher
William Strahan) some observations about the Scottish parliamentary
union with England. He wrote that nothing appeared 'to me more
excusable than the disaffection of Scotland at that time,' yet he went
on to state as an obvious truth that union with England 'was a measure
from which infinite Good has been derived to this country.'[463] Smith
argued that the union failed as a quick fix. 'The trade to the Plantations
was, indeed, opened to them,' he wrote, 'but that was a trade which
they knew nothing about: the trade they were acquainted with, that to
France, Holland and the Baltic, was laid under new embarrassments
which almost totally annihilated the two first and most important

branches of it.'[464] Smith did not mention Darien, but the Scottish experience there illustrated his assertion that Scottish merchants knew nothing about trade with the 'Plantations' in America.[465] Smith concluded his letter by asking Strahan to 'remember me to the Franklins', meaning Benjamin Franklin and his son William, who had visited Glasgow in the autumn of 1759. When Franklin took the lead at the Albany Congress which met in New York in 1754 in response to demands by the British Board of Trade that North American colonies coordinate their efforts to defend themselves from French and Indian attack, his plans for union drew on the ideas of many Scots involved in British government in America who favoured a greater degree of union in British North America. Even before Albany, Franklin had taken up Archibald Kennedy's pamphlet, *The Importance of Gaining and Preserving the Friendship of the Indians to the British Interest Considered*. American historians have sometimes argued that Franklin's ideas for a British union in America were influenced by the success of the Iroquois Indian confederation.[466] Yet Ned Landsman has pointed out how Kennedy and others who influenced Franklin's thinking on union were Scots, such as James Alexander, Cadwallader Colden, John Mitchell, William Livingston and William Smith, most of who were based in New York and thus involved in the cutting edge of frontier conflict with the French and their native allies.[467] The idea of American union thus 'was originally a British invention', and reflected the disproportionate number of Scots who promoted the idea. Franklin ended up proposing at Albany that Parliament at Westminster legislate for a unified British North American government. Twenty years later an American 'Continental Congress' in Philadelphia would do so.[468]

Franklin failed with his unionist proposals at the Albany Congress, but the experience of conflict with the French and their Indian allies along the full extent of the American frontier, from what later became Maine to what was already Georgia, was to act as the catalyst for American unionism as a means of mutual defence, which by 1765 became directed at the British Empire rather than the French. Victory against the French, paradoxically, did not reinforce the case for extending the British union to British North America. It meant that the British imperial authority became identified as a new threat against which all the British colonies in North America should unite. Franklin became associated with the debate over whether American representation in the Westminster Parliament might provide the answer to increasing conflict between British North America and Britain itself. One reason for this association was Franklin's status as the most famous American in Britain and his long residence there as a colonial agent. Indeed, at one point in the late 1760s he hoped for minor office in the British administration of Lord Grafton.[469] Franklin's correspondence with the Scottish judge Lord Kames following his visit to Scotland in 1759 included discussion of an American union with Britain on the Scottish model of union with England. 'I have lived so great a Part of my Life in Britain,' Franklin wrote to Kames, 'and have formed so many Friendships in it, that I love it and wish its Prosperity, and therefore wish to see that Union on which alone I think it can be secur'd and establish'd.' However, as early as 1767, Franklin doubted if union with Britain was the answer for America. 'I am fully persuaded with you,' Franklin wrote, 'that a consolidating Union, by a fair and equal Representation of all the Parts of this Empire in Parliament, is the only firm Basis on which its political Grandeur and Stability can be founded,' but he doubted English willingness to concede this to America as they had to the Scots in 1707.[470]

Franklin, on the basis of the Stamp Act controversy of 1765, was convinced that English opinion would never acknowledge equality of status with American colonies, just as it was obvious by 1767 that the union of 1707 had certainly not resulted in English recognition of Scots as their equals within that union.[471] Lord Halifax, one of Grenville's Secretaries of State, had referred to Americans as 'foreigners' in 1763. The Irish Parliament, indeed, Franklin wrote to Kames, once wished for union with England (referring to the Protestant Irish Parliament's petition for union in 1703), 'but now rejects it'. Franklin argued that soon America would as well, if they were not given 'fair and equal Representation'. The English Parliament had had nothing to do with the establishment of British North America: 'when our Planters arrived they purchas'd the lands of the Natives without putting King or Parliament to any Expence,' just as the Company of Scotland planned to do at Darien.[472] What would the advantages of union be for America, Franklin asked Kames?

Scotland and Ireland are differently circumstanc'd,' he wrote. 'Confin'd by the Sea, they can scarcely increase in Numbers, Wealth and Strength so as to overbalance England. But America, an immense Territory, favour'd by Nature with all Advantages of Climate, Soil, great navigable Rivers and Lakes, &c must become a great Country, populous and mighty.[473]

This was one of the reasons Kames's kinsman, David Hume, in 1775 declared himself 'an American in my Principles, and wish we would let them alone to govern or misgovern themselves as they think proper.'[474]

As John Pocock has written perceptively, 'like Adam Smith in Scotland and Josiah Tucker in England, Hume desired American independence for the strictly Tory reason ... that empire had come to be a radical burden on the structure of British politics.'[475] In other words, victory over the French in North America had come at the cost of political stability in Britain itself, including the endemic Scotophobia that had prevented Hume and many of his fellow Scots from obtaining the full benefit of being citizens living under the unwritten British constitution. If the loss of empire safeguarded British liberty by removing the source of political faction and violent popular politics in London as well as Boston, to Hume that was a price worth paying.[476]

The American Revolution as a crisis of British unionism

Not all Scots agreed with Hume. From the perspective of many Scots, the union of 1707 was about access to overseas trade for the purposes of economic development. To lose the expanded British North American empire so soon after winning it from the French meant that Britain was ceasing to expand dynamically and faced the threat of stagnation and decline. Franklin's pamphlet *Observations concerning the Increase of Mankind* of 1751 had 'helped popularise the notion that the rapid rate of population growth in the colonies would lead inevitably to more Britons living in America than in Britain.'[477] There were Scots who argued that it was the exploits of the famous Scottish Highland regiments during the French and Indian Wars (or Seven Years War) in North America that had brought about final victory, most notably in the conquest of what had been considered the impregnable French fortress of Quebec. Others claimed that it had been Scottish merchants, most noticeably through their spectacular domination of the America tobacco trade with Europe, who had developed and released the full economic potential of the British American colonies.[478]

William Robertson had planned to follow his successful histories of Scotland and early modern Europe (*The History of the Reign of Charles V*) with a history of America, and published his history of the Spanish in America in 1777. The planned additional volume on the British in North America was reduced to two final chapters on Virginia and New England in the seventeenth century that were included in a posthumous edition. Robertson made this decision as a result of the contemporary political crisis in America.[479] For Robertson, stadial history as the history of human progress had not run its true course, as British liberties led to popular licentiousness in British North America. In the chapters on

North America that his son revised for publication in the 1796 and subsequent editions of the *History of America*, he referred to Virginians in the seventeenth century as having 'nourished in secret a spirit of discontent' toward metropolitan authority, and in the final chapter on New England he wrote about the formation there in the seventeenth century (in 1643) of 'a league of perpetual confederacy, offensive and defensive; an idea familiar to several leading men in the colonies, as it was framed in imitation of the famous bond of union among the Dutch provinces.'[480] Robertson added that 'in this transaction the colonies of New England seem to have considered themselves as independent societies, possessing all the rights of sovereignty, and free from the control of any superior power.' For the young Charles Francis Adams, reading in 1830, Robertson's inclination was 'rather to slur than to praise' the American colonies.[481] It was ironic that his *History of America* was viewed in Europe as Robertson's masterpiece (in Jean Suard's French translation), coinciding of course with the French intervention in the conflict that would prove so decisive in the destruction of British North America as it had come into existence in 1763.[482] Robertson's health was destroyed by his efforts to finish the book, and death threats from a pro-American mob in Scotland angered by his support for religious toleration for Roman Catholics in Scotland led to his withdrawal from public affairs in Scotland after 1778.[483]

Adam Smith's *Wealth of Nations*, published in 1776, famously discussed British union with British North America (and Ireland) in positive terms. 'There is not the least probability that the British constitution would be hurt by the union of Great Britain with her colonies,' Smith wrote. 'That constitution, on the contrary, would be completed by it, and seems to be imperfect without it,' he continued, although he acknowledged that such a union would be difficult to achieve. It was not 'insurmountable', however, with the difficulties arising 'not from the nature of things, but from the prejudices and opinions of the people both on this and the other side of the Atlantic.'[484] Smith echoed Franklin in arguing that so rapid had been the economic development of America that 'in the course of little more than a century, perhaps, the produce of American might exceed that of British taxation' and that 'the seat of empire would then naturally remove itself to that part of the empire which contributed most to the general defence and support of the whole.'[485]

Smith agreed with Hume regarding the destructive effect of political faction, but argued that American union with Britain would prevent the emergence of 'rancourous and virulent factions' in America, whereas failure to agree a union with Britain would condemn 'the inhabitants of Ireland' to perpetual political instability. He predicted that American independence would eventually lead to civil war there 'in the course of little more than a century.'[486] In his advocacy of transatlantic union, Smith echoed some of the more visionary passages in Andrew Fletcher of Saltoun's contributions to the political debate which occurred in Scotland between 1702 and 1707 over the issue of parliamentary union with England, as well as his own *Theory of Moral Sentiments*. Destructive political factions 'in all great countries' occurred 'in the centre of the empire' rather than in its provinces. The metropolis of an empire was 'the principal seat of the great scramble of faction and ambition', while the distance of provincials from the metropolis made 'them more indifferent and impartial spectators in the conduct of all.' Smith argued that political faction meant less in Scotland than England for that very reason, and that if Ireland became part of a British union, 'it would probably prevail less than in Scotland.'[487] Smith concluded by agreeing with Hume that it might be better to divorce Britain from its American colonies if 'the provinces of the British empire cannot be made to contribute towards the support of the whole empire,' but warned that in such a case Britain would have to 'endeavour to accommodate her future views and designs to the real mediocrity of her circumstances.'[488]

Those favouring a British transatlantic union were overtaken by events, in that French intervention in the American conflict in 1778, followed by declarations of war by Spain and the Netherlands on Britain in 1779 and 1780, transformed what had been a British internal conflict into a return match to the British victory of 1763 in North America. The intervention of European rivals ensured the independence of most of British North America although it also led to the return of Spain as a colonial power on the North American continent. By the time the great debate over the post-independence political constitution for the United States of America had been concluded, the advent of the French Revolution had transformed the wider British and European contexts in which American independence had taken place. When the Peace of Paris of 1783 agreed the terms of American independence, the chief British negotiator was a Scot, Richard Oswald, who saw his major task as endeavouring to preserve the commercial dependence of the former British colonies on British merchants. In this he followed Smith, who wrote to William Eden in December 1783 that 'if the Americans really mean to subject the goods of all different nations to the same duties, and to grant them the same indulgences, they set an example of good sense which all other nations ought to imitate', arguing that the United States should be allowed to continue to trade with Britain's remaining American colonies without restraint.[489]

Both the Scottish signatories of the American Declaration of Independence, Wilson and Witherspoon, were not disciples of Oswald and Smith, unlike Franklin, who had helped negotiate the 1783 Treaty of Paris as one of the American negotiators. Ezra Stiles of Connecticut had written about Wilson and Witherspoon in the US Congress as 'strongly national' (meaning Scottish) and observed that Witherspoon claimed 'that Scotland has manifested the greatest Spirit for Liberty as a nation, in that their History is full of their calling kings to account & dethroning them when arbitrary and tyrannical.'[490]

Both Wilson and Witherspoon were American 'unionists', or in contemporary American terms, Federalists. They believed that individual former British colonies had to yield a significant part of the independent sovereignty they had won from Britain as newly independent states after 1783 to a national government of the United States. Neither Wilson nor Witherspoon ever declared publicly that their American unionism had anything to do with their experience of Scottish unionism before their emigration to America, but given the association of Scots with British imperialism in America during the American Revolution this was hardly surprising. The essential distinction for interpreting their American political careers is that along with many of their American contemporaries they came to the conclusion that they no longer wished to remain British. Once independence was achieved it was that conviction, rather than any sense of common ethnic origins, that came to define American identity.

Ned Landsman has commented that Witherspoon anticipated Jefferson in arguing for an American unionism that was expansionary, enabling the United States to become a continental power, just as Franklin had predicted it would.[491] The obvious contrast with British unionism, which centralized all sovereignty in a single supreme parliament at Westminster by insisting on 'incorporating' union, was not mentioned. Later this would change in Britain once the American model of unionism had demonstrated its success by surviving a potentially catastrophic Civil War in the middle of the nineteenth century. British unionism became more federal by the later nineteenth century both in terms of the growth of 'Home Rule' politics in Britain and Ireland and in the use of federal unionism in establishing devolved colonial government in Canada, Australia and South Africa. Eventually the concept would extend in a very different manner to the West Indies and India, as the British wrestled with the challenges of imperial and Commonwealth government in the twentieth century. Although it is not always acknowledged openly, this originated in British recognition of the success of American unionism after 1865.

Scottish and American Romanticism

In a somewhat scathing insight, Daniel Walker Howe has written that 'in America, the Scottish Enlightenment came to a kind of fulfilment denied it at home.'[492] Scots such as Smith provided ideas that were adopted by the younger Pitt and his Scottish lieutenant Henry Dundas at the end of the eighteenth century, and the following generation of Scottish Whigs generated many of the ideas that provided the basis for reinventing the unwritten British Constitution in 1832. In America, however, 'the leading intellectuals were the statesmen' until the American Constitution itself developed in a different direction after the election of Andrew Jackson as President in 1828. Howe has argued that the generation who made the American Revolution and Constitution (including James Wilson and John Witherspoon) benefited from 'a combination of intellectual and political empowerment that was rare, if not unique, in the annals of history.'[493] To some extent then, like the debate over the use of ideas drawn from the leading intellectuals of the Scottish Enlightenment in the Declaration of Independence, by stating this Howe retreated into the traditional ideas of American exceptionalism. Ideas do not belong to nations but to all humanity. That is part of the power of the language of the US Declaration of Independence and the American Constitution, as well as some of the best of the work published by Scots in the eighteenth century under the influence of the European Enlightenment as a movement for human freedom.

Neither Americans or Scots had a monopoly on human virtue in the eighteenth century, but both at that moment in history were provincial societies bound to the same English metropolis and were experiencing the challenges of modernizing under its influence. As Franklin pointed out to Kames, however, while British North America and Scotland were about equal in population, the geographical context of their relation to England and Westminster was vastly different.[494] What made the Scots exceptional in the eighteenth century was that the English had, far from unanimously, agreed to become British with them. Literary scholars such as Andrew Hook have taken the idea of an exceptional Scottish impact on the creation (or invention) of America into an area unexplored by historians, by arguing that the Scottish contribution to European Romanticism was of far greater importance as an influence on how America came to imagine and attempt to define itself than the abstract ideas of Hume and Smith. Certainly the Scottish 'Common Sense' philosophers, such as Thomas Reid, who attempted to respond to the challenges Hume's philosophy posed to Christian belief had a significant impact on American thought.[495] After all, Benjamin Rush suggested 'Common Sense' as the title for Thomas Paine's famous pamphlet in favour of the American Revolution partly as a result of the Presbyterian influences he encountered while a medical student at Edinburgh.[496]

The impact of the success of Sir Walter Scott's epic poems and novels on American literature and the American reading public has been widely acknowledged, but Hook has argued (with considerable support from other literary scholars) that it was not only Scott who transmitted Scottish literary Romanticism into American culture. James Macpherson's Ossianic poetry, Jane Porter's novel *The Scottish Chiefs*, the poetry of Robert Burns and other Scottish literary works also influenced Romanticism in America and the first American literary Renaissance in the early nineteenth century.[497] Yet the question of an American national literature related to the emergence of successful American writers, 'since American *readers* clearly inhabited a transatlantic literary world, consuming large quantities of British [and Scottish] literature made even larger by the absence of international copyright.'[498] Of course Americans did not only read British books that were Scottish. Irish and English authors were read widely as well. The young Abraham Lincoln read Bunyan's *Pilgrim's Progress*, Defoe's *Robinson Crusoe*, Watts's *Hymns* and the King James Bible.[499] But what made Scottish poetry and prose particularly evocative to an American readership was that it was written by British people who were not English. Scots remained British subjects, unlike Americans, but they had created, and were still creating, a literature that was not English, even if it used the English language as its medium of expression.[500] The Scots also created an imaginative literature that sought to define the nation through the romantic grandeur of its landscape. If the Scots lacked the grand cathedrals of England, they possessed vast cathedrals of nature in a mountainous landscape that literally dwarfed that of England. If Scottish castles were ruins standing as gaunt testimony to English military superiority, Scottish traditions of resistance to English political subjugation found a ready audience in America. Jane Porter's *The Scottish Chiefs* was Andrew Jackson's favourite book.[501] When the runaway Maryland slave Fred

Bailey asked those who sheltered him in New Bedford, Massachusetts, to choose him a new name, he was given the name of 'Douglas' from Sir Walter Scott's *Lady of the Lake*. As Frederick Douglass (his spelling of his surname) wrote in 1855, his friends were 'pleased to regard me as a suitable person to wear this, one of Scotland's many famous names,' although he felt that it was those who took risks to give him refuge who, 'better than I, illustrated the virtues of the great Scottish chief.'[502] Scotland had become part of the American literary imagination, at least until the American Civil War. It was that war that altered irrevocably the cultural relationship between America and Scotland as they began to follow increasingly contrasting cultural trajectories over the course of the second half of the nineteenth century.

Notes

Introduction

1. See Jenni Calder, *Scots in the USA* (2006), 191, and Alan MacDermid, 'Woodrow Wilson had Scottish strength', *The Herald*, 18 November 2003. For the original context see Woodrow Wilson, *Papers of Woodrow Wilson*, ed. Arthur S Link et al., Vol. 12 (1972), 53.
2. Quoted in Richard B Sher, *Church and University in the Scottish Enlightenment* (1985), 3.
3. Wilson, *Papers*, Vol. 14 (1972), 306–307.
4. Arthur Herman, *How the Scots Invented the Modern World* (2001), 390, 393; David Hoeveler, Jr, *James McCosh and the Scottish Intellectual Tradition* (1981), 344–48; Wilson, *Papers*, Vol. 12, (1972), 152.
5. RD Anderson, *Education & Opportunity in Victorian Scotland* (1983, reprinted with corrections and an additional bibliography, 1989), 288.
6. Alexander Murdoch, *British Emigration 1603–1941* (2004), chapters 8 and 9; William E Van Vugt, *British Buckeyes: The English, Scots and Welsh in Ohio, 1700–1900* (2006); Peter E Rider and Heather McNabb, eds, *A Kingdom of the Mind: How the Scots Helped Make Canada* (2006).
7. Rosemary Gibson, ed., *The Darien Adventure* (1998), 18, citing National Library of Scotland, Adv MS 83.7.5, f64: 'likeways that without negroes it will be impossible to clear the ground or make any progress in planting.'
8. For example, see RH Campbell, *Scotland Since 1707* (Second Edition, 1985), esp. 39–43.
9. TM Devine, *Scotland's Empire 1600–1815* (2003), chapters 4 and 10 (published in the US by Smithsonian Books in 2004 as *Scotland's Empire & the Shaping of the Americas*); TM Devine, 'Industrialisation', in TM Devine, CH Lee and GC Peden, eds, *The Transformation of Scotland: The Economy Since 1700* (2005), 51–56.
10. See Graeme Morton and RJ Morris, 'Civil Society, Governance and Nation, 1832–1914' in RA Houston and WWJ Knox, eds, *The New Penguin History of Scotland* (2001), esp. 361–62. For 'Scottish Democracy' see Laurance J Saunders, *Scottish Democracy 1815–1840* (1950) and George E Davie, *The Democratic Intellect* (second edn, 1964).
11. Iain Whyte, *Scotland and the Abolition of Black Slavery 1756–1838* (2006).
12. Helen M Finnie, 'Scottish Attitudes Towards American Reconstruction' (University of Edinburgh Ph.D., 1975).
13. Colin G Calloway, *White People, Indians, and Highlanders: Tribal Peoples and Colonial Encounters in Scotland and America* (2008).
14. Bernard Aspinwall, *Portable Utopia: Glasgow and the United States 1820–1920* (1984). See Alexander Murdoch, 'From Sauchiehall to 42nd', *Cencrastus*, No. 20 (Spring 1985), 49–50.

1 Scotland and America in the Seventeenth Century

15. Richard Middleton, *Colonial America: A History, 1565–1776* (third edn, 2002), 67–68.
16. Peter GB McNeill and Hector L MacQueen, eds, *Atlas of Scottish History to 1707* (1996), 154.
17. Quoted in TM Devine, *Scotland's Empire 1600–1815* (2003), 2.
18. John G Reid, *Sir William Alexander and North American Colonization: A Reappraisal* (1990), 11–12 quoting *An Encouragement to Colonies*, 38–39.
19. CH McIllwaine, ed., *The Political Works of James I* (1918), 22.
20. Reid, *Sir William Alexander*, 12.
21. NES Griffiths, *From Migrant to Acadian: A North American Border People, 1604–1755* (2005), 463.
22. See Allan I Macinnes, *The British Revolution, 1629–1660* (2005), chapter 6.
23. See Theodora Keith, 'Scottish Trade with the Plantations Before 1707', *Scottish Historical Review*, Vol. 6 (1909), 32–48.
24. Macinnes, *British Revolution*, 199–200, 221–22.
25. TM Devine, 'The Cromwellian Union and the Scottish Burghs' in John Butt and JT Ward, eds, *Scottish Themes: Essays in Honour of Professor S.G.E. Lythe* (1976), 11. Reprinted in TM Devine, *Exploring the Scottish Past: Themes in the History of Scottish Society* (1995), 1–16.
26. David Dobson, *Scottish Emigration to Colonial America, 1607–1785* (1994), 31–32.
27. Devine, 'Cromwellian Union', 11.
28. Dobson, *Scottish Emigration*, 33–34.
29. George Pratt Insh, *Scottish Colonial Schemes 1620–1686* (1922), 114, 256.
30. Dobson, *Scottish Emigration*, 36.
31. TC Smout, 'The Glasgow Merchant Community in the Seventeenth Century', *Scottish Historical Review*, Vol. 47 (1968), 56.
32. Devine, 'Cromwellian Union', 12.
33. Smout, 'Glasgow Merchant Community', 56, 65.
34. RDS Jack, 'Urquhart [Urchard], Sir Thomas, of Cromarty' in *Oxford DNB*.
35. Smout, 'Glasgow Merchant Community', 56. Also see TC Smout, 'The Early Scottish Sugar Houses, 1660–1720', *Economic History Review*, Vol. 14 (1961), 240–53.
36. Macinnes, *British Revolution*, 234. Also see Brian Levack, *The Formation of the British State: England, Scotland and the Union 1603–1707* (1987).
37. Macinnes, *British Revolution*, 234. Also see Allan I Macinnes, *Union and Empire: The Making of the United Kingdom in 1707* (2007), chapter 6: 'The Transatlantic Dimension'.
38. Donna Merwick, *Possessing Albany, 1630–1710: The Dutch and English Experience* (1990).
39. Hugh Ouston, 'York in Edinburgh: James VII and the Patronage of Learning in Scotland, 1679–1688' in John Dwyer, et al., eds, *New Perspectives on the Politics and Culture of Early Modern Scotland* ([1982]), 133.
40. Pratt Insh, *Scottish Colonial Schemes*, 124.
41. Ibid., 126.
42. Ibid., 124–25.

43. Ibid.
44. Ibid., 127.
45. Ibid.
46. Smout, 'Glasgow Merchant Community', 70.
47. David Harris Sacks, *The Widening Gate: Bristol and the Atlantic Economy, 1450–1700* (1991), 362.
48. RH Campbell, 'The Enlightenment and the Economy' in RH Campbell and Andrew S Skinner, eds, *The Origins and Nature of the Scottish Enlightenment* (1982), 14–15.
49. Campbell, 'The Enlightenment and the Economy', 15.
50. Ned C Landsman, *Scotland and Its First American Colony, 1683–1765* (1985), 103–104.
51. Ibid.
52. Gordon DesBrisay, 'Barclay, Robert, of Ury' [sic] in *Oxford DNB*.
53. Landsman, *Scotland and Its First American Colony*, 105, 122–23.
54. Ibid., 126.
55. Linda G Fryer, 'Documents Relating to the Formation of the Carolina Company in Scotland, 1682', *South Carolina Historical Magazine*, Vol. 99 (1998), 114.
56. Ibid., Also see Pratt Insh, *Scottish Colonial Schemes*, chapter 6.
57. Eric J Graham and Tom Barclay, 'Ayr and the "Scots Lots" in the Americas 1682–1707', *History Scotland*, Vol. 3, No. 4 (2003), 23; Fryer, 'Carolina Company', 116. Also see Tom Barclay and Eric J Graham, *Early Transatlantic Trade of Ayr, 1640–1730* (2005).
58. Pratt Insh, *Scottish Colonial Schemes*, 125–27.
59. Quoted in Fryer, 'Carolina Company', 116.
60. Ibid., 123.
61. Pratt Insh, *Scottish Colonial Schemes*, 203.
62. Fryer, 'Carolina Company', 123–24.
63. Pratt Insh, *Scottish Colonial Schemes*, 202.
64. Landsman, *Scotland and Its First American Colony*, 111–12, 123–24. The *Oxford English Dictionary* definition of 'quitrent' includes the following: 'a nominal rent paid (esp. in former British Colonial territories to the Crown) as an acknowledgement of tenure.'
65. Fryer, 'Carolina Company', 126.
66. Pratt Insh, *Scottish Colonial Schemes*, 125–26.
67. Ibid.
68. Ibid.
69. David Hume, *The Letters of David Hume*, ed. JYT Greig (1932), Vol. 2, 230–31 (Letter 449).
70. See David Armitage, 'The Scottish Vision of Empire: Intellectual Origins of the Darien Venture' in John Robertson, ed., *A Union for Empire: Political Thought and the Union of 1707* (1995) and Colin Kidd, *Union and Unionisms: Political Thought in Scotland, 1500–2000* (2008), 65, 77–78.
71. David Armitage, *The Ideological Origins of the British Empire* (2000), 160.
72. Douglas Watt, *The Price of Scotland: Darien, Union and the Wealth of Nations* (2007), xviii.
73. Ibid., 171.

74. As indeed became the case for some Scots before and after the Darien expeditions. See Eric J Graham, *Seawolves: Pirates and the Scots* (2005) and the review of the book by Steve Murdoch in *The Scottish Historical Review*, Vol. 87 (2008), 341–43.
75. Watt, *Price of Scotland*, 171; James William Kelly, 'Wafer, Lionel' in *Oxford DNB*.
76. Pratt Insh, ed., *Papers Relating to the Ships and Voyages of the Company of Scotland Trading to Africa and the Indies 1696–1707* (1924), 74.
77. Ibid., 76.
78. Pratt Insh, *The Company of Scotland Trading to Africa and the Indies* (1932), 57.
79. Watt, *Price of Scotland*, 35–36.
80. Sonia P Anderson, 'Rycaut, Sir Paul' in the *Oxford DNB*.
81. Watt, *Price of Scotland*, 100.
82. Ibid., 160, 188–89.
83. AE Murphy, *John Law: Economic Theorist and Policy-Maker* (1997).
84. Watt, *Price of Scotland*, 184. Also see Jeffrey Stephen, 'The Presbytery of Caledonia: An Early Scottish Mission', *History Scotland*, Vol. 9 No. 1 (2009), 14–19.
85. Watt, *Price of Scotland*, 80–81.
86. W Douglas Jones, '"The Bold Adventurers": A Quantitative Analysis of the Darien Subscription List (1696)', *Scottish Economic and Social History*, Vol. 21 (2001), 30–31.
87. Bridget McPhail, 'Through a Glass Darkly: Scots and Indians Converge at Darien', *Eighteenth-Century Life*, Vol. 18 (1994), 132.
88. Christopher Storrs, 'Disaster at Darien (1698–1700)? The Persistence of Spanish Imperial Power on the Eve of the Demise of the Spanish Habsburgs', *European History Quarterly*, Vol. 24 (1999), 25.
89. Francis Borland, *The History of Darien* (1779).
90. Armitage, 'Scottish Vision of Empire', 112.
91. Ibid. Also see Colin Kidd, 'Seton, Sir William, of Pitmedden' in the *Oxford DNB*.
92. Armitage, 'Scottish Vision of Empire', 104 n22.

2 Emigration in the Eighteenth Century

93. David Dobson, 'Seventeenth-Century Scottish Communities in the Americas' in Alexia Grosjean and Steve Murdoch, eds, *Scottish Communities Abroad in the Early Modern Period* (2005), 105–31.
94. Aaron Fogleman, 'From Slaves, Convicts, and Servants to Free Passengers', *Journal of American History*, Vol. 85 (1998).
95. TC Smout, NC Landsman and TM Devine, 'Scottish Emigration in the Seventeenth and Eighteenth Centuries' in Nicholas Canny, ed., *Europeans on the Move: Studies in European Migration, 1500–1800* (1994), 98.
96. David Dobson, *Scottish Emigration to Colonial America* (1994), 83.
97. Iain CC Graham, *Colonists from Scotland: Emigration to North America, 1707–1783* (1956), 109. A digitized text of the broadside used for the text published in the *Maryland Historical Magazine* referenced by Graham is now

available through Eighteenth Century Collections Online, accessed 22 January 2009. The ESTC number for the original broadside held by the British Library is T096401.

98. Dobson, *Scottish Emigration to Colonial America*, 89, 104.
99. Linda Colley, *Captives: Britain, Empire and the World 1600–1850* (2003), 188–92; Ferenc M Szasz, 'Peter Williamson and the Eighteenth Century Scottish-America Connection', *Northern Scotland*, Vol. 19 (1999), 47–61.
100. A Roger Ekirch, 'The Transportation of Scottish Criminals to America during the Eighteenth Century', *Journal of British Studies*, Vol. 24 (1985), 373.
101. David Stevenson, 'Burt, Edmund (d. 1755) in the *Oxford DNB*; [Edmund Burt] *Letters from a Gentleman in the North of Scotland to his Friend in London* (1754), Vol. I, 46–48.
102. The *Oxford English Dictionary* defines a wadsetter as either one who mortgages land they own to others, or, more commonly, one who holds lands by paying money that can be redeemed by the owner on payment of the capital, and a tacksman as one who holds a lease of land or other property and 'in the Highlands, a middleman who leases directly from the proprietor of the estate a large piece of land which he sublets in small farms.' See *OED* online edition accessed 1 September 2009.
103. Graham, *Colonists from Scotland*, 77–80; Robert AA McGeachy, 'Captain Lauchlin Campbell and Early Argyllshire Emigration to New York', *Northern Scotland*, Vol. 19 (1999), 21–46; Allan Macinnes, *Clanship, Commerce and the House of Stuart, 1603–1788* (1996), 225.
104. Alan Taylor, *American Colonies: The Settling of North America* (2001), 133–34, 218, 224; McGeachy, 'Captain Lauchlin Campbell', 23, quoting *The Case of Lieutenant Donald Campbell, and the other Children of the Deceased Capt. Lauchlin Campbell, of the Province of New York* [1767], Eighteenth Century Collections Online, accessed 22 January 2009. Copies in the British Library and the New York Historical Society.
105. McGeachy, 'Captain Lauchlin Campbell', 31–32.
106. Alfred R. Hoermann, *Cadwallader Colden* (2002), 185–87; Graham, *Colonists from Scotland*, 78–80; McGeachy, 'Captain Lauchlin Campbell', 28.
107. William Smith, *Information to Emigrants, Being the Copy of a Letter from a Gentleman in North America* [1773]. Eighteenth Century Short Title Catalogue N007683. Eighteenth Century Collections Online digitized image of Library of Congress copy, accessed 22 January 2009.
108. McGeady, 'Captain Lauchlin Campbell', 27.
109. Middleton, *Colonial America* (third edn, 2002), 377.
110. Dobson, *Scottish Emigration to Colonial America*, 116–17; Anthony W Parker, *Scottish Highlanders in Colonial Georgia* (1997), 20.
111. Dobson, Ibid., 119–21; Parker, Ibid., 61–67, 83–86 quoted in Calloway, *White People, Indians and Highlanders*, 203.
112. William Ferguson, 'The Problems of the Established Church in the West Highlands and Islands in the Eighteenth Century', *Records of the Scottish Church History Society*, Vol. 17 (1972), 24–25; Bruce Lenman, *The Jacobite Clans of the Great Glen 1650–1784* (1984), 21.
113. National Archives of Scotland, CH2/312/4/61.
114. Parker, *Scottish Highlanders in Colonial Georgia*. 27, 92.

115. Betty Wood, 'Oglethorpe, James Edward' in the *Oxford DNB*.
116. David Brion Davis, *The Problem of Slavery in Western Culture* (1966, revd prbk edn 1988), 147–48; also see Betty Wood, *Slavery in Colonial Georgia 1730–1775* (1984), 30.
117. Harvey H Jackson, 'The Darien Antislavery Petition of 1739 and the Georgia Plan', *William and Mary Quarterly*, Third Series, Vol. 34 (1977), 618–19; Parker, *Scottish Highlanders in Colonial Georgia*, 73 and Appendix C.
118. Davis, *Problem of Slavery*, 374–78.
119. Ibid., 145.
120. Jackson, 'The Darien Antislavery petition', 618.
121. Wood, *Slavery in Colonial Georgia*, 201.
122. Ibid., 191–92, 201–203.
123. Alex[ander] Murdoch, 'Emigration from the Scottish Highlands', *British Journal for Eighteenth-Century Studies*, Vol. 21 (1998), 165–66; Duane Meyer, *The Highland Scots of North Carolina, 1732–1776* (1961), 79, 82, although Meyer is more speculative in his observations about possible immigration from the Scottish Highlands to North Carolina before 1739.
124. William S Powell, 'Johnston, Gabriel (1698–1752)' in the *Oxford DNB*; A Roger Ekirch, *"Poor Carolina": Politics and Society in Colonial North Carolina, 1729–1776* (1981), 66–111.
125. Robert J Cain, ed., *Records of the Executive Council 1735–1754* (The Colonial Records of North Carolina, Second Series), Vol. VIII (1988), xix.
126. Ibid; Alexander Murdoch, *British Emigration, 1603–1914* (2004), 43–44.
127. Cain, ed., *Records of the Executive Council, 1735–1754*, 237–38.
128. Landsman, *Scotland and its First American Colony*, 214–15, 223–26.
129. TH Breen, 'Persistent Localism: English Social Change and the Shaping of New England Institutions', *William and Mary Quarterly*, Third Series, Vol. 32 (1975), 3–28; Richard Beeman, *Varieties of Political Experience in Eighteenth-Century America* (2004). I am grateful to Dr Alan F Day for directing me to Breen's article.
130. For example, that migration which formed the subject of Marianne McLean, *The People of Glengarry: Highlanders in Transition, 1745–1820* (1991), chapter 6.
131. Bernard Bailyn, *Voyagers to the West: Emigration from Britain to America on the Eve of the Revolution* (1986).
132. Murdoch, *British Emigration*, 47–48, 59.
133. Ibid., Chapter 15.
134. Archibald Menzies, *Proposals for Peopling His Majesty's Southern Colonies on the Continent of America* (1763), 4pp. Eighteenth Century Short Title Catalogue Number T212286. There is a copy in the National Library of Scotland.
135. Annette M Smith, *Jacobite Estates of the Forty-Five* (1982), 66, 100.
136. Bailyn, *Voyagers to the West*, 451–52.
137. Quoted in Alexander Murdoch, *The People Above: Politics and Administration in Mid-Eighteenth Century Scotland* (1980, reissued 2003), 102. 'si sua bona NORUNT,' is a (mis)quotation from Virgil's *Georgics* (2.458) discussed in Lecture 11 of Adam Smith's *Lectures on Rhetoric and Belles Lettres* praising the virtues of rural life and quoting Virgil as 'O Fortunati nimium sua si bona norunt.'

138. Quoted in Bailly, *Voyagers to the West*, 436, from National Archives of Scotland, GD 248/49/2, 7 March 1764.

139. David Hancock, *Citizens of the World: London Merchants and the Integration of the British Atlantic Community, 1735–1785* (1995), 161.

140. National Archives of Scotland, GD 146, Box 12.

141. These are issues that are addressed implicitly in Barbara DeWolfe, ed., *Discoveries of America: Personal Accounts of British Emigrants to America during the Revolutionary Era* (1997).

142. DeWolfe, *Discoveries of America*, 172–73.

143. Ibid., 174.

144. Ibid., 178.

145. Eugene R Fingerhut, 'The Assimilation of Immigrants on the Frontier of New York 1764–1776' (Columbia University Ph.D., 1962), 209–10.

146. Ibid. I am grateful to Ned Landsman for recommending this dissertation to my attention.

147. McLean, *People of Glengarry*, 88–96, 229 n23; Bailly, *Voyagers to the West*, 576–85.

148. Compare Bailly, *Voyagers to the West* with McLean, *People of Glengarry* or JM Bumsted, *The People's Clearance 1770–1815* (1982).

149. For Red River see Marjory Harper, *Adventurers & Exiles: The Great Scottish Exodus* (2003), 119–21. For Scotland and Canada see Marjory Harper, *Emigration from North-East Scotland, Volume 2, Beyond the Broad Atlantic* (1988).

150. McLean, *People of Glengarry*, 5, 97.

151. Andrew Mackillop, *'More Fruitful Than the Soil': Army, Empire and the Scottish Highlands, 1715–1815* (2000), 181.

152. Bumsted, *People's Clearance*, 1.

153. Benjamin Franklin, *The Papers of Benjamin Franklin*, ed. William Willcox, Vol. 19 (1975), 6–7 (13 January 1772). Also see Richard B Sher, 'An "Agreable and Instructive Society": Benjamin Franklin and Scotland', in John Dwyer and Richard B Sher, eds, *Sociability and Society in Eighteenth-Century Scotland* (1993), 190, first published in Vol. 15 (1991) of the journal *Eighteenth-Century* Life. Also see J Hector St John de Crèvecoeur, *Letters From an American Farmer*, ed. Albert E Stone 'History of Andrew, The Hebridean', (1981 edn of text first published 1782). 90–105,

154. McLean, *People of Glengarry*, illustrates this point.

155. Mackillop, *More Fruitful Than the Soil*, 181.

156. Ibid., 180; Whitfield J. Bell, Jr, 'Scottish Emigration to America: A Letter of Dr Charles Nisbet to John Witherspoon, 1784', *William and Mary Quarterly*, Third Series, Vol. 11 (1954), 283 n14.

157. Bell, 'Scottish Emigration to America', 283.

158. Ibid., 284–86.

159. Ned C Landsman, 'Presbyterians and Provincial Society: The Evangelical Enlightenment in the West of Scotland, 1740–1775' in Dwyer and Sher, eds, *Sociability and Society in Eighteenth-Century Scotland*, 206.

160. Bell, 'Scottish Emigration to America', 287.

161. Murdoch, *British Emigration*, 68–69. For 'redundant population', see Donald Winch, *Riches and Poverty: An Intellectual History of Political Economy in Britain, 1750–1834* (1996), 277.

162. *Caledonian Mercury*, 20 October 1791, 3, columns 2–3.
163. Ibid.
164. National Archives of Scotland, RH2/4/64, f300 (17 August 1792). It was not preserved among the Campbeltown Customs House records in the NAS but in the Home Office papers at The National Archives at Kew in London. NAS RH2/4/64 consists of photostatic copies of some of those papers.
165. National Archives of Scotland, GD 51/5/52/1–7, First Report on Emigration of the Highland Society of Scotland, 12 January 1802.
166. Mackillop, *'More Fruitful Than the Soil'*, 180–81, 193–95; Ian Adams and Meredyth Somerville, *Cargoes of Despair and Hope: Scottish Emigration to North America 1603–1803* (1993), 135–41; Bailyn, *Voyagers to the West*, 46–54, 398.
167. Bumsted, *People's Clearance*, 148.
168. Ibid., 141; Oliver MacDonagh, *A Pattern of Government Growth 1800–1860: The Passenger Acts and Their Enforcement* (1961), 56–57.
169. MacDonagh, *A Pattern of Government Growth*, 64.
170. Ibid., 62.
171. Bumsted, *People's Clearance*, 145–48.
172. Fogleman, 'From Slaves, Convicts, and Servants to Free Passengers,' 61–66.

3 Sugar and Tobacco: 'Let Glasgow Flourish'

173. Douglas J Hamilton, *Scotland, the Caribbean and the Atlantic World, 1750–1820* (2005); Richard B Sheridan, 'The Role of the Scots in the Economy and Society of the West Indies' in V Rubin and A Tuden, eds, *Comparative Perspectives on Slavery in New World Plantations* (1977).
174. Hilary McD Beckles, 'The "Hub of Empire": the Caribbean and Britain in the Seventeenth Century' in Nicholas Canny, ed., *The Origins of Empire*, The Oxford History of the British Empire Vol. I (1998); Devine, *Scotland's Empire*, chapter 10; Hamilton, *Scotland, the Caribbean and the Atlantic World*.
175. Beckles, 'Hub of Empire', 218; Armitage, *Ideological Origins of the British Empire*, 160.
176. Beckles, 'Hub of Empire', 221; Macinnes, *Union and Empire*, 149.
177. Dobson, *Scottish Emigration to Colonial America*, 57, 64; Macinnes, *Union and Empire*, 157, 165–66.
178. Beckles, 'Hub of Empire', 230.
179. Kenneth G Davies, *The North Atlantic World in the Seventeenth Century* (1974), 74.
180. Robert M Weir, '"Shaftesbury's Darling": British Settlement in the Carolinas at the Close of the Seventeenth Century' in Canny, ed., *Origins of Empire*, 385.
181. Watt, *Price of Scotland*, 7; although David Armitage in 'Paterson, William', in the *Oxford DNB* relates that 'the first reliable record of his activities records his membership of the Merchant Taylors' Company on 16 November 1681.'

182. Virginia DeJohn Anderson, 'New England in the Seventeenth Century' in Canny, ed., *Origins of Empire*, 209, 216.
183. Watt, *Price of Scotland*, 155–56, 191.
184. Dobson, *Scottish Emigration to Colonial America*, 75.
185. Murdoch, 'Emigration from the Scottish Highlands', 166; Hamilton, *Scotland, the Caribbean and the Atlantic World*, 5, 55–56.
186. Murdoch, *British Emigration*, 42; Alexander Murdoch, 'A Scottish Document Concerning Emigration to North Carolina in 1772', *North Carolina Historical* Review, Vol. LXVII No. 4 (October 1990), 444.
187. Dobson, *Scottish Emigration to Colonial America*, 75.
188. Richard B Sheridan, 'The Formation of Caribbean Plantation Society, 1689–1748' in PJ Marshall, ed., *The Eighteenth Century*, The Oxford History of the British Empire Vol. II (1998), 398.
189. Hamilton, *Scotland, the Caribbean and the Atlantic World*, 45, 85, 94.
190. Richard B Sheridan, 'The Rise of a Colonial Gentry: A Case Study of Antigua, 1730–1775', *Economic History Review*, Second Series, Vol. 18 (1965).
191. Stuart Nisbet, 'The Sugar Adventurers of Glasgow 1640–1740', *History Scotland*, Vol. 9 No. 3 (May/June 2009), 28–33.
192. Hamilton, *Scotland, the Caribbean and the Atlantic World*, 45; Hamilton, 'Scottish Trading in the Caribbean: The Rise and Fall of Houstoun and Co.', in Ned C Landsman, ed., *Nation and Province in the First British Empire: Scotland and the Americas, 1600–1800* (2001), 98–100.
193. Hamilton, *Scotland, the Caribbean and the Atlantic World*, 199. Also see the brief entry for 'Garthland' in Francis H Groome, ed., *Ordnance Gazetteer of Scotland: A Survey of Scottish Topography, Statistical, Biographical, and Historical* (1886).
194. Hamilton, 'Scottish Trading in the Caribbean', 99–100.
195. TM Devine, 'An Eighteenth Century Business Elite: Glasgow West India Merchants, c.1750–1815', *Scottish Historical Review*, Vol. 57 (1978), 42. Also see chapter 4, 'Mercantile Connections' in Hamilton, *Scotland, the Caribbean and the Atlantic World*, 84–111.
196. See TM Devine, 'Colonial Commerce and the Scottish Economy, c1730–1815' in LM Cullen and TC Smout, eds, *Comparative Aspects of Scottish and Irish Economic and Social History 1600–1900* ([1977]), 181; TM Devine, 'The American War of Independence and Scottish Economic History' in Owen Dudley Edwards and George Shepperson, eds, *Scotland, Europe and the American Revolution* (1976), 62–64, reprinted in Devine, *Exploring the Scottish Past* (1995), 99–104.
197. See Hamilton, *Scotland, the Caribbean and the Atlantic World*, 84–111; Hamilton, 'Scottish Trading in the Caribbean', 94–126.
198. Devine, 'An Eighteenth Century Business Elite', 40; Devine, 'Colonial Commerce and the Scottish Economy', 181–82.
199. Hamilton, *Scotland, the Caribbean and the Atlantic World*, 93.
200. TM Devine, *The Tobacco Lords* (1975), 92–98; Devine, 'Industrialisation', in Devine, Lee and Peden, eds, *The Transformation of Scotland*, 52–54.
201. TM Devine, 'The Colonial Trades and Industrial Investment in Scotland, c.1700–1815' *Economic History Review*, Vol. 29 (1976), 1–13. Reprinted in Pieter Emmer and Femme Caastra, eds, *The Organization of Interoceanic*

Trade in European Expansion, 1450–1800 (1996), 299–311, especially 5, 10 (303, 308 in reprinted edition).

202. JR Ward, 'The British West Indies, 1748–1815' in PJ Marshall, ed., *The Eighteenth Century*, 421–24; Iain Whyte, *Scotland and the Abolition of Black Slavery, 1756–1838* (2006), 165–66; Hamilton, *Scotland, the Caribbean and the Atlantic World*, 17, 98.
203. Hamilton, *Scotland, the Caribbean and the Atlantic World*, 101–106; Hamilton, 'Scottish Trading in the Caribbean', 115–18.
204. Whyte, *Scotland and the Abolition of Black Slavery*, chapters 2 and 5 in particular.
205. Michael Fry, 'Dundas, Henry, first Viscount Melville' in the *Oxford DNB*.
206. Michael Duffy, *Soldiers, Sugar and Seapower: The British Expeditions to the West Indies and the War Against Revolutionary France* (1987), 5–33, especially 7; Hamilton, *Scotland, the Caribbean and the Atlantic World*, 180–85.
207. Roger Norman Buckley, *Slaves in Red Coats: The British West India Regiments, 1795–1815* (1979), 14–29.
208. This was similar to British colonial enterprise in Canada and Ireland in principle if not in particulars. See Alexander Murdoch, 'Henry Dundas, Scotland and the Union with Ireland, 1792–1801' in Bob Harris, ed., *Scotland in the Age of the French Revolution* (2005), 125–39; Philip Lawson, *Imperial Challenge: Quebec and Britain in the Age of the American Revolution* (1989).
209. Duffy, *Soldiers, Sugar and Seapower*, 142–49, 237–38, 259–63.
210. Buckley, *Slaves in Red Coats*, particularly 140–44; Duffy, *Soldiers, Sugar and Seapower*, 363–67.
211. Hamilton, 'Scottish Trading in the Caribbean', 116.
212. Hamilton, *Scotland, the Caribbean and the Atlantic World*, 104–106.
213. Hamilton, 'Scottish Trading in the Caribbean', 115–18.
214. Whyte, *Scotland and the Abolition of Black Slavery*, 65, 85, 145–46, 165–68, 175, 179, 202, 214, 230, 234, 240, 248–49. The minutes of the Glasgow West India Association are held by the Mitchell Library Glasgow and have been made available in a microfilm edition by Microform Academic Publishers (www.microform.co.uk/guides/scotland.pdf, accessed 13 January 2009).
215. Andrew Hook, *Scotland and America 1750–1835* (1975), 9–11, 13; Andrew Hook, *From Goosecreek to Gandercleugh: Studies in Scottish-American Literary and Cultural History* (1999), 9.
216. TC Smout, *Scottish Trade on the Eve of Union, 1660–1707* (1963), 177–78. Also see the references to early trade involving tobacco on the Clyde in TM Devine and Gordon Jackson, eds, *Glasgow Volume I: Beginnings to 1830* (1995), 49, 72.
217. Gordon Jackson, 'Glasgow in Transition, c1660–c1740' in Devine and Jackson, eds, *Glasgow*, 73, 76.
218. Jacob M Price, 'The Rise of Glasgow in the Chesapeake Tobacco Trade, 1707–1775', *William and Mary Quarterly*, Third Series, Vol. 11 (1954), reprinted most recently in Jacob M Price, *Tobacco in Atlantic Trade: The Chesapeake, London and Glasgow, 1675–1775* (1995), chapter 1, which retains the pagination of the original publication.

219. Alastair J Durie, 'The Markets for Scottish Linen, 1730–1775', *Scottish Historical Review*, Vol. 52 (1973), 41: 'Ninety per cent of all linen exported from Scottish ports went to America or the West Indies.'
220. Jacob M Price, 'Glasgow, the Tobacco Trade, and the Scottish Customs, 1707–1730', *Scottish Historical Review*, Vol. 63 (1984), 14, 29, reprinted in Jacob M Price, *Overseas Trade and Traders :Essays on Some Commercial, Financial and Political Challenges Facing British Atlantic Merchants, 1660–1775* (1996), chapter 9, which retains the pagination of the original publication.
221. Ibid., 15–16.
222. Ibid., 17.
223. Ibid., 18–19.
224. Ibid., 21; Jacob M Price, *France and the Chesapeake: A History of the French Tobacco Monopoly, 1674–1791, and of Its Relationship to the British and American Tobacco Trades* (1973), Vol. I, 321.
225. Price, 'Glasgow, the Tobacco Trade and Scottish Customs', 21.
226. Ibid., 22.
227. R.C. Nash, 'The English and Scottish Tobacco Trades in the Seventeenth and Eighteenth Centuries: Legal and Illegal Trade', *Economic History Review*, Second Series, Vol. 35 (1982), 359.
228. Price, 'Glasgow, the Tobacco Trade and the Scottish Customs', 25, citing 'Samuel Sandys' Memoranda' in *The Parliamentary Diary of Sir Edward Knatchbull*, 119.
229. Price, 'Glasgow, the Tobacco Trade and the Scottish Customs', 27–28.
230. Ibid., 32, 35.
231. Price, 'The Rise of Glasgow in the Chesapeake Tobacco Trade', 180–81; Price, *France and the Chesapeake* published a table of British tobacco imports 1708–92 providing separate figures for Scotland and England in Vol. II, 843–45. Also see the most recent summaries by TM Devine in *Scotland's Empire*, 69–93 and *The Transformation of Scotland*, 29–30, 52–53.
232. See Price's *France and the Chesapeake*. Also see Philipp Robinson Rössner, *Scottish Trade with German Ports 1700–1770* (2008).
233. Devine, *The Tobacco Lords*. This remains the most authoritative account, updated in TM Devine, 'The Golden Age of Tobacco' in TM Devine and Gordon Jackson, eds, *Glasgow*, 139–83.
234. Devine, 'Golden Age of Tobacco', 149.
235. Price, *France and the Chesapeake*, Vol. I, 620–23.
236. Devine, 'Golden Age of Tobacco', 174.
237. Monica Clough, 'Murdoch, George' in the *Oxford DNB*.
238. *Observations on the culture of the tobacco-plant, with the manner in which it is cured, adopted to the climate of the west of Scotland* (1782), National Library of Scotland.
239. Devine, 'Golden Age of Tobacco', 175.
240. Devine, *Tobacco Lords*, 158–59.
241. Hancock, *Citizens of the World*, 386, 395; Charles R Ritcheson, '"To An Astonishing Degree Unfit for the Task": Britain's Peacemakers, 1782–1783' in Ronald Hoffman and Peter Albert, eds, *Peace and the Peacemakers: The Treaty of 1783* (1986), 70–100.
242. Devine, *Tobacco Lords*, 159.

243. Christopher A Whatley, *The Industrial Revolution in Scotland* (1997), 24-30; T.M. Devine, 'Scotland' in Roderick Floud and Paul Johnson, eds, *The Cambridge Economic History of Modern Britain* (2004), Vol. I, 399.
244. Allan Kulikoff's *Tobacco and Slaves: the Development of Southern Cultures in the Chesapeake, 1680–1800* (1986), 97–98. Kulikoff gives the Prince George's County Wills and Land Records 1725–1735 as his source, but does not identify 'Murdock' and 'Buchanan' as anything other than 'outsiders'.
245. See note 34 above.
246. Kulikoff, *Tobacco and Slavery*, 118, 123–24, 152, 226–27; Devine, *Tobacco Lords*, 59–60; Devine, *Scotland's Empire*, 73–74.
247. This account is based on Whyte, *Scotland and the Abolition of Black Slavery, 1756–1838*, 11–35. Willie Orr wrote a pioneering account of legal cases relating to black slaves in Scotland published under the title 'Slave Labours' in *The Scotsman*, Weekend Section, 30 June 1982. There is a reference to 'Robert Shedden' as a Scottish tobacco merchant in Devine, *Tobacco Lords*, 106, citing RW Coakley, 'The Two James Hunters of Fredericksburg', *The Virginia Magazine of History and Biography*, Vol. 56 (1948), 121.
248. Whyte, *Scotland and the Abolition of Black Slavery*, 14, 17, 259.
249. Ibid., 21. For Jamie's previous name of 'Shanker', see paragraph three of the National Archives of Scotland website feature article, 'the Montgomery slavery case, 1756', www.nas.gov.uk/about/070823.asp accessed 15 January 2009.
250. Whyte, *Scotland and the Abolition of Black Slavery*, 17, 28, 30–31. Professor John Cairns of the School of Law at the University of Edinburgh has suggested that the remarkable denunciation of slavery in George Wallace, *A System of the Principles of the Law of Scotland* (1760), was based on the issues raised by the Sheddan/Montgomery case of 1756 (Inaugural Lecture University of Edinburgh 6 December 2000). Wallace's work was plagiarized for the 1765 entry on 'Traite des Nêgres' by Ouis, Chevalier de Jaucourt, in Diderot's *Encyclopédie*. See Davis, *The Problem of Slavery in Western Culture* (rev. prbk edn, 1988), 416 n72.
251. Jacob M Price, 'Buchanan & Simson, 1759–1763: A Different Kind of Glasgow Firm Trading to the Chesapeake', *William and Mary Quarterly*, Third Series, Vol. 40 (1983), 29–30, reprinted in Price, *Tobacco in Atlantic Trade*, which retains the original pagination of the publication. Also see Hamilton, *Scotland, the Caribbean and the Atlantic World*, 99–100.
252. TM Devine, 'Introduction' in TM Devine, ed., *A Scottish Firm in Virginia 1767–1777: W. Cuninghame and Co.* (1984), xvii–xviii.
253. Ibid., 133–34.
254. Ibid., 134. See Kulikoff, *Tobacco and Slaves*, 359–63, on separation of slave families in Chesapeake society.
255. James Oldham, 'New Light on Mansfield and Slavery', *Journal of British Studies*, Vol. 27 (1988), 45–68; James Oldham, 'Murray, William, first earl of Mansfield' in the *Oxford DNB*.
256. Whyte, *Scotland and the Abolition of Black Slavery*, 9–10, 21–22. For the incentive to apprentice slaves to learn a craft see Hamilton, *Scotland, the Caribbean and the Atlantic World*, 36.
257. Whyte, *Scotland and the Abolition of Black Slavery*, 17.

258. Ibid., 18.
259. Whyte, *Scotland and the Abolition of Black Slavery*, 36. See William Donaldson, 'Tannahill, Robert' in the *Oxford DNB*, which records that after Tannahill was drowned in 1810, 'the body was recovered by Peter Burnet [sic] – Black Peter – an African-American friend of the family.'
260. James Boswell, *Life of Johnson*, edited by George Birkbeck Hill, revised and enlarged by LF Powell (1934), Vol. 3, 200–201. Also see Whyte, *Scotland and the Abolition of Black Slavery*, 18–19.
261. Devine, 'An Eighteenth Century Business Elite', 49–53.
262. Hamilton, 'Scottish Trading in the Caribbean', 94–126.
263. Whyte, *Scotland and the Abolition of Black Slavery*, 60.
264. Andrea Levy's novel, *Small Island* (2004), used the Jamaican term for other British Caribbean islands as a telling analogy for modern Britain. See www.andrealevy.co.uk accessed 14 January 2009.
265. Hamilton, *Scotland, the Caribbean and the Atlantic World*, 196.
266. Gad Heuman, 'The British West Indies', in Andrew Porter, ed., *The Nineteenth Century*, The Oxford History of the British Empire, Vol. III (1999), 472.
267. Hamilton, *Scotland, the Caribbean and the Atlantic World*, chapter 8.
268. Heuman, 'The British West Indies', 483.
269. Hamilton, *Scotland, the Caribbean and the Atlantic World*, chapter 8. Of course wealth was repatriated to Scotland from the East Indies as well, see George K McGilvary, *East India Patronage and the Scottish State: The Scottish Elite and Politics in the Eighteenth Century* (2008).

4   Slavery and Scotland

270. Christopher A Whatley, 'The Dark Side of the Enlightenment? Sorting Out Serfdom' in TM Devine and JR Young, eds, *Eighteenth Century Scotland: New Perspectives* (1999), 259–74.
271. JR Ward, *British West Indian Slavery, 1750–1834: the Process of Amelioration* (1988), 3–4 citing *Wealth of Nations*, Book I, chapter 8.
272. Ibid.
273. David Hume, *Essays, Moral, Political and Literary*, ed. Eugene F Miller (Revd Edn 1987), 208, with a note on a variant reading on 629. See Emma Rothschild, 'David Hume and the Seagods of the Atlantic' in Susan Manning and Francis D Cogliano, eds, *The Atlantic Enlightenment* (2008), 91–95.
274. [Thomas Jefferson] *Notes on the State of Virginia* ([Paris] 1782 [1784]), 257–58, accessed via Eighteenth Century Collections Online, 16 January 2009.
275. Whyte, *Scotland and the Abolition of Black Slavery*, 55; Richard B Sher, *Church and University in the Scottish Enlightenment* (1985), 63–64.
276. William Robertson, *The History of America* (Paris, 1828, English edn), 416, 484.
277. Whyte, *Scotland and the Abolition of Black Slavery*, 60, 71.
278. Ibid., 51–52, 58, 60. See Simon Schama, *Rough Crossings: Britain, The Slaves and The American Revolution* (2005).
279. Richard B Sher and Alexander Murdoch, 'Patronage and Party in the Church of Scotland, 1750–1800' in Norman McDougall, ed., *Church, Politics and Society: Scotland 1408–1929* (1983), 201–203, 206.

280. Whyte, *Scotland and the Abolition of Black Slavery*, 74; Bob Harris, *The Scottish People and the French Revolution* (2008), 40, 231.
281. Whyte, *Scotland and the Abolition of Black Slavery*, 74, 78, 92.
282. Ibid., 77.
283. Ibid., 85.
284. Ibid., 84.
285. Ibid., 85.
286. Ibid., 97–99.
287. Harris, *The Scottish People and the French Revolution*, 40, 51–52.
288. Iain Whyte, 'The Anti-Slave Trade Tour of William Dickson in 1792', *Scottish Local History*, No. 72 (Spring 2008), 10.
289. Michael Fry, *The Dundas Despotism* (1992), 199–201.
290. Murdoch, 'Henry Dundas, Scotland and the Union with Ireland', 125–39.
291. James A Rawley, 'Dalzel [formerly Dalziel], Archibald' in the *Oxford DNB*.
292. Archibald Dalzel, *The History of Dahomy, an Inland Kingdom of Africa* (1793), xxiv–xxv.
293. Quoted in White, *Scotland and the Abolition of Black Slavery*, 154.
294. John Ehrman, *The Younger Pitt: The Consuming Struggle* (1996), 425–36, especially 431; Whyte, *Scotland and the Abolition of Black Slavery*, 99–100, 118, 122, 132; Hamilton, *Scotland, the Caribbean and the Atlantic World*, 185–90; JR Oldfield, *Popular Politics and British Anti-Slavery* (1995), 64, 186; Andrew Porter, 'Trusteeship, Anti-Slavery and Humanitarianism' in Andrew Porter, ed., *The Nineteenth Century*, 203.
295. Linda Colley, *Britons: Forging the Nation 1707–1837* (1992), 358–59.
296. Howard Temperley, *British Antislavery 1833–1870* (1972), 24–29, 39, 80, 210–14, 218, 220, 226–27, 237, 244, 246–47; C Duncan Rice, *The Scots Abolitionists 1833–1861* (1981).
297. Whyte, *Scotland and the Abolition of Black Slavery*, 165-173.
298. Rice, *Scots Abolitionists*, 146, citing George Shepperson, 'Writings on Scottish-American History: A Brief Survey', *William and Mary Quarterly*, Third Series, Vol. 11 (1954), 173.
299. Whyte, *Scotland and the Abolition of Black Slavery*, 158; David Steuart of Garth, *Sketches of the Character, Manners, and Present State of the Highlanders of Scotland* (Second Edn, 1822 reprinted 1977), Vol. I, 212.
300. Whyte, *Scotland and the Abolition of Black Slavery*, 159–60, 163, 164.
301. Ibid., quoting the minutes of the Glasgow West India Association.
302. Ibid., 173–74.
303. Gordon Pentland, *Radicalism, Reform and National Identity in Scotland, 1820–1833* (2008), 167.
304. Whyte, *Scotland and the Abolition of Black Slavery*, 179–80.
305. Pentland, *Radicalism, Reform and National Identity*, 167. This could be a satire on the enthusiasms of the Scottish abolitionist Andrew Thomson, author of *Slavery not Sanctioned but Condemned by Christianity* (Edinburgh 1829) and *Substance of the Speech Delivered at the Meeting of the Edinburgh Society for the Abolition of Slavery* (Edinburgh 1830). See Whyte, *Scotland and the Abolition of Black Slavery*, 190–98.
306. Pentland, *Radicalism, Reform and National Identity*, 167–68.
307. Whyte, *Scotland and the Abolition of Black Slavery*, 183, 187, 202, 207–208.

308. Ibid; Pentland, *Radicalism, Reform and National Identity in Scotland*, 166–68.
309. IGC Hutchison, *A Political History of Scotland 1832–1924: Parties, Elections and Issues* (1986, reissued 2003), chapters 1 and 2.
310. Harper, *Adventurers & Exiles*, 285–87, 364–65; Harper, *Emigration from North-East Scotland*, Vol. I, 28–29, 51, 76, 92, 115, 319–31, 339, 347–48.
311. Jackie Kay, 'Missing Faces', *Saturday Guardian Review*, 24 March 2007, 21.
312. Rice, *Scots Abolitionists*, chapter 1.
313. Hook, *Scotland and America 1750–1835*, chapter 5; Hook, *From Goosecreek to Gandercleugh*, chapters 1, 8 and 9.
314. See in particular Lorraine Peters, 'Scotland and the American Civil War: A Local Perspective' (University of Edinburgh Ph.D. thesis, 1999) and her article 'The Impact of the American Civil War on the Local Communities of Southern Scotland', *Civil War History*, Vol. 49 (2003), 133–52.

5 Scotland and Native Peoples in the Americas

315. Arthur H Williamson, 'Scots, Indians and Empire: The Scottish Politics of Civilization 1519–1609', *Past and Present*, Number 150 (February 1996), 46–83. Buchanan never went to Brazil, but some Scots did. In 1557 Nicolas Durand de Villegagnon, leader of a French expedition to Brazil in 1555, welcomed reinforcements from Geneva to Villegagnon island in the bay of Rio de Janeiro 'surrounded by his Scottish bodyguard'. See Robert Knecht, 'France's Fiasco in Brazil', *History Today* (December 2008), 37 column 3.
316. Ibid., quoting Buchanan from Vol. I, 9 in the Aikman English translation of 1827, also discussed in Williamson, *Scottish National Consciousness in the Age of James VI* (1979), 124.
317. Williamson, 'Scots, Indians and Empire', 63–64.
318. Ibid.; Murdoch, *British Emigration*, 13–15; Julian Goodare and Michael Lynch, 'The Scottish State and its Borderlands' in Julian Goodare and Michael Lynch, eds, *The Reign of James VI* (2000), 186–207.
319. Williamson, 'Scots, Indian and Empire', 63–64, quoting *The Register of the Privy Council of Scotland*, ed. J Hill Burton and D Masson (1877–1933), Vols VI, VII, VIII.
320. Armitage, *Ideological Origins of the British Empire*, 59–60; John G Reid, 'The Conquest of "Nova Scotia"', in Ned Landsman, ed., *Nation and Province in the British Empire* (2001), 42–44.
321. Dobson, *Scottish Emigration to Colonial America*, 26.
322. Ibid., citing PL Barbour, *The Jamestown Voyage Under the First Charter, 1606–1609* (1969), Vol. I, 117, and WN Sainsbury, ed., *Calendar of State Papers, Colonial Series, 1574–1660* (1860), 363, 428, 441, 462, 498.
323. Dobson, *Scottish Emigration to Colonial America*, 27.
324. Arthur H Williamson, 'George Buchanan, Civic Virtue and Commerce', *Scottish Historical Review*, Vol. 75 (1996), 36.
325. NES Griffiths and John G Reid, 'New Evidence on New Scotland, 1629', *William and Mary Quarterly*, Third Series, Vol. 49 (1992), 415, 498–89.
326. Pratt Insh, *Scottish Colonial Schemes*, 169.

327. Williamson, 'Scots, Indians and Empire'; Steve Murdoch, *Britain, Denmark-Norway and the House of Stuart, 1603–1660* (2000); Steve Murdoch, *Network North: Scottish Kin, Commercial and Covert Associations in Northern Europe 1603–1746* (2006).

328. Bridget McPhail, 'Through a Glass Darkly', 129–47.

329. Robert Wodrow, *Early Letters of Robert Wodrow*, ed. LW Sharp (1937), Letter 5, 12–15 and Letter 35, 78–80.

330. David Armitage, 'Making the Empire British: Scotland in the Atlantic World 1542–1707', *Past and Present*, No. 155 (May 1997), 34–63

331. Quoted in Sir Alan Burn, *History of the British West Indies* (1954), 418. See James Falkner, 'Parke, Daniel' in the *Oxford DNB*. I am grateful to Professor Michael Lynch for this reference.

332. Parker, *Scottish Highlanders in Colonial Georgia*, 74–75.

333. Ibid., 82–93.

334. Murdoch, 'Emigration from the Scottish Highlands to America', 166. This is noted in Calloway, *White People, Indians and Highlanders,* 177.

335. Cain, ed., *Records of the Executive Council, 1735–1754*, xvii.

336. Macleod Muniments, Dunvegan Castle, Isle of Sky, Alexander Morison of Skiniden to an unknown correspondent concerned with administration of the Macleod estates, 18 March 1771. See Murdoch, *British Emigration*, 66; Kenneth Morgan, 'Trelawny, Edward' in the *Oxford DNB*. Morison's Loyalist claim in The National Archives [of the UK] at Kew in London. John WM Bannerman, *The Beatons: A Medical Kindred in the Classical Gaelic Tradition* (1986), 122–24; Royal Highland Society of Scotland, Sederunt Book No. 3, 171–73.

337. Parker, *Scottish Highlanders in Colonial Georgia*, 44–45; Dobson, *Scottish Emigration to Colonial America*, 119.

338. Donald E Meek, 'Scottish Highlanders, North American Indians and the SSPCK: Some Cultural Perspectives', *Records of the Scottish Church History Society*, Vol. 23 Part 2 (1990), 385–88, 396. Note that the comment on 388 that there is no record of John Macleod's work in Georgia and that he may later have gone to *North* Carolina is incorrect. See Parker, *Scottish Highlanders in Colonial Georgia*, 44–46, 78, 83. Also see Calloway, *White People, Indians and Highlanders*, 75.

339. Ibid., 388–89.

340. Ibid., 386, 389, 393.

341. Ibid., 393–94; Margaret Connell Szasz, *Scottish Highlanders and Native Americans: Indigenous Education in the Eighteenth-Century Atlantic World* (2007), chapters 7–8.

342. Dobson, *Scottish Emigration to Colonial America*, 104–105; Edward J Cashin, *Lachlan McGillivray, Indian Trader: The Shaping of the Southern Colonial Frontier* (1992), 7, 20, 34–37, 42–43, 51, 81–82, 256; Calloway, *White People, Indians and Highlanders*, 118–19, 155, 204.

343. Cashin, *Lachlan McGillivray*, 34, 36–37.

344. Dobson, *Scottish Emigration to Colonial America*, 105.

345. W Stitt Robinson, *James Glen: From Scottish Provost to Royal Governor of South Carolina* (1996), 44, 53; John Oliphant, *Peace and War on the Anglo-Cherokee Frontier, 1756-63* (2001), chapter 1.

346. James Merrell, *The Indians' New World: Catawbas and Their Neighbors from European Contact Through the Era of Removal* (1989), 150.

347. Oliphant, *Peace and War on the Anglo-Cherokee Frontier, 1756–63*, 11.

348. See Emma Rothschild, *Economic Sentiments: Adam Smith, Condorcet and the Enlightenment* (2001), 9–12.

349. Alex[ander] Murdoch, 'James Glen and the Indians' in Andrew Mackillop and Steve Murdoch, eds, *Military Governors and Imperial Frontiers c1600–1800* (2003), 146, citing National Archives of Scotland, GD 45/2/1, Letterbook of James Glen, April 1748, 76–77, James Glen to 'My Lord', 26 July 1748.

350. Allan I Macinnes, *Clanship, Commerce and the House of Stuart, 1603–1788* (1996), 217; James Hunter, *Culloden and the Last Clansman* (2001), 182–89.

351. Robinson, *James Glen*, 120–23; Calloway, *White People, Indians and Highlanders*, 98, 101.

352. Murdoch, 'James Glen and the Indians', 156; Calloway, *White People, Indians and Highlanders*, 98.

353. Murdoch, 'James Glen and the Indians', 156–57.

354. See Hans Delbrück, *The Dawn of Modern Warfare*, translated by Walter J Renfroe, Jr, History of the Art of War, Vol. IV (1990), 280.

355. Robinson, *James Glen*, 120.

356. Oliphant, *Peace and War on the Anglo-Cherokee Frontier*, chapters 3–6.

357. See Calloway, *White People, Indians and Highlanders*, 95.

358. Ned C Landsman, 'The Provinces and the Empire: Scotland, the American Colonies and the Development of British Provincial Identity' in Lawrence Stone, ed., *An Imperial State at War: Britain from 1688 to 1815* (1994), 267; Matthew Dziennik, '200 acres of free ground: the Transatlantic uses of the Highland military, 1756–1783', draft chapter from a projected University of Edinburgh Ph.D., 'the Highland Military/Soldier in the British Atlantic World, 1754–1783'; Calloway, *White People, Indians, and Highlanders*, 151–53; Oliphant, *Peace and War on the Anglo-Cherokee Frontier*, 201–204.

359. Ibid, 116, 119, 132. For the Stono Rebellion see Gary B Nash, *Red, White & Black: The Peoples of Early America* (Third Edn, 1992), 185, 293–94.

360. John R Alden, *John Stuart and the Southern Colonial Frontier* (1944), 68–69.

361. Ibid., 159–64; Troy O Bickham, 'Stuart, John (1718–1779)' in the *Oxford DNB*.

362. J Russell Snapp, *John Stuart and the Struggle for Empire on the Southern Frontier* (1996), 55–57.

363. David Hume, *The Letters of David Hume*, ed. JYT Greig, Vol. I, 403 (6 October 1763).

364. William Ferguson, *The Identity of the Scottish Nation: An Historic Quest* (1998), 244.

365. Snapp, *John Stuart*, 57.

366. Mark Towsey, 'Reading the Scottish Enlightenment' (University of St Andrews Ph.D. thesis, 2007), citing National Archives of Scotland, GD 248/37/4/3.

367. Joyce Chaplin, *An Anxious Pursuit: Agricultural Innovation and Modernity in the Lower South, 1730–1815* (1993), 30–37, 49–50.

368. Snapp, *John Stuart*, 32, 42, 123.

369. Ibid., 87, 148; Alden, *John Stuart*, 305–306.

370. Ibid., 198; Cashin, *Lachlan McGillivray*, 297; Calloway, *White People, Indians and Highlanders*, 152–53.
371. Snapp, *John Stuart*, 198, 202–205, 207–208, citing Allen Candler, et al., eds, *Colonial Records of the State of Georgia*. Vol. IX (1904–16), Part 2, 162–66.
372. William S Coker and Thomas D Watson, *Indian Traders of the Southeastern Spanish Borderlands: Panton, Leslie & Company and John Forbes & Company, 1783–1847* (1986), especially chapter 7.
373. Snapp, *John Stuart*, 210–11.
374. Daniel Walker Howe, *What Hath God Wrought: The Transformation of America, 1815–1848* (2007), 8–18.
375. See chapters 5 and 6 of Calloway, *White People, Indians and Highlanders*. See James Hunter, *Glencoe and the Indians* (1996).

6 The Spiritual Connection

376. Landsman, 'Presbyterians and Provincial Society', 206–207; Ned C Landsman, 'Witherspoon and the Problem of Provincial Identity in Scottish Evangelical Culture' in Richard B Sher and Jeffrey R Smitten, eds, *Scotland and America in the Age of Enlightenment* (1990), 38–42.
377. WR Ward, *The Protestant Evangelical Awakening* (1992), 353.
378. Perry Miller, *The New England Mind: From Colony to Province* (1953); John Clive and Bernard Bailyn, 'England's Cultural Provinces: Scotland and America', *William and Mary Quarterly*, Third Series, Vol. 11 (1954).
379. See Virginia DeJohn Anderson, 'New England in the Seventeenth Century', 193–17; Toby Barnard, 'Restoration or Initiation?' in Jenny Wormald, ed., *The Seventeenth Century*, a volume in 'The Short Oxford History of the British Isles' (2008), 117–48.
380. Hall, 'Mather, Cotton' in the Oxford DNB, citing Kenneth Silverman, *The Life and Times of Cotton Mather* (1984), xvii.
381. Most notably, Wodrow's *Analecta: or Materials for a History of Remarkable Providences Mostly Relating to Scotch Ministers and Christians*, ed. Matthew Leishman (1842–1843), 4 volumes.
382. Hall, 'Mather, Cotton' in the *Oxford DNB*.
383. Ned C Landsman, *From Colonials to Provincials: American Thought and Culture, 1680–1760* (1997), 12.
384. Wodrow, *Early Letters of Robert Wodrow* (1937), 4 February 1706.
385. Robert Wodrow, *The Correspondence of the Rev. Robert Wodrow*, ed. Thomas McCrie (1842–1843), Volume I, 387, Letter CXV, Mather to Wodrow, 1712.
386. Ibid., 388–89, Letter CXVI, Wodrow to Mather, 8 December 1713.
387. Ibid., Vol. II, 424, Letter CXXX, Mather to Wodrow, '6d.8m.1718' for quotation; Vol. III, 18–21, Letter XI, Wodrow to Mather, 18 March 1723, on Mather's subscription to Wodrow's *History*.
388. Ibid, Vol. II, 426, Letter CXXXI, Wodrow to Mather, 29 January 1719.
389. William Ferguson, *Scotland: 1689 to the Present* (1968), 178.
390. Ward, *Protestant Evangelical Awakening*, 266–67, 353.
391. Thomas S Kidd, *The Great Awakening* (2007), xiv.

392. See, for example, Mechal Sobel, *The World They Made Together: Black and White Values in Eighteenth-Century Virginia* (1987).
393. Boyd Stanley Schlenther, 'Whitefield, George' in the *Oxford DNB*.
394. Ward, *Protestant Evangelical Awakening*, 270, 285–86.
395. Landsman, *Scotland and Its First American Colony*, 180–84.
396. Ward, *Protestant Evangelical Awakening*, 270–72.
397. John B Franz, 'Tennent, Gilbert' in the *Oxford DNB*, which identifies Tennent's parents as 'Scottish Presbyterians who had emigrated to Ireland.' It is still common to see his father's place of birth given as Ireland.
398. Schlenther, 'Whitefield, George' in the *Oxford DNB*.
399. Ward, *Protestant Evangelical Awakening*, 325, citing Wodrow, *Correspondence*, Vol. I, 55–58.
400. John R McIntosh, *Church and Theology in Enlightenment Scotland: The Popular Party, 1740–1800* (1998), 27.
401. Ward, *Protestant Evangelical Awakening*, 329–30.
402. Ibid, 336–37.
403. Ned C Landsman, 'Evangelists and Their Hearers: Popular Interpretation of Revivalist Preaching in Eighteenth-Century Scotland', *Journal of British Studies*, Vol. 28 (1989), 122–23, 126–27.
404. Ibid.; Ward, *Protestant Evangelical Awakening*, 336–37. Also see TC Smout, 'Born Again at Cambuslang: New Evidence on Popular Religion and Literacy in Eighteenth-Century Scotland', *Past and Present*, No. 97 (1982); McIntosh, *Church and Theology in Enlightenment Scotland*, 64–65, 68.
405. Ward, *Protestant Evangelical Awakening*, 337.
406. Ibid., 332–33, 338–39; McIntosh, *Church and Theology in Enlightenment Scotland*, chapters 4 and 5.
407. Ward, *Protestant Evangelical Awakening*, 339–40.
408. Ned C Landsman, 'Erskine, John' in the *Oxford DNB*.
409. John Erskine, *Shall I Go to War with my American Brethren?* (Second Edn, 1776), 9–10.
410. Ibid., 18.
411. Ibid., 20.
412. Ibid., 10.
413. Ibid., v, 14.
414. Ned C Landsman, 'Witherspoon, John' in the *Oxford DNB*.
415. Richard B Sher, 'Introduction' in Sher and Smitten, eds, *Scotland and America in the Age of the Enlightenment*, 15.
416. Daniel Walker Howe, 'Why the Scottish Enlightenment was Useful to the Framers of the American Constitution', *Comparative Studies in Society and History*, Vol. 31 (1989), 582.
417. See McIntosh, *Church and Theology in Enlightenment Scotland*, 155–60; Robert Kent Donovan, *No Popery and Radicalism: Opposition to Roman Catholic Relief in Scotland, 1778–1782* (1987).
418. J Steven Watson, *The Reign of George III* (1960), 280–81; Lindsay Paterson, *The Autonomy of Modern Scotland* (1994), 38, 45. Also see Stewart J Brown, *Thomas Chalmers and the Godly Commonwealth* (1982), 301–302,
419. Compare Kidd, *The Great Awakening*, which focuses on the colonial period, with Howe, *What Hath God Wrough*, chapter 5: 'Awakenings of Religion'.

420. Benjamin L Carp, 'Fire of Liberty: Firefighters, Urban Voluntary Culture, and the Revolutionary Movement', *William and Mary Quarterly*, Third Series, Vol. 58 (2001), 781–818.

421. Leigh Eric Schmidt, *Holy Fairs: Scottish Communions and American Revivals in the Early Modern Period* (1989), 59. For the different nature of the Great Awakening in the Middle Colonies as distinct from New England, see Marilyn J Westerkamp, *Triumph of the Laity: Scots-Irish Piety and the Great Awakening* (1988). I am grateful to Professor Ned Landsman for first directing me to Professor Westerkamp's work.

422. Schmidt, *Holy Fairs*, 60–65.

423. Donald E. Meek, 'The Pulpit and the Pen: Clergy, Orality and Print in the Scottish Gaelic World' in Adam Fox and Daniel Woolf, eds, *The Spoken Word: Oral Culture in Britain, 1500–1800* (2002), 97; H Scott, *Fasti Ecclesiae Scotlcanae: The Succession of Ministers in the Church of Scotland from the Reformation* (Second Edn, 1915–1923), Vol. IV, 63, which notes the publication of Crawford's sermons in Fayetteville.

424. Meek, 'The Pulpit and the Pen', 97.

425. The pamphlet survives in an apparently unique copy held by the First Presbyterian Church of Fayetteville, from which a photocopy has been made and is held by the Southern Studies Collection at the University of North Carolina at Chapel Hill; Meek, 'Pulpit and the Pen', 97–98. For Gaelic-speakers, this evangelical culture did not completely supplant more traditional beliefs as has been demonstrated by Ronald Black in '"The Nine": A Scottish Gaelic Charm in the North Carolina State Archives,' *The North Carolina Historical Review*, Vol. 84 (2007), 37–58.

426. Patrick Griffin, *The People with No Name: Ireland's Ulster Scots, America's Scots Irish, and the Creation of a British Atlantic World 1689–1764* (2001), 2, 175–76 n5.

427. Andrew Carnegie, *Autobiography* (1920), 22.

428. Peter Krass, *Carnegie* (2002), 423, 441–42.

429. John Coffey, 'Democracy and Popular Religion: Moody and Sankey's Mission to Britain 1873–1875' in Eugenio F Biagini, ed., *Citizenship and Community: Liberals, Radicals and Collective Identities in the British Isles 1865–1931* (1996), 95.

430. Hutchison, *A Political History of Scotland*, 136; Andrew L. Drummond and James Bulloch, *The Church in Late Victorian Scotland, 1874–1900* (1978), 13.

431. Andrew L Drummond and James Bulloch, *The Church in Victorian Scotland, 1843–1874* (1975), 184.

432. Coffey, 'Democracy and Popular Religion', 100.

433. Ibid; Drummond and Bulloch, *Church in Victorian Scotland*, 188.

434. Coffey, 'Democracy and Popular Religion', 100; Drummond and Bulloch, *Church in Late Victorian Scotland*, 9, which gives the variant quotation: 'What would John Knox think of the like of yon?'

435. Ibid, 309.

436. Ibid., 13.

437. Ibid. Bulloch based the final texts of his history of the church in Scotland on an earlier unpublished text by Drummond, who thus was the author most likely to have spoken to those who had been 'converted' under the influence of Moody's and Sankey's evangelicalism.

438. Coffey, 'Democracy and Popular Religion', 106.
439. Discussed in ibid; quotation from *The Scotsman*, 18 December 1873 accessed electronically via 'The Scotsman Archive', 5 November 2008.
440. DW Bebbington, 'Moody, Dwight Lyman, also including 'Ira David Sankey' in the *Oxford DNB*. Sankey was born in 1840 at Edinburgh (sometimes rendered Edinboro) Pennsylvania. Bebbington argues that 'Moody and Sankey probably represent the chief cultural influence of the United States on Britain during the nineteenth century.'
441. Hutchison, *A Political History of Scotland*, 137, quoting publications of the Association of 1875 and 1924.

Epilogue: 'The Scottish Invention of the USA'

442. Hook's essay was republished as the introductory chapter in *From Goosecreek to Gandercleugh*, see 9.
443. Landsman, 'The Provinces and the Empire', 278.
444. Although after the success of *Inventing America*, he joined the faculty at Northwestern University, Illinois: www.northwestern.edu/faculty/wills.htm accessed 7 January 2009.
445. Hook, 'The Scottish Invention of the USA' in *From Goosecreek to Gandercleugh*, 10–18; Daniel Walker Howe, 'Why the Scottish Enlightenment Was Useful to the Framers of the American Constitution', 572.
446. David Armitage, *The Declaration of Independence: A Global History* (2007), 9.
447. Edward J Cowan, *'For Freedom Alone': The Declaration of Arbroath, 1320* (2003), 146.
448. Edward J Cowan, 'Declaring Arbroath' in Geoffrey Barrow, ed., *The Declaration of Arbroath* (2003), 20. A considerably different (and characteristically nuanced) discussion of Jefferson's 'Declaration' in relation to Scotland has been advanced by Susan Manning in *Fragments of Union: Making Connections in Scottish and American Writing* (2002), chapter 4, especially 188–95.
449. Benedict Anderson, *Imagined Communities* (rev. edn, 1991), 2, 145, 147. Anderson was born in China, educated in England, is an Irish citizen, and held an academic post in the United States when he first published his study in 1983.
450. Cowan, *'For Freedom Alone'*, 122.
451. Cowan, 'Declaring Arbroath', 21.
452. Neal Ascherson, *Stone Voices: The Search for Scotland* (rev. edn, 2003), 265, in which the Christian names of Wilson and Witherspoon are transposed. See Cowan, 'Declaring Arbroath', 72 and John Simpson, 'James Wilson and the Making of Constitutions' in Thomas J Barron, Owen Dudley Edwards and Patricia J Storey, eds, *Constitutions and National Identity: Proceedings of the Conference on 'The Making of Constitutions and the Development of National Identity' held in honour of Professor George Shepperson at the University of Edinburgh 3–6 July 1987* (1993), 45–61.
453. Cowan, 'Declaring Arbroath', 14.
454. Hugh Brogan, *The Longman History of the United States of America* (1985), 136–80. The 'American' Declaratory Act of 1766 was based on the 'Irish'

Declaratory Act passed at Westminster in 1720, see Roy Foster, *Modern Ireland: 1600–1972* (1988), 162.

455. Alexander Murdoch, *British History 1660–1832: National Identity and Local Culture* (1998), 45.

456. Cowan, 'Declaring Arbroath', 26.

457. Charles Ivar McGrath, 'The "Union" Representation of 1703 in the Irish House of Commons: a Case of Mistaken Identity?' *Eighteenth-Century Ireland*, Vol. 23 (2008), 11–35; Allan Macinnes, *Union and Empire*, chapter 5.

458. Ibid., 137–38.

459. Colin Kidd, 'Religious Realignment Between the Restoration and Union' in John Robertson, ed., *A Union for Empire: Political Thought and the Union of 1707* (1995); Colin Kidd, 'Constructing a Civil Religion: Scots Presbyterians and the Eighteenth-Century British State' in James Kirk, ed., *The Scottish Churches and the Union Parliament* (2001)'; Karin Bowie, *Scottish Public Opinion and the Anglo-Scottish Union, 1699–1707* (2007), chapters 6–7; Derek J Patrick, 'The Kirk, Parliament and the Union, 1706–7', in Stewart J Brown and Christopher A Whatley, eds, *Union of 1707: New Dimensions* (2008).

460. Macinnes, *Union and Empire*, 239.

461. Murdoch, *British History*, 56.

462. This draws on some of the cultural ideas of 'Hugh MacDiarmid' about Scottish national identity. See Catherine Kerrigan, *Whaur Extremes Meet: the Poetry of Hugh MacDiarmid 1920–1934* (1983).

463. Smith, Adam, *Correspondence*, ed. Ernest Campbell Mossner and Ian Simpson Ross, (1977), 67–68 (4 April 1760). See Patricia Henlund, 'Strahan, William' in the *Oxford DNB*.

464. Smith, *Correspondence*, 67–68.

465. Alexander Murdoch, 'The Legacy of Unionism in Eighteenth-Century Scotland' in TM Devine, ed., *Scotland and the Union 1707–2007* (2008), 85.

466. Gordon S Wood, *The Americanization of Benjamin Franklin* (2004), 72–74, 259 n31.

467. Ned C Landsman, 'The Provinces and the Empire', 267–73; Landsman, 'The Legacy of British Union for the North American Colonies' in John Robertson, ed., *A Union for Empire* (1995), 302, 307–309.

468. Landsman, 'The Provinces and the Empire', 267.

469. Wood, *Americanization*, 133–34.

470. Benjamin Franklin, *The Papers of Benjamin Franklin*, ed. William Willcox, Vol. 14 (1970), 65, 69 (25 February 1767).

471. Wood, *Americanization*, 113, refers curiously to the inability of Scots in the eighteenth century 'to retain any strong sense of nationhood.'

472. Franklin, *Papers*, Vol. 14, 67–68.

473. Edmund Morgan, *Benjamin Franklin* (2002), 160–64.

474. JGA Pocock, 'Hume and the American Revolution: The Dying Thoughts of a North Briton', chapter 7 in JGA Pocock, *Virtue, Commerce and History* (1985), 127.

475. Ibid., adding the caveat: 'Tory, that is, as that word would be used in the generation following his own.'

476. Ibid. Also see Bernard Bailyn, *Voyagers to the West*, 283 n247: 'the workers' extreme discontent, emigration, and American political resistance merged in the minds of government officials and fed the fear that the entire fabric of civil society was threatened.'
477. Landsman, 'The Legacy of British Union', 308.
478. Landsman, 'The Provinces and the Empire', 267; Murdoch, *People Above*, 132.
479. Karen O'Brien, 'Robertson's Place in the Development of Eighteenth-Century Narrative History' in Stewart J Brown, ed., *William Robertson and the Expansion of Empire* (1997), 75.
480. I consulted the one volume edition (in English) published by Bauday in Paris, 1828, 457–526.
481. Owen Dudley Edwards, 'Robertsonian Romanticism and Realism' in Brown, ed., *William Robertson and the Expansion of Empire*, 107.
482. Jeffrey R Smitten, 'Robertson, William' in the *Oxford DNB*.
483. Donovan, *No Popery and Radicalism*.
484. Adam Smith, *An Inquiry into the Nature and Causes of the Wealth of Nations*, ed. RH Campbell et al. (1976), Vol. 2, 624–25 (Book IV, chapter 7, Part Third).
485. Ibid., 625–26. Also see Peter S Onuf, 'Adam Smith and the Crisis of the American Union' in Manning and Cogliano, eds, *The Atlantic Enlightenment*.
486. Smith, *Wealth of Nations*, Vol. 2, 625, 944–45.
487. Ibid., 945 and n91 on that page. For Andrew Fletcher's visionary unionism see John Robertson, 'Introduction' to Andrew Fletcher of Saltoun, *Political Works* ed. John Robertson (1997), xxv–xxviii.
488. Ibid., 947.
489. Smith, *Correspondence*, 271, Letter 233.
490. Cowan, 'For Freedom Alone', 131, citing Vernum L Collins, *President Witherspoon* (1925), Vol. 2, 188–89. Also see Daniel Walker Howe, 'John Witherspoon and the Transatlantic Enlightenment' in Manning and Cogliano, eds, *The Atlantic Enlightenment* (2008).
491. Landsman, 'The Legacy of British Union', 316–17.
492. Howe, 'Why the Scottish Enlightenment Was Useful to the Framers of the American Constitution', 580.
493. Ibid., 580–81.
494. Franklin, *Papers*, Vol. 14, 69.
495. Manning, *Fragments of Union*, 240.
496. Rush, Benjamin, *Autobiography*, ed. George W Corner (1948), 114, 323. See Manning, *Fragments of Union*, 21. My former student Lorna Bain (now Howat) first suggested this connection to me. Paine's *Common Sense: A Letter to the Fourteen Incorporations of Edinburgh* was published in Edinburgh in 1777, see Alexander Murdoch, 'The Importance of Being Edinburgh: Management and Opposition in Edinburgh Politics, 1746–1784', *Scottish Historical Review*, Vol. 62 (1983), 6, 12.
497. Hook, 'Scottish Invention of the USA', 22.
498. Howe, *What Hath God Wrought*, 636.
499. Ibid., 616, 637.

500. Including the Scots language as a distinctive linguistic tradition within the English language most broadly defined.
501. Hook, 'Scottish Invention of the USA', 22.
502. Frederick Douglass, *Autobiographies*, ed. Henry Louis Gates Jr (1994), 92–93, 354, 1053. May and Nathan Johnson were a black couple who ran a catering business in New Bedford, Massachusetts, who gave shelter to the runaway slave Frederick Bailey, who had arrived in New Bedford using the surname Johnson to avoid detection (1053 in *Autobiographies*). Lord James of Douglas, unjustly outlawed, was the hero of Scott's poem.

Bibliography

Entries in the *Oxford Dictionary of National Biography* (2004, and in progress in its electronic form) are listed individually.

Adams, Ian, and Meredyth Somerville, Cargoes of Despair and Hope: Scottish Emigration to North America 1603–1803 (1993)

Alden, John R, *John Stuart and the Southern Colonial Frontier* (1944)

[Americanus, Scotus] *Informations Concerning the Province of North Carolina* (1773)

Anderson, Benedict, *Imagined Communities* (rev. edn 1991)

Anderson, RD, *Education and Opportunity in Victorian Scotland* (rev. prbk edn 1989, first published 1983)

Anderson, Sonia P, 'Rycaut, Sir Paul' in the *Oxford DNB*.

Anderson, Virginia DeJohn, 'New England in the Seventeenth Century' in Nicholas Canny, ed., *The Origins of Empire*, The Oxford History of the British Empire, Vol. I (1998)

Armitage, David, 'The Scottish Vision of Empire: Intellectual Origins of the Darien Venture' in John Robertson, ed., *A Union for Empire: Political Thought and the Union of 1707* (1995)

Armitage, David, 'Making the Empire British: Scotland in the Atlantic World 1542–1707', *Past and Present*, No. 155 (May 1997)

Armitage, David, *The Ideological Origins of the British Empire* (2000)

Armitage, David, 'Paterson, William' in the *Oxford DNB*.

Armitage, David, *The Declaration of Independence: A Global History* (2007)

Ascherson, Neal, *Stone Voices: The Search for Scotland* (rev. edn, 2003)

Aspinwall, Bernard, *Portable Utopia: Glasgow and the United States 1820–1920* (1984)

Bailyn, Bernard, *Voyagers to the West: Emigration from Britain to America on the Eve of the Revolution* (1986)

Bannerman, John WM, *The Beatons: A Medical Kindred in the Classical Gaelic Tradition* (1986)

Barclay, Tom, and Eric J Graham, *Early Transatlantic Trade of Ayr, 1640–1730* (2005)

Barnard, Toby, 'Restoration or Initiation?' in Jenny Wormald, ed., *The Seventeenth Century*, a volume in 'The Short Oxford History of the British Isles' (2008)

Bebbington, DW, 'Moody, Dwight Lyman' in the *Oxford DNB*.

Beckles, Hilary McD, 'The "Hub of Empire": the Caribbean and Britain in the Seventeenth Century' in Nicholas Canny, ed, *The Origins of Empire*, The Oxford History of the British Empire, Vol. I (1998)

Beeman, Richard, *Varieties of Political Experience in Eighteenth-Century America* (2004)

Bell, Whitfield J, Jr, 'Scottish Emigration to America: A Letter of Dr Charles Nisbet to John Witherspoon, 1784', *William and Mary Quarterly*, Third Series, Vol. 11 (1954)

Bickham, Troy O, 'Stuart, John (1718–1779)' in the *Oxford DNB*.

Black, Ronald, ed, *To the Hebrides: Samuel Johnson's Journey to the Western Islands of Scotland and James Boswell's Journal of a Tour to the Hebrides* (2007)

Black, Ronald, '"The Nine": A Scottish Gaelic Charm in the North Carolina State Archives,' *The North Carolina Historical Review*, Vol. 84 (2007)

Borland, Francis, *The History of Darien* (1779)

Boswell, James, *Life of Johnson*, ed. George Birkbeck Hill, rev. LF Powell, 6 vols (1934–52)

Bowie, Karin, *Scottish Public Opinion and the Anglo-Scottish Union, 1699–1707* (2007)

Breen, TH, 'Persistent Localism: English Social Change and the Shaping of New England Institutions', *William and Mary Quarterly*, Third Series, Vol. 32 (1975)

Brock, William R, *Scotus Americanus: A Survey of the Sources for Links Between Scotland and America in the 18th Century* (1982)

Brogan, Hugh, *The Longman History of the United States of America* (1985)

Brown, Stewart J, *Thomas Chalmers and the Godly Commonwealth* (1982)

Buckley, Roger Norman, *Slaves in Red Coats: The British West India Regiments, 1795–1815* (1979)

Bumsted, JM, *The People's Clearance 1770–1815* (1982)

Burn, Sir Alan, *History of the British West Indies* (1954)

[Burt, Edmund] *Letters from a Gentleman in the North of Scotland to his Friend in London* (1754)

Cain, Robert J, ed., *Records of the Executive Council 1735–1754*, Colonial Records of North Carolina), Second Series, Vol. VIII (1988)

Calder, Jenni, *Scots in the USA* (2006)

Calloway, Colin G, *White People, Indians and Highlanders: Tribal Peoples and Colonial Encounters in Scotland and America* (2008)

Campbell, RH, 'The Enlightenment and the Economy' in RH Campbell and Andrew S Skinner, eds, *The Origins and Nature of the Scottish Enlightenment* (1982)

Campbell, RH, *Scotland Since 1707* (second edn, 1985)

Carnegie, Andrew, *Autobiography* (1920)

Carp, Benjamin L, 'Fire of Liberty: Firefighters, Urban Voluntary Culture, and the Revolutionary Movement', *William and Mary Quarterly*, Third Series, Vol. 58 (2001)

Cashin, Edward J, *Lachlan McGillivray, Indian Trader: The Shaping of the Southern Colonial Frontier* (1992)

Chaplin, Joyce, *An Anxious Pursuit: Agricultural Innovation and Modernity in the Lower South 1730–1815* (1993)

Clive, John, and Bernard Bailyn, 'England's Cultural Provinces: Scotland and America', *William and Mary Quarterly*, Third Series, Vol. 11 (1954)

Clough, Monica, 'Murdoch, George' in the *Oxford DNB*.

Coffey, John, 'Democracy and Popular Religion: Moody and Sankey's Mission to Britain 1873–1875' in Eugenio F Biagini, ed., *Citizenship and Community: Liberals, Radicals and Collective Identities in the British Isles, 1865–1931* (1996)

Coker, William S, and Thomas D Watson, *Indian Traders of the Southeastern Spanish Borderlands: Panton, Leslie & Company and John Forbes & Company, 1783–1847* (1986)

Colley, Linda, *Britons: Forging the Nation 1707–1837* (1992)

Colley, Linda, *Captives: Britain, Empire and the World 1600–1850* (2003)

Cowan, Edward J, *'For Freedom Alone': The Declaration of Arbroath* (2003)

Cowan, Edward J, 'Declaring Arbroath' in Geoffrey Barrow, ed., *The Declaration of Arbroath* (2003)

Cowan, Edward J, 'Tartan Day in America' in Celeste Ray, ed., *Transatlantic Scots* (2005)

Crèvecoeur, J Hector St John de, *Letters From an American Farmer*, ed. Albert E Stone 'History of Andrew, The Hebridean' (1981 edn of text first published 1782), 90–105

Dalzel, Archibald, *The History of Dahomy, an Inland Kingdom of Africa* (1793)

Davie, George E, *The Democratic Intellect* (second edn, 1964)

Davies, Kenneth G, *The North Atlantic World in the Seventeenth Century* (1974)

Davis, David Brion, *The Problem of Slavery in Western Culture* (rev. prbak edn 1988, first published 1966)

Dean, Dennis R, 'Muir, John (1838–1914)' in the *Oxford DNB*.

Delbrück, Hans, *The Dawn of Modern Warfare*, translated by Walter J Renfroe, Jr, History of the Art of War, Vol. IV (1990)

DesBrisay, Gordon, 'Barclay, Robert, of Ury' in the *Oxford DNB*.

Devine, TM, *The Tobacco Lords* (1975, reissued 1990)

Devine, TM, 'Introduction' in TM Devine, ed., *A Scottish Firm in Virginia 1767–1777: W. Cuninghame and Co.* (1984), xvii–xviii.

Devine, TM, 'The Colonial Trades and Industrial Investment in Scotland, c.1700–1815', *Economic History Review*, Vol. 29 (1976), reprinted in Pieter Emmer and Femme Caastra, eds, *The Organization of Interoceanic Trade in European Expansion, 1450–1800* (1996)

Devine, TM, 'The Cromwellian Union and the Scottish Burghs' in John Butt and JT Ward, eds, *Scottish Themes: Essays in Honour of Professor SGE Lythe* (1976), reprinted in TM Devine, *Exploring the Scottish Past: Themes in the History of Scottish Society* (1995)

Devine, TM, 'The American War of Independence and Scottish Economic History' in Owen Dudley Edwards and George Shepperson, eds, *Scotland, Europe, and the American Revolution* (1976), reprinted in TM Devine, *Exploring the Scottish Past: Themes in the History of Scottish Society* (1995)

Devine, TM, 'Colonial Commerce and the Scottish Economy, c1730–1815' in LM Cullen and TC Smout, eds, *Comparative Aspects of Scottish and Irish Economic and Social History 1600–1900* ([1977])

Devine, TM, 'An Eighteenth Century Business Elite: Glasgow West India Merchants, c.1750–1815', *Scottish Historical Review*, Vol. 57 (1978)

Devine, TM, 'The Golden Age of Tobacco' in TM Devine and Gordon Jackson, eds, *Glasgow Volume I: Beginnings to 1830* (1995)

Devine, TM, *Scotland's Empire 1600–1815* (2003) published in the US under the title *Scotland's Empire and the Shaping of the Americas* in 2004.

Devine, TM 'Scotland' in Roderick Floud and Paul Johnson, eds, *The Cambridge Economic History of Modern Britain* (2004), Vol. I

Devine, TM, 'Industrialisation', in TM Devine, CH Lee and GC Peden, eds, *The Transformation of Scotland: The Economy Since 1700* (2005)

Devine, TM, 'Scottish Elites and the Indian Empire, 1700–1815' in TC Smout, ed., *Anglo-Scottish Relations from 1603–1900* (2005)

DeWolfe, Barbara, ed., *Discoveries of America: Personnel Accounts of British Emigrants to America During the Revolutionary Era* (1997)

Dobson, David, *Scottish Emigration to Colonial America, 1607–1785* (1994)

Dobson, David, 'Seventeenth-Century Scottish Communities in the Americas' in Alexia Grosjean and Steve Murdoch, eds, *Scottish Communities Abroad in the Early Modern Period* (2005)

Donaldson, William, 'Tannahill, Robert' in the *Oxford DNB*.

Donovan, Robert Kent, *No Popery and Radicalism: Opposition to Roman Catholic Relief in Scotland, 1778–1782* (1987)

Douglass, Frederick, *Autobiographies*, ed. Henry Louis Gates, Jr (1994)

Drummond, Andrew L, and James Bulloch, *The Church in Victorian Scotland, 1843–1874* (1975)

Drummond, Andrew L, and James Bulloch, *The Church in Late Victorian Scotland, 1874–1900* (1978)

Duffy, Michael, *Soldiers, Sugar and Seapower: The British Expeditions in the West Indies and the War Against Revolutionary France* (1987)

Durie, Alastair J, 'The Markets for Scottish Linen, 1730–1775', *Scottish Historical Review*, Vol. 52 (1973)

Dziennik, Matthew, '200 acres of free ground: the Transatlantic uses of the Highland military, 1756–1783', draft chapter from a projected University of Edinburgh Ph.D., 'the Highland Military/Soldier in the British Atlantic World, 1754–1783'

Edwards, Owen Dudley, and George Shepperson, eds, *Scotland, Europe and the American Revolution* (1976)

Edwards, Owen Dudley, 'Robertsonian Romanticism and Realism' in Stewart J Brown, ed., *William Robertson and the Expansion of Empire* (1997)

Ehrman, John, *The Younger Pitt: The Consuming Struggle* (1996)

Ekirch, A Roger, *"Poor Carolina": Politics and Society in Colonial North Carolina, 1729–1776* (1981)

Ekirch, A Roger, 'The Transportation of Scottish Criminals to America during the Eighteenth Century', *Journal of British Studies*, Vol. 24 (1985)

Erskine, John, *Shall I Go to War with my American Brethren?* (second edn 1776)

Falkner, James, 'Parke, Daniel' in the *Oxford DNB*.

Ferguson, William, *Scotland: 1689 to the Present* (1968)

Ferguson, William, 'The Problems of the Established Church in the West Highlands and Islands in the Eighteenth Century', *Records of the Scottish Church History Society*, Vol. 17 (1972)

Ferguson, William, *The Identity of the Scottish Nation: An Historic Quest* (1998)

Fingerhut, Eugene R, 'The Assimilation of Immigrants on the Frontier of New York 1764–1776' (Columbia University Ph.D., 1962)

Finnie, Helen M, 'Scottish Attitudes Towards American Reconstruction' (University of Edinburgh Ph.D., 1975)

Fletcher, Andrew, of Saltoun, *Political Works*, ed. John Robertson (Cambridge Texts in the History of Political Thought, 1997)

Fogleman, Aaron, 'From Slaves, Convicts, and Servants to Free Passengers', *Journal of American History*, Vol. 85 (1998)

Foster, Roy, *Modern Ireland: 1600–1972* (1988)

Franklin, Benjamin, *The Papers of Benjamin Franklin*, ed. William Willcox, Vol. 14 (1970)

Franklin, Benjamin, *The Papers of Benjamin Franklin*, ed. William Willcox, Vol. 19 (1975)

Franz, John B, 'Tennent, Gilbert' in the *Oxford DNB*.

Fry, Michael, *The Dundas Despotism* (1992)

Fry, Michael et al., *Scotland and the Americas 1600–1800* (1995)

Fry, Michael, 'Dundas, Henry, First Viscount Melville' in the *Oxford DNB*.

Fryer, Linda G, 'Documents Relating to the Formation of the Carolina Company in Scotland, 1682', *South Carolina Historical Magazine*, Vol. 99 (1998)

Gibson, Rosemary, ed., *The Darien Adventure* (1998)

Goodare, Julian, and Michael Lynch, 'The Scottish State and Its Borderlands' in Julian Goodare and Michael Lynch, eds, *The Reign of James VI* (2000)

Graham, Eric J, and Tom Barclay, 'Ayr and the "Scots Lots" in the Americas 1682–1707', *History Scotland*, Vol. 3, No. 4 (2003)

Graham, Eric J, *Seawolves: Pirates and the Scots* (2005)

Graham, Ian CC, *Colonists from Scotland: Emigration to North America, 1707–1783* (1956)

Greene, Jack P, *Pursuits of Happiness: The Social Development of Early Modern British Colonies and the Formation of American Culture* (1988)

Griffin, Patrick, *The People With No Name: Ireland's Ulster Scots, America's Scots Irish, and the Creation of a British Atlantic World 1689–1764* (2001)

Griffiths, NES, and John G Reid, 'New Evidence on New Scotland, 1629', *William and Mary Quarterly*, Third Series, Vol. 49 (1992)

Griffiths, NES, *From Migrant to Acadian: A North American Border People, 1604–1755* (2005)

Groome, Francis H, ed., 'Garthland' in *Ordnance Gazetteer of Scotland: A Survey of Scottish Topography, Statistical, Biographical, and Historical* (1886).

Hall, Michael G, 'Mather, Cotton' in the *Oxford DNB*.

Hamilton, Douglas J, 'Scottish Trading in the Caribbean: The Rise and Fall of Houston and Co.', in Ned C Landsman, ed., *Nation and Province in the First British Empire: Scotland and the Americas, 1600–1800* (2001)

Hamilton, Douglas J, *Scotland, the Caribbean and the Atlantic World, 1750–1820* (2005)

Hancock, David, *Citizens of the World: London Merchants and the Integration of the British Atlantic Community, 1735–1785* (1995)

Handley, Stuart, 'Gordon, Lord Adam' in the *Oxford DNB*.

Harper, Marjory, *Emigration from North-East Scotland* (1988)

Harper, Marjory, *Adventurers & Exiles: The Great Scottish Exodus* (2003)

Harris, Bob, *The Scottish People and the French Revolution* (2008)

Henlund, Patricia, 'Strahan, William' in the *Oxford DNB*.

Herman, Arthur, *How the Scots Invented the Modern World* (2001), published in the UK under the title *The Scottish Enlightenment* in 2002.

Heuman, Gad, 'The British West Indies' in Andrew Porter, ed., *The Nineteenth Century*, The Oxford History of the British Empire, Vol. III (1999)

Hoermann, Alfred R, *Cadwallader Colden* (2002)

Hoeveler, Jr, David, *James McCosh and the Scottish Intellectual Tradition* (1981)

Hook, Andrew, *Scotland and America 1750–1835* (1975)

Hook, Andrew, *From Goosecreek to Gandercleugh: Studies in Scottish-American Literary and Cultural History* (1999)

Howe, Daniel Walker, 'Why the Scottish Enlightenment was Useful to the Framers of the American Constitution', *Comparative Studies in Society and History*, Vol. 31 (1989)

Howe, Daniel Walker, *What Hath God Wrought: The Transformation of America 1815–1848* (2007).

Howe, Daniel Walker, 'John Witherspoon and the Transatlantic Enlightenment' in Susan Manning and Francis D Cogliano, eds, *The Atlantic Enlightenment* (2008)

Hume, David, *The Letters of David Hume*, ed. JYT Greig, (1932), 2 vols.

Hume, David, *Essays, Moral, Political and Literary*, ed. Eugene F Miller (rev. edn 1987)

Hunter, James, *Glencoe and the Indians* (1996).

Hunter, James, *Culloden and the Last Clansman* (2001)

Hutchison, IGC, *A Political History of Scotland 1832–1924: Parties, Elections and Issues* (1986, reissued 2003)

Jack, RDS, 'Urquhart [Urchard], Sir Thomas, of Cromarty' in the *Oxford DNB*.

Jackson, Gordon, 'Glasgow in Transition, c1660–c1740' in TM Devine and Gordon Jackson, eds, *Glasgow Volume I: Beginnings to 1830* (1995)

Jackson, Harvey H, 'The Darien Antislavery petition of 1739 and the Georgia Plan', *William and Mary Quarterly*, Third Series, Vol. 34 (1977)

Jefferson, Thomas, *Notes on the State of Virginia* (1782 [1784])

Jones, W Douglas, '"The Bold Adventurers": A Quantitative Analysis of the Darien Subscription List (1696)', *Scottish Economic and Social History*, Vol. 21 (2001)

Kay, Jackie, 'Missing Faces', *Saturday Guardian Review*, 24 March 2007

Keith, Theodora, 'Scottish Trade with the Plantations Before 1707', *Scottish Historical Review*, Vol. 6 (1909)

Kelly, James William, 'Wafer, Lionel' in the *Oxford DNB*.

Kerrigan, Catherine, *Whaur Extremes Meet: the Poetry of Hugh MacDiarmid 1920–1934* (1983)

Kidd, Colin, 'Religious Realignment Between the Restoration and Union' in John Robertson, ed., *A Union for Empire: Political Thought and the Union of 1707* (1995)

Kidd, Colin, 'Constructing a Civil Religion: Scots Presbyterians and the Eighteenth-Century British State' in James Kirk, ed., *The Scottish Churches and the Union Parliament* (2001)

Kidd, Colin, 'Seton, Sir William, of Pitmedden' in the *Oxford DNB*.

Kidd, Colin, *Union and Unionisms: Political Thought in Scotland, 1500–2000* (2008)

Kidd, Thomas S, *The Great Awakening* (2007)

Knecht, Robert, 'France's Fiasco in Brazil', *History Today* (December 2008)

Krass, Peter, *Carnegie* (2002)

Kulikoff, Allan, *Tobacco and Slaves: the Development of Southern Culture in the Chesapeake, 1680–1800* (1986)

Landsman, Ned C, *Scotland and Its First American Colony, 1683–1765* (1985).

Landsman, Ned C, 'Evangelists and Their Hearers: Popular Interpretation of Revivalist Preaching in Eighteenth-Century Scotland', *Journal of British Studies*, Vol. 28 (1989)

Landsman, Ned C, 'Witherspoon and the Problem of Provincial Identity in Scottish Evangelical Culture' in Richard B Sher and Jeffrey R Smitten, eds, *Scotland and America in the Age of Enlightenment* (1990)

Landsman, Ned C, 'Presbyterians and Provincial Society: The Evangelical Enlightenment in the West of Scotland, 1740–1775' in John Dwyer and Richard B Sher, eds, *Sociability and Society in Eighteenth-Century Scotland* (1993)

Landsman, Ned C, 'The Provinces and the Empire: Scotland, the American Colonies and the Development of British Provincial Identity' in Lawrence Stone, ed., *An Imperial State at War: Britain from 1688 to 1815* (1994)

Landsman, Ned C, 'The Legacy of British Union for the North American Colonies' in John Robertson, ed., *Union for Empire: Political Thought and the Union of 1707* (1995)

Landsman, Ned C, *From Colonials to Provincials: American Thought and Culture, 1680–1760* (1997)

Landsman, Ned C, ed., *Nation and Province in the First British Empire: Scotland and the Americas, 1600–1800* (2001)

Landsman, Ned C, 'Erskine, John' in the *Oxford DNB*.

Landsman, Ned C, 'Witherspoon, John' in the *Oxford DNB*.

Lawson, Philip, *The Imperial Challenge: Quebec and Britain in the Age of the American Revolution* (1989)

Lenman, Bruce, *The Jacobite Clans of the Great Glen* (1984, reissued 1995)

Levack, Brian, *The Formation of the British State: England, Scotland and the Union 1603–1707* (1987)

Levy, Andrea, *Small Island* (2004)

MacDermid, Alan, 'Woodrow Wilson had Scottish strength', *The Herald*, 18 November 2003.

MacDonagh, Oliver, *A Pattern of Government Growth 1800–1860: the Passenger Acts and Their Enforcement* (1961)

Macinnes, Allan I, *Clanship, Commerce and the House of Stuart, 1603–1788* (1996)

Macinnes, Allan I, *The British Revolution, 1629–1660* (2005)

Macinnes, Allan I, *Clanship, Commerce and the House of Stuart, 1603–1788* (1996)

Macinnes, Allan I, *Union and Empire: The Making of the United Kingdom in 1707* (2007)

Mackillop, Andrew, *'More Fruitful Than the Soil': Army, Empire and the Scottish Highlands, 1715–1815* (2000)

Mackillop, Andrew, 'The Highlands and the Returning Nabob: Sir Hector Munro of Navar, 1760–1807' in Marjory Harper, ed., *Emigrant Homecomings: The Return Movement of Emigrants, 1600–2000* (2005)

Manning, Susan, *Fragments of Union: Making Connections in Scottish and American Writing* (2002)

Manning, Susan and Francis D Cogliano, eds, *The Atlantic Enlightenment* (2008)

McGeachy, Robert AA, 'Captain Lauchlin Campbell and Early Argyllshire Emigration to New York', *Northern Scotland*, Vol. 19 (1999)

McGilvary, George K, *East India Patronage and the Scottish State: The Scottish Elite and Politics in the Eighteenth Century* (2008)

McGrath, Charles Ivar, 'The "Union" Representation of 1703 in the Irish House of Commons: a Case of Mistaken Identity?' *Eighteenth-Century Ireland*, Vol. 23 (2008)

McIllwaine, CH, ed., *The Political Works of James I* (1918)

McIntosh, John R, *Church and Theology in Enlightenment Scotland: The Popular Party, 1740–1800* (1998)

McLean, Marianne, *The People of Glengarry: Highlanders in Transition, 1745–1820* (1991)

McNeill, Peter GB, and Hector L MacQueen, eds, *Atlas of Scottish History to 1707* (1996)

McPhail, Bridget, 'Through a Glass Darkly: Scots and Indians Converge at Darien', *Eighteenth-Century Life*, Vol. 18 (1994)

Meek, Donald E, 'Scottish Highlanders, North American Indians and the SSPCK: Some Cultural Perspectives', *Records of the Scottish Church History Society*, Vol. 23 Part 2 (1990)

Meek, Donald E, 'The Pulpit and the Pen: Clergy, Orality and Print in the Scottish Gaelic World' in Adam Fox and Daniel Woolf, eds, *The Spoken Word: Oral Culture in Britain, 1500–1800* (2002)

Menzies, Archibald, *Proposals for Peopling His Majesty's Southern Colonies on the Continent of America* (1763)

Merrell, James, *The Indians' New World: Catawbas and Their Neighbors from European Contact Through the Era of Removal* (1989)

Merwick, Donna, *Possessing Albany, 1630–1710: The Dutch and English Experience* (1990)

Meyer, Duane, *The Highland Scots of North Carolina, 1732–1776* (1961)

Middleton, Richard, *Colonial America: A History, 1565–1776* (third edn, 2002)

Miller, Perry, *The New England Mind: From Colony to Province* (1953)

Morgan, Edmund, *Benjamin Franklin* (2002)

Morgan, Kenneth, 'Trelawny, Edward' in the *Oxford DNB*.

Morton, Graeme, and RJ Morris, 'Civil Society, Governance and Nation, 1832–1914' in RA Houston and WW Knox, eds, *The New Penguin History of Scotland* (2001)

Murdoch, Alexander, *The People Above: Politics and Administration in Mid-Eighteenth Century Scotland* (1980, reissued 2003)

Murdoch, Alexander, 'The Importance of Being Edinburgh: Management and Opposition in Edinburgh Politics, 1746–1784', *The Scottish Historical Review*, Vol. 62 (1983)

Murdoch, Alexander, 'A Scottish Document Concerning Emigration to North Carolina in 1772', *North Carolina Historical Review*, Vol. LXVII No. 4 (1990)

Murdoch, Alex[ander], 'Emigration from the Scottish Highlands to America in the Eighteenth Century', *British Journal for Eighteenth-Century Studies*, Vol. 21 (1998)

Murdoch, Alexander, *British History 1660–1832: National Identity and Local Culture* (1998)

Murdoch, Alex[ander], 'James Glen and the Indians' in Andrew Mackillop and Steve Murdoch, eds, *Military Governors and Imperial Frontiers c1600–1800* (2003)

Murdoch, Alexander, *British Emigration, 1603–1914* (2004)

Murdoch, Alexander, 'Henry Dundas, Scotland and the Union with Ireland, 1792–1801' in Bob Harris, ed., *Scotland in the Age of the French Revolution* (2005)

Murdoch, Alexander, 'The Legacy of Unionism in Eighteenth-Century Scotland' in TM Devine, ed., *Scotland and the Union 1707–2007* (2008)

Murdoch, Steve, *Britain, Denmark-Norway and the House of Stuart, 1603–1660* (2000)

Murdoch, Steve, *Network North: Scottish Kin, Commercial and Covert Associations in Northern Europe 1603–1746* (2006)

Murphy, AE, *John Law: Economic Theorist and Policy-Maker* (1997)

Nash, Gary B, *Red, White & Black: The Peoples of Early America* (third edn, 1992)

Nash, RC, 'The English and Scottish Tobacco Trades in the Seventeenth and Eighteenth Centuries: Legal and Illegal Trade', *Economic History Review*, Second Series, Vol. 35 (1982)

Nelson, Paul D, *General James Grant: Scottish Soldier and Royal Governor of East Florida* (1993)

Nisbet, Stuart, 'The Sugar Adventurers of Glasgow 1640–1740', *History Scotland*, Vol. 9 No. 3 (May/June 2009).

O'Brien, Karen, 'Robertson's Place in the Development of Eighteenth-Century Narrative History' in Stewart J Brown, ed., *William Robertson and the Expansion of Empire* (1997)

Oldfield, JR, *Popular Politics and British Anti-Slavery* (1995)

Oldham, James, 'New Light on Mansfield and Slavery', *Journal of British Studies*, Vol. 27 (1988)

Oldham, James, 'Murray, William, first earl of Mansfield' in the *Oxford DNB*.

Oliphant, John, *Peace and War on the Anglo-Cherokee Frontier, 1756–63* (2001)

Onuf, Peter S, 'Adam Smith and the Crisis of the American Union' in Susan Manning and Francis D Cogliano, eds, *The Atlantic Enlightenment* (2008)

Orr, Willie, 'Slave Labours', *The Scotsman*, Weekend Section, 30 June 1982.

Ouston, Hugh, 'York in Edinburgh. James VII and the Patronage of Learning in Scotland, 1679–1688' in John Dwyer, Roger A Mason and Alexander Murdoch, eds, *New Perspectives on the Politics and Culture of Early Modern Scotland* ([1982])

Parker, Anthony W, *Scottish Highlanders in Colonial Georgia: The Recruitment, Emigration, and Settlement at Darien, 1735–1748* (1997)

Paterson, Lindsay, *The Autonomy of Modern Scotland* (1994)

Patrick, Derek J, 'The Kirk, Parliament and the Union, 1706–7' in Stewart J Brown and Christopher A Whatley, eds, *Union of 1707: New Dimensions* (2008)

Pentland, Gordon, *Radicalism, Reform and National Identity in Scotland, 1820–1833* (2008)

Peters, Lorraine, 'Scotland and the American Civil War: A Local Perspective' (University of Edinburgh Ph.D. thesis, 1999)

Peters, Lorraine, 'The Impact of the American Civil War on the Local Communities of Southern Scotland', *Civil War History*, Vol. 49 (2003)

Pocock, JGA, 'Hume and the American Revolution: The Dying Thoughts of a North Briton' in JGA Pocock, *Virtue, Commerce and History* (1985)

Porter, Andrew, 'Trusteeship, Anti-Slavery and Humanitarianism' in Andrew Porter, ed., *The Nineteenth Century*, The Oxford History of the British Empire, Vol. III (1999)

Powell, William S, 'Johnston, Gabriel (1698–1752)' in the *Oxford DNB*.

Pratt Insh, George, *Scottish Colonial Schemes 1620–1686* (1922)

Pratt Insh, George, ed., *Papers Relating to the Ships and Voyages of the Company of Scotland Trading to Africa and the Indies 1696–1707* (1924)

Pratt Insh, George, *The Company of Scotland Trading to Africa and the Indies* (1932)

Price, Jacob M, 'The Rise of Glasgow in the Chesapeake Tobacco Trade, 1707–1775', *William and Mary Quarterly*, Third Series, Vol. 11 (1954), reprinted most recently in JM Price, *Tobacco in Atlantic Trade: The Chesapeake, London and Glasgow 1675–1775* (1995)

Price, Jacob M, *France and the Chesapeake: A History of the French Tobacco Monopoly, 1674–1791, and of Its Relationship to the British and American Tobacco Trades* (1973)

Price, Jacob M, 'Buchanan & Simson, 1759–1763: A Different Kind of Glasgow Firm Trading to the Chesapeake', *William and Mary Quarterly*, Third Series, Vol. 40 (1983), reprinted in Jacob M Price, *Tobacco in Atlantic Trade: The Chesapeake, London and Glasgow 1675–1775* (1995)

Price, Jacob M, 'Glasgow, the Tobacco Trade, and the Scottish Customs, 1707–1730', *Scottish Historical Review*, Vol. 63 (1984), reprinted in Jacob M Price, *Overseas Trade and Traders: Essays on Some Commercial, Financial and Political Challenges Facing the British Atlantic Merchants, 1660–1775* (1996)

Rawley, James A, 'Dalzel [*formerly* Dalziel], Archibald' in the *Oxford DNB*.

Reid, John G, *Sir William Alexander and North American Colonization: A Reappraisal* (1990)

Reid, John G, 'The Conquest of "Nova Scotia": Cartographic Imperialism and the Echoes of a Scottish Past' in Ned C Landsman, ed., *Nation and Province in the First British Empire: Scotland and the Americas, 1600–1800* (2001)

Rice, C Duncan, *The Scots Abolitionists 1833–1861* (1981)

Rider, Peter E, and Heather McNabb, eds, *A Kingdom of the Mind: How the Scots Helped Make Canada* (2006)

Ritcheson, Charles R., '"To An Astonishing Degree Unfit for the Task": Britain's Peacemakers, 1782–1783' in Ronald Hoffman and Peter Albert, eds, *Peace and the Peacemakers: The Treaty of 1783* (1986)

Robertson, William *History of America* (Paris, 1828, English edn)

Robinson, W Stitt, *James Glen: From Scottish Provost to Royal Governor of South Carolina* (1996)

Rössner, Philipp Robinson, *Scottish Trade with German Ports 1700–1770* (2008)

Rothschild, Emma, *Economic Sentiments: Adam Smith, Condorcet and the Enlightenment* (2001)

Rothschild, Emma, 'David Hume and the Seagods of the Atlantic' in Susan Manning and Francis D Cogliano, eds, *The Atlantic Enlightenment* (2008)

Royal Highland Society of Scotland, Sederunt Book No. 3.

Rush, Benjamin, *Autobiography*, ed. George W Corner (1948)

Sacks, David Harris, *The Widening Gate: Bristol and the Atlantic Economy, 1450–1700* (1991)

Saunders, Laurance J, *Scottish Democracy 1815–1840* (1950)

Schama, Simon, *Rough Crossings: Britain, The Slaves and the American Revolution* (2005)

Schlenther, Boyd Stanley, 'Whitefield, George' in the *Oxford DNB*.

Schmidt, Leigh Eric, *Holy Fairs: Scottish Communions and American Revivals in the Early Modern Period* (1989)

Scott, H, *Fasti Ecclesiae Scoticanae: The Succession of Ministers in the Church of Scotland from the Reformation* (second edn, 1915–1923), Vol. IV, 63

Shepperson, George, 'Writings on Scottish-American History', *William and Mary Quarterly*, Third Series, Vol. 11 (1954)

Sher, Richard B, and Alexander Murdoch, 'Patronage and Party in the Church of Scotland, 1750–1800' in Norman McDougall, ed., *Church, Politics and Society: Scotland 1408–1929* (1983)

Sher, Richard B, *Church and University in the Scottish Enlightenment* (1985)

Sher, Richard B, 'Introduction' in Richard B Sher and Jeffrey R Smitten, eds, *Scotland and America in the Age of the Enlightenment* (1990)

Sher, Richard B, 'An "Agreable and Instructive Society": Benjamin Franklin and Scotland' in John Dwyer and Richard B Sher, eds, *Sociability and Society in Eighteenth-Century Scotland* (1993)

Sheridan, Richard B, 'The Rise of a Colonial Gentry: A Case Study of Antigua, 1730–1775', *Economic History Review*, Second Series, Vol. 18 (1965)

Sheridan, Richard B, 'The Role of the Scots in the Economy and Society of the West Indies' in V Rubin and A Tuden, eds, *Comparative Perspectives on Slavery in the New World Plantations* (1977)

Sheridan, Richard B, 'The Formation of Caribbean Plantation Society, 1689–1748' in PJ Marshall, ed., *The Eighteenth Century*, The Oxford History of the British Empire, Vol. II (1998)

Simpson, John, 'James Wilson and the Making of Constitutions' in Thomas J Barron, Owen Dudley Edwards and Patricia J. Storey, eds, *Constitutions and National Identity: Proceedings of the Conference on 'The Making of constitutions and the Development of National Identity' held in honour of Professor George Shepperson at the University of Edinburgh 3–6 July 1987* (1993)

Smith, Adam, *An Inquiry into the Nature and Causes of the Wealth of Nations*, ed. RH Campbell et al., 2 vols. (1976)

Smith, Adam, *Correspondence*, ed. Ernest Campbell Mossner and Ian Simpson Ross (1977)

Smith, Annette M, *Jacobite Estates of the Forty-Five* (1982)

[Smith, William] *Information to Emigrants, Being the Copy of a Letter from a Gentleman in North America* [1773]

Smitten, Jeffrey R, 'Robertson, William' in the *Oxford DNB*.

Smout, TC, 'The Early Scottish Sugar Houses, 1660–1720', *Economic History Review*, Vol. 14 (1961)

Smout, TC, *Scottish Trade on the Eve of Union, 1660–1707* (1963)

Smout, TC, 'The Glasgow Merchant Community in the Seventeenth Century', *Scottish Historical Review*, Vol. 47 (1968)

Smout, TC, 'Born Again at Cambuslang: New Evidence on popular Religion and Literacy in Eighteenth-Century Scotland', *Past and Present*, No. 97 (1982)

Smout, TC, Ned C Landsman and TM Devine, 'Scottish Emigration in the Seventeenth and Eighteenth Centuries' in Nicholas Canny, ed., *Europeans on the Move: Studies in European Migration, 1500–1800* (1994)

Snapp, J Russell, *John Stuart and the Struggle for Empire on the Southern Frontier* (1996)

Sobel, Mechal, *The World They Made Together: Black and White Values in Eighteenth-Century Virginia* (1987)

Stephen, Jeffrey, 'The Presbytery of Caledonia: An Early Scottish Mission', *History Scotland*, Vol. 9 No. 1 (2009)

Steuart, David, of Garth, *Sketches of the Character, Manners, and Present State of the Highlanders of Scotland* (second edn, 1822, reprinted 1977)

Stevenson, David, 'Burt, Edmund (d. 1755)' in the *Oxford DNB*.

Storrs, Christopher, 'Disaster at Darien (1698–1700)? The Persistence of Spanish Imperial Power on the Eve of the Demise of the Spanish Habsburgs', *European History Quarterly*, Vol. 24 (1999)

Szasz, Ferenc M, 'Peter Williamson and the Eighteenth Century Scottish-American Connection', *Northern Scotland*, Vol. 91 (1999)

Szasz, Margaret Connell, *Scottish Highlanders and Native Americans: Indigenous Education in the Eighteenth-Century Atlantic World* (2007)

Taylor, Alan, *American Colonies: The Settling of North America* (2001)

Temperley, Howard, *British Antislavery 1833–1870* (1972)

Towsey, Mark, 'Reading the Scottish Enlightenment' (University of St Andrews Ph.D. thesis, 2007)

Van Vugt, William E, *British Buckeyes: The English, Scots and Welsh in Ohio, 1700–1900* (2006)

Ward, JR, *British West Indian Slavery, 1750–1834: the Process of Amelioration* (1988)

Ward, JR, 'The British West Indies, 1748–1815' in PJ Marshall, ed., *The Eighteenth Century*, The Oxford History of the British Empire, Vol. II (1998)

Ward, WR, *The Protestant Evangelical Awakening* (1992)

Watson, J Steven, *The Reign of George III* (1960)

Watt, Douglas, *The Price of Scotland: Darien, Union and the Wealth of Nations* (2007).

Weir, Robert M, '"Shaftesbury's Darling": British Settlement in the Carolinas at the Close of the Seventeenth Century' in Nicholas Canny, ed., *The Origins of Empire*, The Oxford History of the British Empire, Vol. I (1998)

Westerkamp, Marilyn J, *Triumph of the Laity: Scots-Irish Piety and the Great Awakening* (1988)

Whatley, Christopher A, *The Industrial Revolution in Scotland* (1997)

Whatley, Christopher A, 'The Dark Side of the Enlightenment? Sorting Out Serfdom' in TM Devine and JR Young, eds, *Eighteenth Century Scotland: New Perspectives* (1999)

Whyte, Iain, *Scotland and the Abolition of Black Slavery, 1756–1838* (2006)

Whyte, Iain, 'The Anti-Slave Trade Tour of William Dickson in 1792', *Scottish Local History*, No. 72 (Spring 2008)

Williamson, Arthur H, *Scottish National Consciousness in the Age of James VI* (1979)

Williamson, Arthur H, 'Scots, Indians and Empire: The Scottish Politics of Civilization 1519–1609', *Past and Present*, Number 150 (February 1996)

Williamson, Arthur H, 'George Buchanan, Civic Virtue and Commerce', *Scottish Historical Review*, Vol. 75 (1996)

Wilson, Woodrow, *Papers of Woodrow Wilson*, ed. Arthur S Link et al., Vols 12 and 14 (1972)

Winch, Donald, *Riches and Poverty: An Intellectual History of Political Economy in Britain, 1750–1834* (1996)

Wodrow, Robert, *Analecta: or Materials for a History of Remarkable Providences Mostly Relating to Scotch Ministers and Christians*, ed. Matthew Leishman, 4 vols (1842–1843)

Wodrow, Robert, *The Correspondence of the Rev. Robert Wodrow*, 4 vols. ed. Thomas McCrie (1842–1843)

Wodrow, Robert, *Early Letters of Robert Wodrow*, ed. LW Sharp (1937)

Wood, Betty, *Slavery in Colonial Georgia 1730–1775* (1984)

Wood, Betty, 'Oglethorpe, James Edward' in the *Oxford DNB*.

Wood, Gordon S, *The Americanization of Benjamin Franklin* (2004)

Index